German Ordnungspolizei

DIE
POLIZEI
IM FRONTEINSATZ

Combat Operations of the

German Ordnungspolizei

1939-1945

Polizei-Bataillone • SS-Polizei-Regimenter

Rolf Michaelis

Schiffer Military History
Atglen, PA

Book translated by David Johnston
Book Design by Ian Robertson.

Library of Congress Control Number: 2010931216

Printed in China.
ISBN: 978-0-7643-3659-1

This book was originally published in German under the title
Die Einsatz der Ordnungspolizei 1939-1945 by Michaelis-Verlag

We are interested in hearing from authors with book ideas on related topics.

Published by Schiffer Publishing Ltd.
4880 Lower Valley Road
Atglen, PA 19310
Phone: (610) 593-1777
FAX: (610) 593-2002
E-mail: Info@schifferbooks.com.
Visit our web site at: www.schifferbooks.com
Please write for a free catalog.
This book may be purchased from the publisher.
Please include $5.00 postage.
Try your bookstore first.

In Europe, Schiffer books are distributed by:
Bushwood Books
6 Marksbury Avenue
Kew Gardens
Surrey TW9 4JF
England
Phone: 44 (0) 20 8392-8585
FAX: 44 (0) 20 8392-9876
E-mail: Info@bushwoodbooks.co.uk.

Contents

Foreword

"The current European war differs significantly from the World War of 1914-18 in its entire structure, meaning both in its strategic conduct and in the types of weapons employed. This fact made it necessary to assign special military tasks not only to the Wehrmacht, but for the first time to the German Police as well."

So began a publication about the police by the then *SS-Gruppenführer und Generalleutnant der Polizei* Jedicke in 1942.[1] And, in fact, elements of the German Police had taken part in unprecedented actions in which they caused, directly or indirectly, physical or mental harm to tens of thousands of people in Europe. This was of course contrary to the slogan *The Police – Your Friend and Helper*.

While countless publications about the troops of the *Wehrmacht* and the *Waffen-SS* have been printed since 1945, only recently have the first books on the German Police appeared, resulting from the discussion of its role in the Holocaust. This delay may be due on the one hand to the fact that the small size of these units made the creation of a chronicle scarcely justifiable in economic terms, and on the other to the fact that the special operations in which the *Ordnungspolizei* participated made publication seem unwarranted because of the possibility of war crimes trials. This was all the more so because most active police members returned to the police service after the war, and with the birth of the Federal Republic of Germany there was no desire to call the profession into question.

With this work I have attempted to provide an overview of the approximately 100 police battalions and more than 40 police regiments, the majority of which were deployed in the occupied areas.[2]

In a work of this scope errors are unavoidable. I am grateful for any corrections and would especially like to thank Herr Kwasny for his unselfish support.

Berlin, August 2008
Rolf Michaelis

Introduction

After minor actions in Austria and Czechoslovakia, the Second World War brought the first large-scale operations by German police outside the borders of the Reich. The *Ordnungspolizei* had adopted military structures after the Treaty of Versailles restricted the Reichswehr to 100,000 men, and this now benefited the organization. The barracked *Sicherheitspolizei* had been created in Prussia in 1919. Consisting mainly of members of the *Freikorps*, it was disbanded in 1920. Immediately after taking power on 30 January 1933, the National-Socialists began expanding Germany's military potential. As part of this, Hitler ordered the formation of a militarily-organized force of 56,000 men from the roughly 160,000-man *Ordnungspolizei*. The force was given the name "*Landespolizei*."[3] After the introduction of universal military service, on 1 August 1935 large elements of these provincial police were incorporated into the *Wehrmacht*.

On 17 June 1936 the former provincial police were combined into a national police force, the "*Deutschen Polizei*," under the Ministry of the Interior. The force was organized as follows:

Ordnungspolizei (Orpo) Head Office with
- *Schutzpolizei*
- *Gendarmerie*
- *Gemeindepolizei*
- *Land- und Stadtwacht*
- *Feuerschutzpolizei* (from 1938)
- *Luftschutzpolizei* (from 1942)

and

Sicherheitspolizei (Sipo) Head Office with
- *Kriminalpolizei (Kripo)*
- *Geheime Staatspolizei (Gestapo)*
- *Sicherheitsdienst (SD)*

Reichsführer-SS Heinrich Himmler became the head of the *Deutschen Polizei*. *General der Polizei* Kurt Daluege was head of the *Ordnungspolizei* until 1943, when he was succeeded by *General der Polizei* Alfred Wünnenberg. *SS-Gruppenführer* Reinhard Heydrich was head of the *Sicherheitspolizei* until 1942 and was succeeded by *SS-Obergruppenführer* Kaltenbrunner.

By the outbreak of war in 1939, the *Ordnungspolizei*'s strength had been brought back up to about 120,000 members, of whom about 9,000 were concentrated in so-called "*Polizei-Hundertschaften*" in the large cities. In 1938 the so-called "*verstärkte Polizeischutz*" (increased police protection) had been formed to meet the personnel requirements for the tasks that would follow in the event of war. After consultation with the *Wehrmacht*, this was initially formed with almost 92,000 untrained men—from all career groups (no policemen)—from the age classes 1901 – 1909. These reservists were prepared for potential police service on weekends or in one or two multi-day courses. Like the later *Polizei-Bataillonen* (police battalions), training was limited to the use of small arms, marching, guard duties, and a short legal instruction. In the course of mobilization, between September 1939 and July 1940 approximately 30,000 police reservists were called up under the Emergency Service Order[4] to serve as *Wachtmeister* for the formation of about 50 police battalions. Concerning the formation of the police reserve, a contemporary publication from 1942 remarked:

> "*Of course the peacetime forces of the Ordnungspolizei were insufficient to perform all the tasks that came with the war. All of its branches had to be greatly strengthened for the duration of the war, and so the police reserve was formed for this purpose. Men from all stations and professions were called up and schooled and trained for wartime police duties before the war. And so when the war began, the Ordnungspolizei was able to master the important tasks given it. As well as performing all the police duties, the training of these men, who were doing their war service in the ranks of the police, continued. Everywhere today the members of the police reserve are pulling their weight, whether in street duty in the homeland, in site protection, or in the police battalions in Poland, in the occupied western territories or even in the far north of Norway. Side by side with their active comrades they are doing their duty, and their eagerness to serve is unsurpassed.*"

Until 1942 the police battalions consisted of just three companies. With an authorized strength of 693 men,[6] they were organized as follows:

Headquarters	16 men
Signals Platoon	19 men
Motorcycle Platoon	35 men
Armored Car Platoon	17 men
3 companies of 150 men each	450 men
Anti-Tank Platoon (3 37-mm guns)	26 men
Infantry Gun Platoon (2 75-mm guns)	26 men
Transport Column	97 men
Medical Squad	7 men

A police battalion was thus roughly equal in strength to an army battalion, although it must be remembered that their training differed vastly. Restricted by their envisioned duties—primarily the guarding of militarily important objects, patrol duty, and fighting of crime (such as the black market)—there was no military training (such as assault training).[7] The often advanced age and lack of motivation of the draftees resulted in the nominal formation of battalions which had no military potential, as was to be repeatedly shown when they were assigned front line duties.

Because of the need to quickly form new army units, in autumn 1939 an agreement was reached between the *Wehrmacht* and the *Ordnungspolizei* to form the so-called *Polizei-Division*[8] using about 16,000 policemen. In return, the army gave the *Ordnungspolizei* 26,000 untrained recruits from the age classes 1918 – 1920 and 1909 – 1912. The approximately 9,000 men in the 19 – 21 age bracket were taken on as so-called *Polizei-Anwärter*, and the approximately 17,000 in the 27 – 31 age bracket as so-called *Polizei-Wachtmeister d.R.* Together with active police and police reservists, the approximately 10,000 surplus recruits formed *Polizei-Bataillonen 251 – 256* and *301 – 325.*

On 20 August 1940 the total strength of the *Deutschen Polizei* stood at 244,500 members. Of these:

232,500 men were in the ***Ordnungspolizei***, including
176,000 actively serving members of the *Ordnungspolizei*, of which
- 16,000 police in the *Polizei-Division* with the army
- 8,000 men in the *Feldgendarmerie* units in the *Wehrmacht*
- 60,000 men in the approx. 100 police battalions[9]
- 92,500 men in the *Gendarmerie*, *Land- ünd Stadtwacht* and *Feuerschutzpolizei*

56,000 police reservists
12,000 men in the ***Sicherheitspolizei***

In the summer of 1941 a large number of men from the occupied states of the Soviet Union volunteered for military service at Germany's side. In addition to the formation of several so-called *Ost-Bataillone* within the *Wehrmacht*, as per a decree dated 6 November 1941 many of the volunteers were assigned to the *Ordnungspolizei*, where they were concentrated in so-called *Schutzmannschafts-Bataillonen.* Approximately 205 of these battalions were formed with a total of about 100,000 men—mainly from the Baltic States, White Russia, and the Ukraine—and deployed for long or short periods. In general, the Baltic units proved more capable than those from White Russia or the Ukraine.[10]

Losses suffered in actions against partisans or at the front were made good in part by secondments from the police authorities in the Reich, through newly called-up ethnic Germans[11] and additional police reservists—some units were also disbanded. The affected battalions provided replacements for the *SS-Polizei-Division*, which suffered heavy casualties at Leningrad and on the Volkhov.

In 1942 the battalions were concentrated to form *Polizei-Regimenter*, which were renamed *SS-Polizei-Regimenter* one year later. With an authorized strength of about 2,800 men, these were organized as follows:

Regimental Headquarters	22 men
Motorized Signals Company	57 men
Motorcycle Company	124 men
Pioneer Platoon	35 men
3 battalions of 700 men each	2,100 men
13th (Infantry Gun) Company	163 men
14th (Anti-Tank) Company	82 men
15th (Armored) Company	194 men
Workshop Platoon	13 men

In contrast to army regiments, the police regiments were even supposed to have an armored company. This directive could only be realized in part, however, and then only with obsolete French or Italian vehicles. Nominally possessing about the same strength, the police regiments still had less military training than those of the army—despite the modified training manuals. Their members were also frequently older than their army counterparts; consequently, the police regiments were significantly less capable than those of the army.

After the defeat at Stalingrad there was an exchange of personnel similar to the one that had occurred during mobilization in 1939: the *Waffen-SS* released about 7,500 untrained men—mostly from older age classes or ethnic Germans—to the *Ordnungspolizei*, in return receiving at least partially-trained men from the police regiments. Most of these were used to form new units or make good on losses suffered by units of the *Waffen-SS.*

At the same time, the *Ordnungspolizei* began deploying foreign volunteers in regiment-size units. And so, in addition to the existing *Schutzmannschafts-Bataillone*, so-called *Polizei-Schützen-Regimenter* were formed, plus *Polizei-Freiwilligen-Regimenter* in southeastern Europe.

After the collapse of Army Group Center in the summer of 1944, most of these police rifle regiments were disbanded. Effective 1 August 1944, the bulk of the remaining *Schutzmannschafts-Bataillone* were used to form the *30. Waffen-Grenadier-Division der SS (russische Nr. 2).*[14]

Nevertheless, with large numbers of replacements sent from the Reich, the SS police regiments were able to boast a strength of about 60,000 men. During mobilization of the last reserves, on 16 March 1945 units of the *Ordnungspolizei* formed a second police division on the Eastern Front, which on 8 April was attached to the *SS-Führungshauptamt* (operational headquarters) as the *35. SS-Polizei-Grenadier-Division.*[15]

Training on the (sMG) 08/15, a First World War heavy machine-gun.

Range practice with the carbine.

Instruction on the 45-mm Pak 184 (r), a captured Russian anti-tank gun.

One month later the end of the war brought to an end operations by the SS police regiments. Their principal responsibilities had been:

- securing the areas assigned to them specifically:
  - protecting objects and supply lines from attack
  - patrol duty in and outside the cities
  - guard duties, including in POW camps and ghettos
  - anti-partisan operations
- collection of agricultural products and areas and labor forces (so-called *Ostarbeiter*[16])
- resettlement[17] and execution of Jews, gypsies, or persons (also groups of persons) hostile to the Germans from Germany or annexed areas (e.g. the Warthe District or Upper Ukraine) or occupied territories (e.g. France, the Netherlands, USSR, or Hungary)

Not all members of the police were involved in these sometimes criminal actions; however, one can assume that many were at least briefly associated with them, even if it was just escorting transports or participating in confinement measures or gaining knowledge of them.

In Action 1939

In March 1938 five battalion- to regiment-strength *Marschgruppen* (march groups) formed from the active *Polizei-Hundertschaften* in the major cities took part in the entry into Austria. Then, in March 1939, a total of ten police battalions were formed during the occupation of rump-Czechoslovakia. Concentrated in two regiments, they were assigned the police function of maintaining order in the occupied areas. The following units were sent to Bohemia and Moravia:

Polizei-Regiment 1 "Böhmen" (became *Polizei-Regiment 20* in 1942)
- *Polizei-Bataillon I/1 "Jungbunzlau"*
- *Polizei-Bataillon II/1 "Klattau"*
- *Polizei-Bataillon III/1 "Prag"*
- *Polizei-Bataillon IV/1 "Tabor"*
- *Polizei-Bataillon V/1 "Kladno"*
- *Polizei-Bataillon VI/1 "Pardubitz"*

Polizei-Regiment 2 "Mähren" (became *Polizei-Regiment* 21 in 1942)
- *Polizei-Bataillon I/2 "Iglau"*
- *Polizei-Bataillon II/2 "Mährisch-Ostrau"*
- *Polizei-Bataillon III/2 "Hölleschau"*
- *Polizei-Bataillon IV/2 Brünn"*

Seventeen more police battalions were formed during the mobilization in the summer of 1939, and these were concentrated in police groups (regiments):

Polizei-Gruppe 1/AOK 14	FPNr. 00 027*
Polizei-Bataillon I/1	FPNr. 00 869 (later *Polizei-Bataillon* 92)
Polizei-Bataillon II/1	FPNr. 04 703 (later *Polizei-Bataillon* 63)
Polizei-Bataillon III/1	FPNr. 11 307 (later *Polizei-Bataillon* 171)
Polizei-Bataillon IV/1	FPNr. 16 695 (later *Polizei-Bataillon* 81)
Polizei-Bataillon V/1	FPNr. 20 382 (later *Polizei-Bataillon* 62)

Polizei-Gruppe 2/AOK 10	FPNr.	24 093
Polizei-Bataillon I/2		FPNr. 24 062 (later *Polizei-Bataillon 101*)
Polizei-Bataillon II/2		FPNr. 27 065 (later *Polizei-Bataillon 102)*
Polizei-Bataillon III/2		FPNr. 30 225 (later *Polizei-Bataillon 103)*
Polizei-Bataillon IV/2		FPNr. 31 338 (later *Polizei-Bataillon 42*)
Polizei-Bataillon V/2		FPNr. 20 020 (later *Polizei-Bataillon 71*)
Polizei-Gruppe 3/AOK 8		FPNr. 32 433
Polizei-Bataillon I/3		FPNr. 32 649 (later *Polizei-Bataillon 41*)
Polizei-Gruppe 4 z.b.V. Military Commander Posen		FPNr. 34 145
Polizei-Bataillon I/4		FPNr. 34 383 (later *Polizei-Bataillon 61*)
Polizei-Gruppe 5/AOK 4		FPNr. 35 744
Polizei-Bataillon I/5		FPNr. 35 937 (later *Polizei-Bataillon 1*)
Polizei-Gruppe 6		FPNr. 26 514
Polizei-Bataillon I/6		FPNr. 31 274 (later *Polizei-Bataillon 2*)
Polizei-Bataillon II/6		FPNr. 36 361 (later *Polizei-Bataillon 3*)
Polizei-Bataillon III/6		FPNr. 26 800 (later *Polizei-Bataillon 4*)
Polizei-Bataillon IV/6		FPNr. 33 747 (later *Polizei-Bataillon 91*)

*FPNr. = *Feldpostnummer*, or military postal number.

In the summer of 1939 the *Ordnungspolizei* began forming about 80 new battalions in the military districts using police reservists and recruits. The bulk of these were designated as so-called Reserve Police Battalions. The battalion numbers now reflected the responsible *Wehrkreis* (military district), with the exception of *Wehrkreis III* (Berlin). The resulting numbers, some of them high, undoubtedly helped confuse the enemy as to the actual number of German police battalions. Here are several examples of the new designations:

Berlin (WK III)	*Polizei-Bataillone 1, 2, 3, 4* and *5*
Wehrkreis II	*Polizei-Bataillone 21* and *22*
Wehrkreis XVII	*Polizei-Bataillon 171* and *172*

After the end of the campaign in Poland, on 4 November 1939 four police regiments were created for the four districts of the newly-established *Generalgouvernement* (General-Government):

Polizei-Regiment "Warschau" (became *Polizei-Regiment 22* in 1942)
Polizei-Bataillon "Warschau I" (H.Q Berlin) (*Polizei-Bataillon 6*)
Polizei-Bataillon "Warschau II" (H.Q. Berlin) (*Polizei-Bataillon 8*)
Polizei-Bataillon "Warschau III" (H.Q. Munich) (*Polizei-Bataillon 72*)

Polizei-Regiment "Radom" (became *Polizei-Regiment 24* in 1942)
Polizei-Bataillon "Radom" (H.Q. Cologne) (*Polizei-Bataillon 309)*
Polizei-Bataillon "Tschenstochau" (H.Q. Berlin) (*Polizei-Bataillon 310*)
Polizei-Bataillon "Kielce" (H.Q. Hamburg) (*Polizei-Bataillon 305*)

<u>*Polizei-Regiment "Krakau"*</u> (became *Polizei-Regiment 23 in 1942*)
Polizei-Bataillon "Krakau I" (H.Q. Jena) (*Polizei-Bataillon 311*)
Polizei-Bataillon "Krakau II" (H.Q. Breslau) (*Polizei-Bataillon 321*)
Polizei-Bataillon "Tarnow" (H.Q. Bremen) (*Polizei-Bataillon 303*)
Polizei-Bataillon "Reichshof" (H.Q. Vienna) (*Polizei-Bataillon 314*)

<u>*Polizei-Regiment "Lublin"*</u> (became *Polizei-Regiment 25* in 1942)
Polizei-Bataillon "Lublin" (H.Q. Frankfurt/Main) (*Polizei-Bataillon* 306)
Polizei-Bataillon "Zamosc" (H.Q. Stettin) (*Polizei-Bataillon 313*)
Polizei-Bataillon "Biala-Podlaska" (H.Q. Lübeck) (*Polizei-Bataillon 308*)

A member of the *Schutzpolizei* wrote a telling report on police operations in the *Generalgouvernement.*[18] He made no mention, however, of the fact that the area of the Warthe District, in which ethnic Germans from the Baltic States and the Ukraine were resettled, first had to be cleared of its Polish and Jewish inhabitants:[19]

"*In Warsaw there was a police regiment headquarters and several battalion headquarters. The police had established several bases here in Warsaw, and also patrolled actively in order to maintain peace and order in this difficult-to-oversee city with its large ghetto, full of nooks and crannies. This ghetto was one of my first destinations. It was fenced in with barbed wire — at least they were beginning to fence it in at that time — and large signs warned of the danger of epidemic and forbade entrance to that quarter of the city except for official purposes.*

As strange as it sounds, in those March days in 1940 Warsaw was not only the most destroyed city in the east, but also the most full of life. Except where they were blocked by piles of rubble, the streets were full of people. In contrast to the old Reich there was no blackout, the shop windows were lit up, the streetcars were running and were filled to overflowing, the cafes were busy, and in addition to the Polish cinemas there was also a police cinema run by an Ufa projectionist from Berlin.

Before I left the east for good, I paid a visit to what was then Lodsch. The purpose of the visit was to see the transit camp for Wohlhynian and Galician Germans, and also the city's ghetto.

In Przemsyl I had had the opportunity to speak to the Galician Germans soon after they crossed the border, and in Lodsch I was able to augment and complete my material. My plan to also visit the new settlements in the Warthe District later in the spring was wrecked by the action in Norway, which no one could have imagined at the time, but I also saw much in Lodsch. The peasant carts, which had crossed the bridge in Przemsyl and had been unloaded in Jaroslau, were in a wagon park outside Lodsch. The resettlement was in progress. Each day families that had been assembled were called out and transported to their new homes in buses. Other families waited in the various camps in the city and waited for their call."

In autumn 1939 the *Polizei-Bataillone 1, 4, 5, 7, 12, 22, 31*, and *52* were detached for the establishment of the *Polizei-Division* (Police Division) being formed by the army.

Schutzpolizei officers.

In Action 1940

Until September, the year 1940 was characterized in part by the formation of about 80 new police battalions, elements of which were temporarily assigned to occupation duties alongside the "old" police battalions. In addition to those deployed in the Protectorate of Bohemia and Moravia and the *Generalgouvernement*, police battalions were now also sent to Norway, the Netherlands, Alsace-Lorraine, Luxemburg, and the new "Eastern Provinces" of the German Reich (Wartheland and Danzig-West Prussia). In October 1940 there was a second wave of deportations of Jews and Poles from those provinces in the *Generalgouvernement* that had been incorporated into the Reich – for example, approximately 160,000 Jews were sent to the Warsaw ghetto. Deployed were:

	Protectorate of "Bohemia and Moravia"
10 police battalions	144 officers and 5,401 *Wachtmeister**
	Generalgouvernement
13 police battalions[20]	219 officers and 8,245 *Wachtmeister*
	Reichskommissariat for the Occupied Norwegian Territories
6 police battalions	73 officers and 3,270 *Wachtmeister*
	Reichskommissariat for the Occupied Dutch Territories
4 police battalions	58 officers and 2,420 *Wachtmeister*
	Alsace-Lorraine and Luxemburg
3 police battalions	45 officers and 1,10 *Wachtmeister*
	New Eastern Provinces: Danzig-West Prussia and Wartheland
7 police battalions[21]	63 officers and 3,500 *Wachtmeister*
1 mounted police battalion	4 officers and 270 *Wachtmeister*
1 police signals battalion	4 officers and 390 *Wachtmeister*

**Wachtmeister* = police constable

A police officer wrote the following propaganda account of police actions in Norway:[22]

"*On Monday, the 22nd of April 1940, I was advised by telephone that, not only had the final orders been given for a deployment to Norway, but also that a part of the headquarters staff had already left by plane for Oslo. Orders had been issued for the rest of the headquarters and the first deployed battalions to depart on 24 April. On the afternoon of 23 April the head of the Ordnungspolizei, SS-Obergruppenführer und General der Polizei Daluege, bade farewell to the two police battalions in the old Maikäfer barracks on the Chausseestraße in Berlin. In his speech to the men, the general declared that the conditions in Norway were not to be compared to those in Poland. The Norwegians were a people racially related to us, and we were entering the country not to conquer it, but to shield it from the much greater perils of a war which England wanted to bring to the peaceful north. The country had its government, its administration, and its own economic life, which was to be interfered with as little as possible. The German police were to feel as friends and guests in Norway, but when they encountered resistance they were to take action, toughly but fairly. The speech ended with a Sieg Heil to the Führer…*

In the evening, coming from Fredrikshavn (Denmark), we set foot on Norwegian soil for the first time in Larvik. Larvik is a small port and also a seaside resort. The reception was not overly friendly, but also not overtly hostile. And, given the attitude held by the Norwegians for many years, one couldn't ask for much more.

Two schools had been set aside for the two battalions temporarily still in Larvik, and the offices of the Commander of the Ordnungspolizei were initially in the Storthing, the Norwegian parliament building. When the battalions arrived in the following days they were deployed immediately. One battalion stayed in Oslo, while the second was made responsible for the south, the Drammen area. Soon there was a police guard at the Storthing. Police patrolled the city and, after negotiations with the Wehrmacht, the area to be watched over by the police was moved more and more to the north. One extremely important task was added to the police responsibilities: guarding the border with Sweden. This boundary is not natural, it is formed neither by a river nor a chain of mountains; rather, it runs through the middle of a vast wooded area and in general can only be reached by way of secondary roads. On the other side Sweden had fortified its border quite strongly, and to show them that we Germans had no aggressive designs against Swedish territory, the military border guard was to be replaced by a police one.

Then the third battalion assigned to Norway arrived in Oslo and was sent to Trondheim. There too, as everywhere, there is a stark difference between war and peace. Up in Narvik, completely cut off from the south, a small force of paratroopers and sailors is fighting against a superior English force, at Mo there is still an entire Norwegian division, and here in Trondheim there is peace. True, the city has changed. More stores have been boarded up than in Oslo, but the young people of Trondheim still stroll these streets at the usual time just as before, all of the bars are full, and in the hotel's Wintergarten members of the Wehrmacht and Norwegians sit together in the lovely, well-maintained room and listen to the house band that plays every evening."

After the conclusion of the Western Campaign, in June 1940 three police battalions were ordered to Alsace-Lorraine and Luxemburg. In addition to general police duties, large-scale resettlements were carried out there too. The following report reflects the chauvinistic tone—in this case toward the French—encouraged by the state in those days:[23]

"Another time it was a German traffic sentry in Metz who was arrogantly insulted by a Frenchman. In the course of his duties, the sentry pointed out to this questionable figure—hands in his pockets up to the elbows, cigarette in the corner of his mouth and a beret on his right ear—that he was crossing the street illegally. The answer from the Frenchman's mouth was 'Sale Boche' (German swine). But before the policeman could give him a well-deserved boxing of the ears, the offender was already sitting on the ground. Two passing Wehrmacht members had heard his words and immediately given the cheeky Frenchman a stern lecture. Of course he did not escape his well-earned punishment and subsequent deportation. Because of this and much more – for example, the use of the French language and refusal to adapt to their changed circumstances – the French elements, which had swept into this ancient German region in large numbers after 1919, had to be removed. There were large-scale resettlement actions, the main burden of which fell to the police. The representatives of the 'chosen people,' of whom there were obviously many, showed their true colors by singing the Marseillaise…

Parallel to the resettlement of French and Jews, the police also attended to the German population of Lorraine, which had been moved to central France, and saw to it that their return, together with the protection of their belongings, was carried out according to plan. A refugee processing office had been set up in Metz for this purpose, and it was able to process more than 400,000 persons and return them to their homeland."

The report on Luxemburg shows how the racial policies of the time were brought subliminally into the public mind:[24]

"As previously said, pure German blood flows through the veins of the Luxemburg population, for they are of the very same tribe as our people from the Moselle region, and also share with them one and the same dialect. But in spite of this it would be wrong to claim that the Luxembourgers had welcomed their new national-political situation with joy and true frenzies of enthusiasm. On the contrary, they were very reserved at first and took a wait-and-see attitude, in no small part because about half the population was well-disposed toward the French.

After Luxemburg was occupied by German troops and became part of the Greater German Reich, German administration was introduced in this country as it was in Alsace-Lorraine. German police units assumed responsibility for maintaining peace and order, as well as watching over the borders with France and Belgium and that with the Reich—as customs had not yet been removed. Traffic into the Reich was monitored solely to check the flow of goods, while the borders with France and Belgium still had to be sealed to prevent the afflux of Frenchmen and Jews. For this reason, therefore, stronger police forces had to be moved to Luxemburg.

A police battalion entered the city of Luxemburg soon after the ceasefire with France. People lined the streets as the column passed. Most were still quite reserved, and the majority were curiosity seekers who wanted to see the military spectacle of the green-uniformed police entering the city. Only a few raised their arm in the German salute…

Meanwhile, the vanguard with the band had reached the parade square, whose surrounding houses were bedecked with the victorious flags of the Reich. A large crowd of people ringed the decorated square, and when the police battalion marched in smartly to the strains of a stirring German military march, thousands of arms went up in the German salute amid shouts of Heil! This spontaneous outburst probably took the men in the green tunics a little by surprise. Every Reich and ethnic German from near and far had made his way to the square to take part in a German celebration."

At the end of 1940 there were 98 police battalions:

Wehrkreis I	*Polizei-Bataillone 11* and *13*
Wehrkreis II	*Polizei-Bataillon 22*
Wehrkreis III	*Polizei-Bataillone 2, 3, 6, 8, 9, 10, 32* and *33*
Wehrkreis IV	*Polizei-Bataillone 41-45*
Wehrkreis V	*Polizei-Bataillone 51-56*
Wehrkreis VI	*Polizei-Bataillone 61-69*
Wehrkreis VII	*Polizei-Bataillone 72-74*
Wehrkreis VIII	*Polizei-Bataillone 81-85*
Wehrkreis IX	*Polizei-Bataillone 91* and *93*
Wehrkreis X	*Polizei-Bataillone 101-106*
Wehrkreis XI	*Polizei-Bataillone 111* and *112*
Wehrkreis XII	*Polizei-Bataillone 121-123*
Wehrkreis XIII	*Polizei-Bataillon 131-134*
Wehrkreis XVII	*Polizei-Bataillone 171* and *172*
Wehrkreis XVIII	*Polizei-Bataillon 181*
Wehrkreis XX	*Polizei-Bataillone 201-210*
No *Wehrkreis*	*Polizei-Bataillone 251-256*
	Polizei-Bataillone 301-325

Most members of the police battalions and SS police regiments were between 35 and 45 years of age.

Guarding a railway line.

In Action 1941

For the police battalions, the year 1941 began with further resettlement and expulsion operations in the newly-incorporated provinces of Danzig-West Prussia and the Wartheland. In January 1941 Himmler planned the deportation of 831,000 Poles and Jews into the *Generalgouvernement*.[26]

The Balkan campaign in April 1941 and the war against the Soviet Union which began in June brought new responsibilities. On the one hand, the occupied areas—including Carniola (Krain) and southern Styria in southern Europe and the Baltic States and White Russia in eastern Europe—had to be secured and special assignments associated with the "ideological war" carried out.[27] Various police battalions took part in the execution of several thousand Jews, their involvement ranging from guarding the Jews, transporting them to the places of execution, sealing off of the places of execution,[28] and up to participation in the actual executions.[29]

In the "Protectorate of Bohemia and Moravia," the younger active policemen were replaced by older age classes, resulting in a reorganization of the two police regiments:

Polizei-Regiment "Böhmen (became *Polizei-Regiment 20* in 1942)
- *Polizei-Bataillon "Prag"* (H.Q. Cologne) (*Polizei-Bataillon 319*)
- *Polizei-Bataillon "Klattau"* (H.Q. Berlin) (*Polizei-Bataillon 32*)
- *Polizei-Bataillon "Tabor"* (H.Q. Recklinghausen) (*Polizei-Bataillon 312*)
- *Polizei-Bataillon "Jungbunzlau"* (H.Q. Berlin) (*Polizei-Bataillon 320*)
- *Polizei-Bataillon "Pardubitz"* (H.Q. Wuppertal) (*Polizei-Bataillon* 317)

Polizei-Regiment "Mähren" (became *Polizei-Regiment 21* in 1942)
- *Polizei-Bataillon "Brünn* (H.Q. Halle) (*Polizei-Bataillon 315*)
- *Polizei-Bataillon "Iglau"*(H.Q. Vienna) (*Polizei-Bataillon 318*)
- *Polizei-Bataillon "Holleschau"* (H.Q. Gleiwitz) (*Polizei-Bataillon* 84)

In 1941 the police forces deployed in Norway grew to six battalions, and two regimental headquarters were formed to provide standardized command:

Polizei-Regiment "Nord-Norwegen" (became *Polizei-Regiment 26* in 1942)
- *I. Bataillon* (*Polizei-Bataillon 255*)
- *II. Bataillon* (*Polizei-Bataillon 256*)
- *III. Bataillon* (*Polizei-Bataillon 251*)

Polizei-Regiment Süd-Norwegen (became *Polizei-Regiment 27* in 1942)
- *I. Bataillon* (*Polizei-Bataillon 3*)
- *II. Bataillon* (*Polizei-Bataillon 9* later *252*)
- *III. Bataillon* (*Polizei-Bataillon 105* later *253*)

In the Soviet Union, 13 police battalions in rotation were initially concentrated under regimental headquarters assigned to the various army groups:

Heeresgruppe "Nord":	*Polizei-Regiment "Nord"* (FPNr. 38 968)
207. Sicherungs-Division	*Reserve-Polizei-Bataillon 22*
281. Sicherungs-Division	*Reserve-Polizei-Bataillon 53*
285. Sicherungs-Division	*Polizei-Bataillon 319*
Heeresgruppe "Mitte":	*Polizei-Regiment "Mitte"* (FPNr. 42 982)
221. Sicherungs-Division	*Polizei-Bataillon 30*
286. Sicherungs-Division	*Polizei-Bataillon 316*
403. Sicherungs-Division	*Polizei-Bataillon 322*
Heeresgruppe "Süd"	*Polizei-Regiment "Süd"* (FPNr. 36 524)
213. Sicherungs-Division	*Reserve-Polizei-Bataillon 45*
444. Sicherungs-Division	*Polizei-Bataillon 303*
454. Sicherungs-Division	*Polizei-Bataillon 314*
	Polizei-Regiment "z.b.V." (FPNr. 44 870)
	Polizei-Bataillon 304
	Polizei-Bataillon 315
	Polizei-Bataillon 320

Sicherheitspolizei Einsatzgruppen: *Reserve-Polizei-Bataillon* 9 then *Polizei-Bataillon* 3.

With German units hard pressed following the Red Army's winter offensive, in December 1941 the battalions of *Polizei-Regimenter "Nord"* and *"Mitte"* were sent to the front.[30]

In Action 1942

The training given to members of the police force had proven inadequate both for the spreading partisan war in the Soviet Union and the extremely costly front line deployments, and consequently the Commander of the *Ordnungspolizei* amended the manuals and on 16 January 1942 issued the "*Guidelines for Combat Training of the Self-Contained Units of the Ordnungspolizei for the East*." The training given to members of the police force was to become more specific and make the police battalions capable of employment against the "*treacherous Russian foe*." The men were to be instilled with an "*unconditional, tough fighting spirit, which is to be augmented by the ability to adapt to any situation and military skills, especially the ability to use all existing weapons. Those officers and NCOs without combat experience must be instilled with a sound faculty of imagination in the nature of this unconditional life and death struggle. (...) The training must be structured so that after a certain time the fighter is fully familiarized with all possible situations and surprises and mentally prepared for the unique conditions in the east.*"

These pithy sentences show just how poorly the police battalions had been prepared for the imminent operations in the east as well as in Southern Europe, and the improvised means with which an attempt was made to rectify the situation. In addition to its previous responsibilities, in 1942 the *Ordnungspolizei* was also given an increasing number of economic tasks. And so the collection of agricultural products and the procurement of labor forces—so-called "*Ostarbeiter*"—grew steadily in importance.

From a political standpoint, the Wannsee Conference on 20 January 1942 and the decision to adopt a "final solution"

After the campaign in the Balkans in 1941, battalions of the Ordnungspolizei began serving in the areas recently incorporated into the Reich: Krain, Southern Styria, and Carinthia...

...armed with carbines, members of the police patrol the mountains of the southeastern region. It was not until after the invasion of the Soviet Union that the (communist) partisan movement began to grow.

It soon became apparent that motorized, highly-mobile troops were indispensable—at least for actively engaging the partisans. Particularly successful were the police tank companies, which began appearing in the summer of 1942. As a rule these units were equipped with French or Italian vehicles.

to the Jewish question represented a special starting point for the *Ordnungspolizei*. Approximately 180,000 Jews from the German Reich were to be deported to the *Generalgouvernement* or to Theresienstadt.

To create space for this, large elements of the Jewish population—living mainly in the Warsaw ghetto—were murdered in Auschwitz and Belzec.[31] At the end of April 1942 Himmler announced his General Plan "East," which called for at least part of the non-German population of the *Generalgouvernement* (for example, in the Zamosc area) to be depopulated and the area made available for German settlers. The ensuing transports were almost all carried out by the *Ordnungspolizei*.

As a result of transfers to the *SS-Polizei-Division*, which suffered heavy casualties in the constant fierce fighting, and the transfers of personnel to act as core personnel in the numerous foreign *Schutzmannschafts-Bataillone* then being established, in February 1942 the *Ordnungspolizei* had 82 police battalions. These are listed below according to their home bases:

Berlin (WK III)	*Polizei-Bataillone 2, 3, 6, 8, 9,* and *10*
Wehrkreis I	*Polizei-Bataillone 11* and *13*
Wehrkreis II	*Polizei-Bataillon 22*
Wehrkreis III	*Polizei-Bataillone 32* and *33*
Wehrkreis IV	*Polizei-Bataillone 41-45*
Wehrkreis V	*Polizei-Bataillone 51, 53* and *56*
Wehrkreis VI	*Polizei-Bataillone 61-69*
Wehrkreis VII	*Polizei-Bataillone 72* and *74*
Wehrkreis VIII	*Polizei-Bataillone 81-85*
Wehrkreis IX	*Polizei-Bataillone 91* and *93*
Wehrkreis X	*Polizei-Bataillone 101-105*
Wehrkreis XI	*Polizei-Bataillone 111* and *112*
Wehrkreis XII	*Polizei-Bataillone 121-123*
Wehrkreis XIII	*Polizei-Bataillone 131-134*
Wehrkreis XVII	*Polizei-Bataillone 171* and *172*
Wehrkreis XVIII	*Polizei-Bataillone 251-256* and *301-325*

There was another front line deployment for the *Ordnungspolizei* at the end of February 1942. *Bataillone 56, 121, 305, 306*, and *310* were transferred to *Polizei-Kampfgruppe "Jeckeln"* in Siverskaya, mainly by air, relieving elements of the *58. Infanterie-Division*, which were withdrawn from the siege ring around Leningrad near Pushkin.[32]

On 9 July 1942 the Chief of German Police ordered the approximately 82 independent battalions combined into a total of 28 regiments. This measure was not carried out to create more powerful units; instead, it was purely an administrative restructuring. As before, the individual battalions were deployed separately—in some cases far apart—and tactical control by the regimental headquarters was impossible. As an example, two battalions of *SS-Polizei-Regiment 1* were deployed in the Soviet Union and one in Slovenia.

Police units saw further action at the front in late 1942, especially with *Heeresgruppe "Süd"* (Army Group South). In January 1943, between the Don and Donets Rivers, *Polizei-Regimenter 6, 8, 14*, and *15* were all but wiped out.[33] This was due to inadequate armaments, lack of front line experience on the part of NCOs and officers, and the Soviets' marked superiority in winter warfare.

The Deployment of SS Police Regiments in 1942
Legend: 1, 2, 3 = SS-Polizei-Regiment 1, 2, 3

In Action 1943

The year 1943 was marked by the defeat at Stalingrad and the near collapse of the entire southern front, and the end of the *Deutsche Afrika-Korps* in Tunis. The *Ordnungspolizei*'s involvement was limited to the four units named above with about 10,000 men.

In order to provide somewhat trained personnel to help make good the losses suffered by units of the *Waffen-SS* and create new formations, at the beginning of the year the *Ordnungspolizei* released about 7,500 police—to the *SS-Panzer-Grenadier-Division "Götz von Berlichingen,"* for example—and in return received the same number of recruits from *Waffen-SS* contingents.

On 24 February the police regiments were renamed SS police regiments (*SS-Polizei-Regimenter*). This decision by Himmler, justified as "*recognition of your especially brave and successful actions,*" had several motives. On one hand, it was a response to the increasingly difficult actions against the partisans and front line operations against the Red Army, while on the other it enabled Himmler to further merge the SS and the police.[34] Beyond that, it can be seen as a measure to fool enemy intelligence, making good the loss of the *6. Armee* at Stalingrad with new SS regiments.

As well, seven *Polizei-Schützen-Regimenter* (police rifle regiments) were formed effective 29 March 1943. Only the first battalion of each regiment consisted of German police members, while the second and third battalions were made up of about 7,000 foreign volunteers—*Schutzmannschaften*. This was an effort by the *Ordnungspolizei* to at least nominally make good its own losses in the short term.

In May 1943 more than 63,000 members of the *Ordnungspolizei* were deployed outside the Reich:

Generalgouvernement	11,400 men of the *Ordnungspolizei* 2,200 men of the *Sicherheitspolizei*
Senior SS and Police Commander "Russia North"	4,083 men of the *Ordnungspolizei* 800 men of the *Sicherheitspolizei*
Senior SS and Police Commander "Russia Center"	7,000 men of the *Ordnungspolizei* 750 men of the *Sicherheitspolizei*
Senior SS and Police Commander "Russia South"	12,900 men of the *Ordnungspolizei* 2,000 men of the *Sicherheitspolizei*
France	2,000 men[35]
Finland	2,500 men[36]
With eight army security divisions	3,200 men

"Protectorate of Bohemia and Moravia"	in total approx.
Reichskommissariat for the Occupied Netherlands	20,000 men of the
South Styria/South Carinthia	*Ordnungspolizei*

In April-May 1943 the Warsaw ghetto was liquidated as part of the final solution in the *Generalgouvernement*. The Jewish inhabitants resisted with force. Among the units committed to put down the uprising was *SS-Polizei-Regiment 22*.The Minsk ghetto was liquidated in September 1943, and the ghettos in Riga, Kaunas, and Vilna in November. Approximately 50,000 Jews were sent to labor camps in Estonia and Latvia. Not inconsiderable contingents from the *Ordnungspolizei* took part in these actions.

As well, in autumn 1943 various units again saw front line action as part of the *Polizei-Kampfgruppen "von Gottberg"* and *"Jeckeln"* (police battle groups) during the fierce fighting at Nevel. The two battle groups were organized as follows:

Polizei-Kampfgruppe "von Gottberg"
- *SS-Polizei-Regiment 2*
- *SS-Polizei-Regiment 13* (less II. Btl.)
- *SS-Polizei-Regiment 24* (less III. Btl.)
- *1. /9/ /12. Polizei-Panzer-Kompanie*

Polizei-Kampfgruppe "Jeckeln"
Sicherungs-Regiment 113 with
- *III./SS-Polizei-Regiment 9*

Sicherungs-Regiment 773
Polizei-Regiment 1 "Riga"

After four regiments were disbanded at the beginning of the year following the winter battles, at the end of 1943 the *Ordnungspolizei* still boasted 32 regiments,[38] which were deployed as follows:[39]

13 in action in the USSR
5 in France, Norway, and the Netherlands as occupation troops
5 in Serbia, Slovenia, Greece, and Italy as occupation troops
6 in the *Generalgouvernement* as occupation troops
2 in the "Protectorate of Bohemia and Moravia" as occupation troops, 1 being reformed at its home base

The most prominent new formation was *SS-Polizei-Regiment "Bozen"* from South Tyrol, which was employed in Italy.

For some there were Iron Crosses…

…for others wooden crosses.

The Deployment of SS Police Regiments in 1943
Legend: 1, 2, 3 = SS-Polizei-Regiment 1, 2, 3

Operational History 1944

The year 1944 saw the beginning of the collapse of the German Reich. The Soviet winter offensive brought fierce fighting to the entire Eastern Front, but in the spring the *Wehrmacht* managed to stabilize the situation. Further police battle groups were formed during the Soviet summer offensive. They tried to reach East Prussia, at times heavily engaged. The main battle groups were:

Polizei-Kampfgruppe "von Gottberg"
- *SS-Polizei-Regiment 2*
- *SS-Polizei-Regiment 17*
- *SS-Polizei-Regiment 22*
- *Polizei-Schützen-Regiment 31*
- *Polizei-Schützen-Regiment 36*

Polizei-Kampfgruppe "Jeckeln"
- *SS-Polizei-Regiment 9*
- *Polizei-Kampfgruppe "Krukenberg"*
- *Polizei-Kampfgruppe "Knappe"*
- *Polizei-Kampfgruppe "Osis"*[42]

At the beginning of August 1944 *SS-Gruppenführer und Generalleutnant der Polizei* von Gottberg assumed command of a *Korpsabteilung* (corps detachment). The C.O. of *SS-Polizei-Regiment 2* replaced him as commander of the battle group, now designated *Polizei-Brigade "Anhalt."* He was in turn replaced by the commander of *SS-Polizei-Regiment 31* in October, and the unit was renamed *Polizei-Brigade "Hannibal."*

Polizei-Brigade "Anhalt" (later *"Hannibal*)
- *SS-Polizei-Regiment 2*
- *SS-Polizei-Regiment 4* (less II. Btl.)
- *SS-Polizei-Regiment 17* (I. Btl. only)
- *Polizei-Schützen-Regiment 31*
- *Polizei-Schützen-Regiment34* (I. Btl. only)

In the *Generalgouvernement*, the evacuation of the labor and concentration camps before the advancing Red Army began at the end of July 1944. The Lodz ghetto, with its approximately 80,000 Jews, was liquidated at the end of August. In September deportation trains carrying Slovakian Jews began arriving in the *Generalgouvernement*. For the 11 *SS-Polizei-* and *Polizei-Schützen-Regimenter* deployed in the Soviet Union, the end came in the late summer of 1944 after fierce fighting with partisans and regular enemy troops; shattered, the units were disbanded. As a result, at the end of 1944 the *Ordnungspolizei* had left about 24 regiments, deployed as follows:[43]

3 combined as *Polizei-Kampfgruppe "Hannibal"* in East Prussia
3 in Norway and the Netherlands as occupation troops
12 in Slovenia and Italy as occupation troops
4 in the *Generalgouvernement* as occupation troops
1 in the "Protectorate of Bohemia and Moravia" as occupation troops
1 being reformed in Upper Silesia

The Deployment of SS Police Regiments in 1944
Legend: 1, 2, 3 = SS-Polizei-Regiment 1, 2, 3

In Action 1945

At the beginning of 1945, *Polizei-Brigade "Wirth"* was formed using elements of the disbanded police regiments and the remnants of *SS-Polizei-Regimenter 1* and *2*. In mid-March 1945 the newly-established *SS-Polizei-Regimenter 29* and *30*, together with *SS-Polizei-Regiment 14*, formed the *35. SS-Polizei-Division* on the Oder Front. In April 1945, with a strength of about 6,500 men, it was transferred to the *Waffen-SS*.[44] In February, *SS-Polizei-Regiment 8* and the newly-established *Polizei-Regiment 50* formed the *1. Polizei-Jäger-Brigade* within the *Oder-Korps*, and at the same time the *SS-Polizei-Regiment "Brixen"* was sent to the *31. SS-Freiwilligen-Grenadier-Division* in Silesia.

While the units stationed in the south and southeast of Europe attempted to reach the borders of Austria, on the Eastern Front the SS police regiments were engaged in fierce fighting against the Red Army. The units based in Norway and the Netherlands, on the other hand, became POWs of the British without suffering serious casualties.

At war's end the strength of the SS police regiments—including the members of the *35. SS-Polizei-Division* attached to the *Waffen-SS*—stood at about 40,000 men. The members of the *Ordnungspolizei* serving in the regiments had thus dropped by about 1/3 in the previous two years. In addition to the heavy losses in killed,[45] wounded, and missing during 1944, additional members were detached to divisions of the *Waffen-SS* during the lead-up to the Ardennes offensive in late 1944, and also in the spring of 1945 for the Lake Balaton offensive.

May 8, 1945, ended the activities of the SS police regiments, whose deployments and roles must be viewed differently:

1. With respect to the guarding of objects and installations in the occupied western territories, the police units were able to successfully carry out this mission. In southeastern and eastern Europe the units were mostly overextended, and their operational capabilities were seriously degraded in active service because of the age structure and inadequate training and armaments.

2. In special actions against the unarmed (e.g. resettlement, guarding, and liquidation[46] of undesirable groups of people), with few exceptions the performance of the *Ordnungspolizei* lived up to the expectations of the state.

3. In front line operations in the winter of 1941/42 and 1942/43, in autumn 1943, in summer 1944, and in early 1945, the police battalions and SS police regiments represented one of the last reserves. As a rule, the units were unable to carry out the missions assigned to them because of shortcomings in training and command, lack of tactical experience in battle, and poor or inadequate supporting weapons.

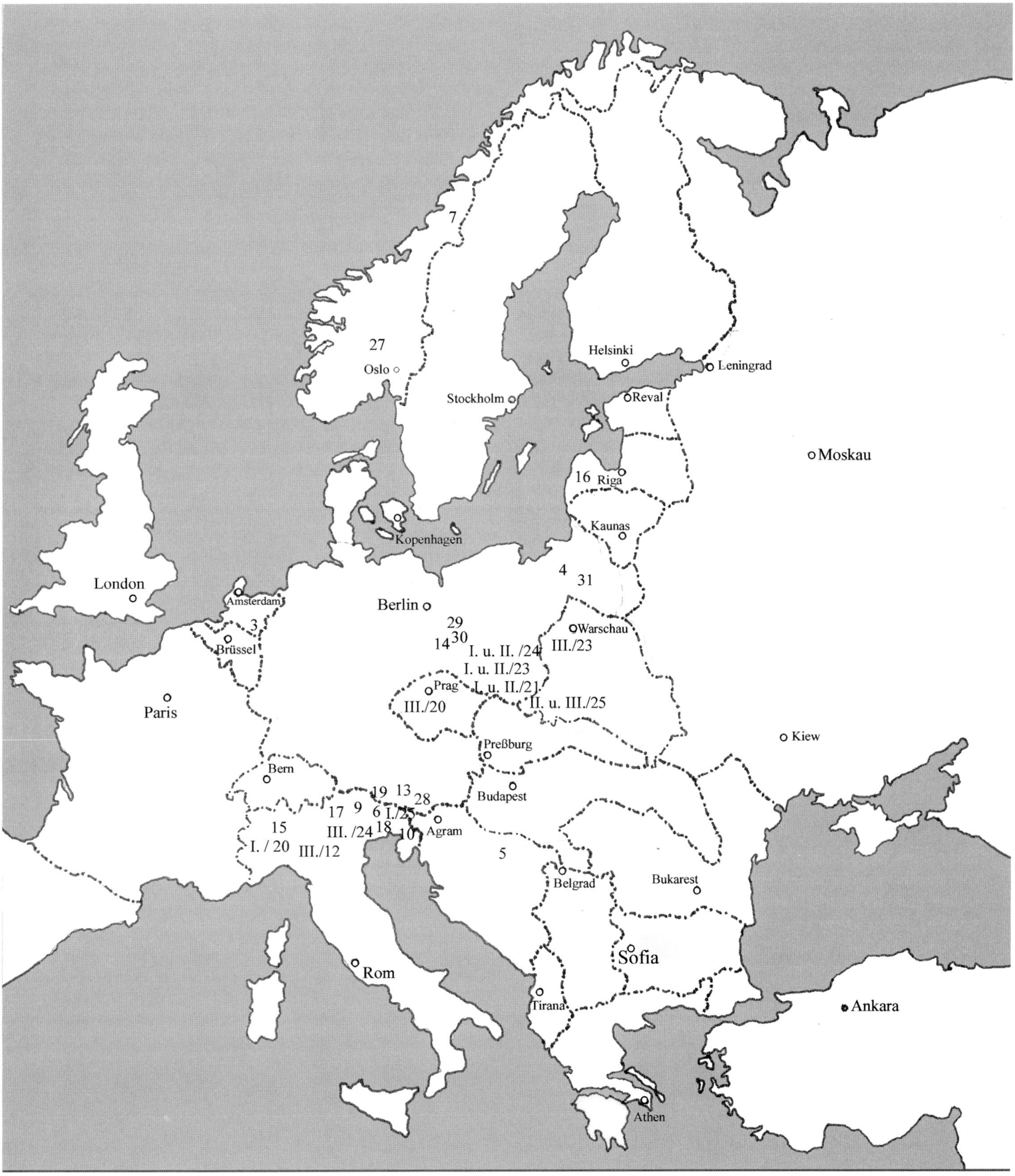

The Deployment of SS Police Regiments in 1945
Legend: 1, 2, 3 = SS-Polizei-Regiment 1, 2, 3

The retreat in 1945 – German police and civilians flee before Tito partisans in the Balkans.

Histories of the Units

The *Polizei-Bataillone*

This chapter provides a chronological listing of the individual police battalions and their employment until formation of the police regiments in 1942. The subsequent histories of these units may be found in the following chapter on the *SS-Polizei-Regimenter*.

At the end of September 1939 the battalions were given numbers which consisted of two parts: the first or first two numbers identified the *Wehrkreis* in which the battalion was established, while the last number was the sequential number of the battalion formed there. An exception to this rule was *Wehrkreis III* in Berlin. The numbers given to its first battalions contained no reference to the *Wehrkreis*. Not until the *Wehrkreis*' 11th, 12th, and 13th battalions were formed was the Arabic number 3 added to the battalion number to differentiate them from those of *Wehrkreis I* in Königsberg.

For deployments outside the borders of the German Reich, the police battalions and later the SS police regiments were assigned a *Feldpostnummer* (field postal number)—the exceptions being the units in the "Protectorate of Bohemia and Moravia" and in the *Generalgouvernement*.

Identification of the battalions as *Polizei-Bataillone* and *Reserve-Polizei-Bataillone* was determined by the personnel composition of the units. Battalions made up primarily of active police officers were classed as *Polizei-Bataillone*, while those made up mainly of police reservists were designated *Reserve-Polizei-Bataillone*. Later in the war the units often became visibly mixed as a result of mergers or transfers. Where another location is not specified, battalions were established in the city/town containing the *Wehrkreis*' seat of government.

Wehrkreis Berlin (III)

Polizei-Bataillon 1 (FPNr. 35 937) was created in Poland in September 1939 through the renaming of *Polizei-Bataillon I/5*. In autumn 1939 the unit became part of the *Polizei-Division*, resulting in its disbandment.

Reserve-Polizei-Bataillon 2 (FPNr. 31 274 + 40 848) was created in Poland at the end of September 1939 through the renaming of *Polizei-Bataillon I/6*. In June 1940 the battalion was transferred to Kongsvinger (Norway) and remained there until May 1942. As part of the restructuring of the *Ordnungspolizei* into *Polizei-Regimenter*, in June 1942 the battalion was sent to the Senior SS and Police Commander "Russia North" and became ***I./Polizei-Regiment 1***.

Polizei-Bataillon 3 (FPNr. 36 381) was created in Poland at the end of September 1939 through the renaming of *Polizei-Bataillon II/6*. The battalion was transferred to Trondheim (Norway) in May 1940, and in April 1942 it went to the Soviet Union, where it relieved *Reserve-Polizei-Bataillon 9*, which was attached to the *Einsatzgruppen* of the *Sicherheitspolizei*. The companies were attached to the following *Einsatzgruppen*

1. Kompanie to *Einsatzgruppe B*
2. Kompanie to *Einsatzgruppe C*
3. Kompanie to *Einsatzgruppe D*
4. Kompanie to *Einsatzgruppe A*

and took part in numerous mass executions in the Soviet Union. Effective 9 July 1942 the battalion became ***II./Polizei-Regiment 1***.

Polizei-Bataillon 4 (FPNr. 26 800) was created in Poland at the end of September 1939 through the renaming of *Polizei-Bataillon III/6*. Used in the formation of the *Polizei-Division*, it was disbanded in autumn 1939.

Polizei-Bataillon 5 (FPNr. 36 187) was also in Poland at the end of September 1939, and in September 1939 it was integrated into the *Polizei-Division* and disbanded.

Polizei-Bataillon 6 (FPNr. 03 316) was created in Poland in September 1939 through the renaming of *Polizei-Bataillon II/5*.[47] From November 1939 to late summer 1940 it was employed as *Polizei-Bataillon "Warschau I"* of the *Polizei-Regiment "Warschau."* Transferred to its home base of Berlin, in April 1941 it was sent back to the *Generalgouvernement* in the Radom area. Assigned to the Senior SS and Police Commander "Russia Center," it was later attached to *Polizei-Regiment "Mitte."* In July 1942 it formed ***I./Polizei-Regiment 13***.

Polizei-Bataillon 7 was not established.

Polizei-Bataillon 8 was established at the end of September 1939, and in November 1939 it formed *Polizei-Bataillon "Warschau II"* of the *Polizei-Regiment "Warschau."* The unit was transferred back to its home base in Berlin in autumn 1940, and from there to Upper Krain in summer 1941. The battalion was disbanded in mid-April 1942 and its personnel assigned to other police units.

Reserve-Polizei-Bataillon 9 (FPNr. 38 393 and 32 850) was established at the end of September 1939, and was stationed in Oslo from June 1940 to April 1941. For the war in Russia a fourth company was formed, and the battalion was distributed among the *Einsatzgruppen* of the *Sicherheitspolizei*:

1. Kompanie	*Einsatzgruppe "A" (Heeresgruppe "Nord")*
2. Kompanie	*Einsatzgruppe "B" (Heeresgruppe "Mitte")*
3. Kompanie	*Einsatzgruppe "C" (Heeresgruppe "Süd")*
4. Kompanie	*Einsatzgruppe "D" (11. Armee)*

The battalion's *1. Kompanie* was deployed mainly in the Baltic States, and took part in mass executions in Hochwald/Bikernieki, near Riga (Latvia), in July/August 1941, and in Krasnogvardeysk (northern Russia) in September. The *2. Kompanie* was in White Russia—at times attached to the *221. Sicherungs-Division*—and participated in shootings in various locations, including Mogilev Minsk, Rudnya, and Kauen. The *3. Kompanie* was deployed in Krivoy Rog, Dnepropetrovsk, and Zaporozhye, and the *4. Kompanie* in the Caucasus. *Reserve-Polizei-Bataillon 9* assembled in April 1942 and moved via Mogilev, Zamosc, and Zakopane to Iglau. From there, in July 1942 it was sent back to Norway to guard the Norwegian-Swedish border. At the same time it became ***III./Polizei-Regiment 27***.

Polizei-Bataillon 10 was established at the end of September 1939 and was in Warsaw from December. Effective 1 March 1942 the battalion was ordered back to Berlin, and a short time later was transferred to the Upper Krain, in the area between Laibach and Kranj. There the battalion became ***III./SS-Polizei-Regiment 1*** in July 1942.

Wehrkreis I (Königsberg)

Reserve-Polizei-Bataillon 11 (FPNr. 47 450), established at the end of September 1939, was in Pultusk[48] in autumn. In November 1939 it was sent to Ostrov, 40 kilometers away, to shoot Polish civilians. After the invasion of the Soviet Union, at the beginning of July 1941 it was attached to the Senior SS and Police Commander "Russia North." Its duties included guarding the Kauen ghetto. In mid-October 1941 elements of the battalion, along with Lithuanian auxiliary police, moved to Smolevichi, about 28 km away (40 km east of Minsk). There, by order of the *707. Infanterie-Division*, it sealed off the area while the Lithuanian volunteers killed every Jew in the city. The same thing was repeated in Slutsk (about 100 km south of Minsk) in cooperation with an *Einsatzkommando* of the *Sicherheitspolizei*. Approximately 300 Jews were killed. The killings continued into December 1941 in Minsk, Rudensk (approx. 40 km SE of Minsk), Uzjany (approx. 130 km NE of Kauen), and Smilovichi (approx. 40 km SE of Minsk). Bolstered by the Lithuanian auxiliary police, the battalion executed mainly Jews, prisoners of war, and (suspected) partisans. In January 1942 two companies were sent to the front in the Velikiye Luki—Nevel and Toropets areas, while the third company remained in the Kauen area. The battalion reassembled in Kauen in May, and in July 1942 it became ***I./Polizei-Regiment 2*** in Tilsit.

Reserve-Polizei-Bataillon 12 was established in September 1939; however, a short time later it was assigned to the *Polizei-Division* then being established.

Reserve-Polizei-Bataillon 13 was established in Schröttersburg at the beginning of 1940, and until the start of the war with Russia it was deployed in *Wehrkreis XX* (Danzig - West Prussia), former Polish territories. Its duties there included guarding the Plock ghetto, and it participated in the shooting of many Jews and Poles. Assigned to the Senior SS and Police Commander "Russia North" in July 1941, from 2 June elements of the battalion took part in mass execution of Jews and communists in the Libau – Priekule – Aipute – Skeden – Ventspils area. In July1942 it became ***II./Polizei-Regiment 2*** in Tilsit.

Wehrkreis II (Stettin)

Polizei-Bataillon 21 was established at the end of September 1939, and for a time was deployed in the *Generalgouvernement*. Assigned to the Senior SS and Police Commander "Russia North" in July 1941, in December the battalion participated in the shooting of as many as 25,000 Jews in the Rumbuli Forest near Riga (Latvia). The battalion was subsequently disbanded.

Reserve-Polizei-Bataillon 22 (FPNr. 20 525 + 47 348) was established at the end of September 1939, and in autumn was located in the *Generalgouvernement*. In 1940 it was used to guard a camp near Thorn which held up to 20,000 prisoners. Many Jews and Poles were executed there. Ordered back to Stettin, the battalion was attached to *Polizei-Regiment "Nord"* for the campaign against Russia. The battalion's three companies were deployed separately. The *1. Kompanie* was deployed in Frauenburg and Goldingen (Latvia) for a time, while the *2. Kompanie* was employed in Riga and the *3. Kompanie* in Mitau. In December 1941 the battalion was assembled in Riga to provide security for extensive mass executions. In January 1942 the battalion again saw action at the front as part of *Polizei-Regiment "Nord."* The regiment was attached to the *81. Infanterie-Division*, part of the *X. Armee-Korps*, between Lake Ilmen and Staraya Russa. In July 1942 it became ***III./Polizei-Regiment 2***.

Wehrkreis III (Berlin)

Reserve-Polizei-Bataillon 31 was established at the beginning of 1940 and was stationed in Litzmannstadt for a short time, helping guard the ghetto there. In 1940 the unit was disbanded.

Reserve-Polizei-Bataillon 32 was established at the beginning of 1940, and in the spring of 1941 it was in the "Protectorate of Bohemia and Moravia," attached to *Polizei-Regiment "Böhmen"* as *Polizei-Bataillon "Klattau."* In

Alexander Zahharov, an ethnic German from Estonia, and other members of Polizei-Bataillon "Ostland" in Frankfurt/Oder in August 1941. In October 1941 the unit became Reserve-Polizei-Bataillon 33.

summer 1941 it was transferred to the *Generalgouvernement* in preparation for deployment to Russia. There it was attached to *Polizei-Regiment "Mitte"* for a time. In September 1941 it took part in executions in Lvov, and at the end of December it marched into the Minsk area. In July 1942 it became ***I./ Polizei-Regiment 21***.

Reserve-Polizei-Bataillon 33 (FPNr. 47 769) was created in October 1941 through the renaming of *Reserve-Polizei-Bataillon "Ostland,"* which had been formed in summer 1941 using Baltic-German volunteers from Estonia. In spring 1942 the unit was transferred into the *Generalkommissariat "Ukraine"* and was employed in the Rovno area. The battalion's duties there included guarding the local ghetto. After use in Kiev the battalion was disbanded in the summer of 1942. Alexander Zahharov recalled:

"I was born on 26 October 1916, the son of a Russian officer and a German mother, and lived in Estonia. As a result of the Hitler-Stalin Pact, while at work at the trust company I was suddenly arrested and, under cover of night, expelled from Estonia as an ethnic German! I initially lived in a refugee and resettlement camp in Mainfranken, and in July 1941 I volunteered for military service along with other ethnic Germans. We had been promised that we would be sent to Estonia to fight the remnants of the Red Army there. Then in August 1941 we were sent to Polizei-Bataillon 'Ostland' in Frankfurt/Oder. In October 1941, however, against our wishes we were sent to the Kiev area instead of to Estonia. There we were assigned to various police precincts. I was attached to the 5th Precinct. We carried out normal police duties there; for example, one time we were notified that a Ukrainian family was regularly selling items of clothing at the market which allegedly had been taken from people who were dead and buried. Things like that happened then. In July 1942 the battalion was disbanded and most of us were transferred to the Estonian SS Legion."

Wehrkreis IV (Dresden)

Reserve-Polizei-Bataillon 41 (FPNr. 32 649) was created from *Polizei-Bataillon I/3* at the end of September 1939 and garrisoned in Leipzig. The unit was assigned to *Wehrkreis XXI* (Warthe District) in Posen under the commander of the *Ordnungspolizei*. During this deployment the battalion executed Poles in Litzmannstadt. Sent back to Leipzig in mid-January 1940, from June to December 1940 the unit was attached to the commander of the *Ordnungspolizei* in the Netherlands. The battalion was back at its garrison from January to March 1941, and from April 1941 to April 1942 it was again deployed in *Wehrkreis XXI* in the Posen – Krasnik area. Its duties included the resettlement of Poles into the *Generalgouvernement*.[49] In May 1942 it was sent into the Zamosc area. There, in July 1942, the battalion became ***I./ Polizei-Regiment 22***.

Reserve-Polizei-Bataillon 42 (FPNr. 31 338 + 03 634) was established in Poland from *Polizei-Bataillon IV/2* at the end of September 1939 and was later attached to *Polizei-Regiment "Radom."* Detachments were frequently sent to Litzmannstadt, Kutno, Posen, Krasnik, Trawniki, and the Zamosc region to execute Jews. Transferred to Arnhem in the Netherlands in mid-December 1940, the battalion was subsequently ordered back to its garrison in Dresden for reorganization. It was sent back to the Netherlands in summer 1941 and took up quarters in Eindhoven. Dispatched to the Senior SS and Police Commander "Russia North" in spring 1942, in July 1942 it became ***I./Polizei-Regiment 17***.

Reserve-Polizei-Bataillon 43 was established at the end of September 1939 and was transferred to Lublin in the *Generalgouvernement* in the autumn, and to Warsaw in December. The battalion was disbanded in 1940.

Reserve-Polizei-Bataillon 44 (FPNr. 39 202 and 33 345) was established in Leipzig in autumn 1939 for use in the *Generalgouvernement*. In November 1939 it took part in the shootings of about 80 Jews in Litzmannstadt. On 10 March 1942 the battalion was transferred back to its garrison in Dresden and then into the area southwest of Kranj, in the Upper Krain. It was active there from 27 December 1941 to 12 January 1942, including participation in a major anti-partisan operation between Laibach and Krain. In July 1942 it was assigned to Oslo and became ***IV./Polizei-Regiment 27***.

Reserve-Polizei-Bataillon 45 (FPNr. 37 718) was established in Aussig in 1940, largely with Sudeten-German volunteers, and was initially deployed in the *Generalgouvernement*. Attached to *Polizei-Regiment "Süd"* for the Russian campaign, between July and November it took part in the shooting of approximately 2,400 Jews at Berdichev, Chorol, Kiev, Shepetovka, and Vinnitsa in the Ukraine. In July 1942 it became ***I./Polizei-Regiment 10***.

Wehrkreis V (Stuttgart)

Polizei-Bataillon 51 (FPNr. 9 414) was established in September 1939, and that autumn was transferred to Pionki, near Radom, in the *Generalgouvernement*. In the summer of 1940 it marched into the Saverne area of Alsace ((NW of Strasbourg). In 1941 it was deployed to the "Protectorate of Bohemia and Moravia," and at the beginning of 1942 to Reichshof (Rzeszow), in the *Generalgouvernement*. In the spring of 1942 the battalion was sent to the Senior SS and Police Commander "Russia South" and in July was renamed ***I./Polizei-Regiment 14***.

***Polizei-Bataillon* 52** was established in Karlsruhe in September 1939, but soon afterwards it was assigned to the formation of the *Polizei-Division* and disbanded.

Reserve-Polizei-Bataillon 53 (FPNr. 39 947) was established in September 1939 and transferred to the "Protectorate of Bohemia and Moravia." In summer 1941 it became *I./Polizei-Regiment "Nord,"* and in January 1942 saw front line action at Staraya Russa, south of Lake Ilmen, as part of the *X. Armee-Korps*. In July 1942 the battalion became ***III./Polizei-Regiment 22*** and remained at the front line in Demyansk until transferred to Warsaw in September 1942.

Polizei-Bataillon 54 was established in September 1939. In June 1940 it was transferred to Strasbourg, in Alsace, and was disbanded soon afterwards.

Polizei-Bataillon 55 was established in September 1939 and transferred to Colmar. Like Bataillon 54, it was disbanded in the summer of 1940.

Polizei-Bataillon 56 (FPNr. 23 418) was established at the beginning of 1940 and assigned to the commander of the *Ordnungspolizei* in Prague. At the end of February 1942 the battalion was air-transported to *Polizei-Kampfgruppe "Jeckeln,"* which was to relieve the *58. Infanterie-Division* near Pushkin in the siege ring around Leningrad.[50] On 9 July 1942 the battalion was renamed ***I./Polizei-Regiment 16***.

Wehrkreis VI (Münster)

Reserve-Polizei-Bataillon 61 (FPNr. 34 383 and 06 545) was established in Poland at the end of September from *Polizei-Bataillon I/4* (garrison Dortmund). It was deployed to guard the Warsaw ghetto, in the course of which there were numerous shootings. It was also tasked with resettling Polish families into the *Generalgouvernement*. In the spring of 1941 the battalion was sent back to its garrison, where it remained until sent back to the *Generalgouvernement* in December. There, in June 1942 it shot 110 Jews as a reprisal for the murders of German policemen and members of the *Wehrmacht*. The battalion was subsequently transferred to the Senior SS and Police Commander "Russia North," relieved a police battalion in *Polizei-Regiment "Nord,"* and in July 1942 became ***I./Polizei-Regiment 9***.

Reserve-Polizei-Bataillon 62 (FPNr. 20 382 and 40 113) was established in Poland at the end of September 1939 from *Polizei-Bataillon V/1* (garrison Essen) and was attached to the commander of the *Ordnungspolizei* in Cracow. From February to September 1940 the battalion was stationed in Königshütte. Then it was transferred to the Lorient area of France, where it was assigned to guard units of *Organisation Todt* constructing the Atlantic Wall. In Dieppe in July 1942 it was renamed ***I./Polizei-Regiment 28 "Todt."*** In August 1942 the battalion helped repulse the Allied commando operation at Dieppe.

Reserve-Polizei-Bataillon 63 (FPNr. 04 703) was established in Poland in September 1939 from *Polizei-Bataillon II/1* (garrison Wuppertal), and in December 1939 it was integrated into *Polizei-Regiment "Krakau."* At the beginning of 1940 the battalion moved to Lorraine. It was attached to the Senior SS and Police Commander "West," and was stationed in the Calais – Lille – Douai – Arras area in northern France. Then, in September the battalion was transferred to Metz.[51] Assigned to Essen in August 1941, it was attached to the commander of the *Ordnungspolizei* in Münster. In March 1942 the unit was transferred to Den Haag (The Hague). There, in July 1942, it became ***III./Polizei-Regiment 14***.

Reserve-Polizei-Bataillon 64 (FPNr. 32 932 + 22 732) was established in Essen at the end of September 1939, and in October was transferred to Leslau for the formation of a fourth company. There the battalion was briefly split up. The *1.* and *3. Kompanie* were sent to Gotenhafen and placed under the commander of the *Ordnungspolizei* in Danzig. The battalion assembled in Graudenz in November 1939 and took part in the resettlement of Poles into the *Generalgouvernement.* At the end of May 1940 the battalion received orders to return to its garrison in Essen, where it was employed in air defense and patrol duties. At the end of July it was sent to Belgrade, where it was temporarily attached to *Einsatzgruppe "E."* It subsequently participated in actions against the Serbian *Chetniks* in the Uzice – Sabac – Klenac – Skela – Semlin area. It also participated in actions against Jews. On 26 September 1941, for example, it took part in the shooting of approximately 6,000 Jews as a reprisal for the murder of German soldiers in Sajmiste. In July 1942 the battalion became ***I./Polizei-Regiment 5***.

Reserve-Polizei-Bataillon 65 "Cholm" (FPNr. 38 608) was established in Recklinghausen in autumn 1939, and in May 1940 was transferred to the Netherlands. After deployment to Assen in November 1940, in December the battalion was ordered back to its garrison. At the end of May 1941 it was assigned to Heilsberg (East Prussia), from where the battalion marched via Tilsit into the Baltic States on 22 June 1941 as part of *Polizei-Regiment "Nord,"* which was attached to the *285. Sicherungs-Division.* Four days later the battalion took up quarters in Kauen and Schaulen and participated in the Lithuanian pogroms, initiated by the Germans, in Kauen, Schaulen, and Raseinen, and later in Pskov. Following the German advance, in September 1941 the battalion arrived in Luga, where its duties included guarding a camp for Soviet prisoners of war. In the course of the Soviet winter offensive, from January to May 1942 the battalion saw front line action near Cholm as part of *Kampfgruppe "Scherer."* At the beginning of June 1942 the battalion was transferred via Luga to Brunowiece, near Cracow. It subsequently took part in the liquidation of the Cracow ghetto as part of *Aktion "Reinhard"* and escorted transports taking Jews to Auschwitz and Belzec. It was renamed ***I./Polizei-Regiment 25*** in the Lublin area.

Reserve-Polizei-Bataillon 66 was established in Cologne at the beginning of 1940, and at the end of the year was transferred to Lorraine (France). At the beginning of August 1940 it was sent to Tilburg, in the Netherlands, and in December was transferred back to its garrison. Sent back to the Netherlands in May 1942, in July 1942 it was renamed ***I./Polizei-Regiment 3*** in The Hague.

Reserve-Polizei-Bataillon 67 was established in Essen in May 1940 and assigned to The Hague in the Netherlands. In February 1942 the battalion was ordered back to its garrison and from there was assigned to Lublin as ***II./Polizei-Regiment 25*** in July 1942.

Reserve-Polizei-Bataillon 68 was established in Cologne in June 1940 and sent to the commander of the *Ordnungspolizei* in The Hague. From 15 December 1940 to 23 April 1941 the battalion was located in Assen. It was then employed in Rotterdam until 10 July 1941, and finally in Amsterdam until the end of the war. It was renamed ***II./Polizei-Regiment 3*** there in July 1942.

Reserve-Polizei-Bataillon 69 (FPNr. 40 937) was established in Cologne in the summer of 1940 and transferred to The Hague in June. In June 1941 it was transferred to the *Generalgouvernement* for the impending invasion of the Soviet Union and expanded to five companies. In September 1941 these were committed separately—in some cases attached to the *Einsatzgruppen*:

1. Kompanie transferred to *Heeresgruppe "Süd,"* and for a time was stationed in Nikolayev and Vinnitsa as part of *Einsatzgruppe "D."*

2. Kompanie was also transferred to *Heeresgruppe "Süd,"* and was deployed in Kiev and Kharkov, as well as Poltava.

3. Kompanie operated within *Heeresgruppe "Mitte"* under *Einsatzkommando 7c* in Brest-Litovsk, Mogilev, Minsk, Slonim, Baranowice, and Smolensk.

4. Kompanie was located in Vilnius (Wilna) with *Heeresgruppe "Nord,"* and its duties included guarding the local ghetto. It also took part in the execution of Jews in Radoszkowicze, Luninecz, and Lachwa.

5. Kompanie was also attached to *Heeresgruppe "Nord,"* but in the Pskov – Luga area, and was employed in the siege line around Leningrad for a time.

In July 1942 it was renamed **III./Polizei-Regiment 17**.

Wehrkreis VII (Munich)

Polizei-Bataillon 71 (FPNr. 20 020) was created in Poland at the end of September 1939 from *Polizei-Bataillon V/2*, and a short time later was attached to *Polizei-Regiment "Radom."* Transferred to *Wehrkreis XX*, the battalion was disbanded in 1940.

Reserve-Polizei-Bataillon 72 was established in September 1939. Initially attached to *Polizei-Regiment "Radom"* in the *Generalgouvernement*, in April 1940 it formed *Polizei-Bataillon "Warschau III"* in *Polizei-Regiment "Warschau."* Ordered back to its garrison in November 1940, in April 1941 the battalion was transferred to Marburg, in Slovenia. There followed operations in the area Bled (German Veldes, approx. 50 km NW of Laibach) – Sostanj (German Schönstein, approx. 25 km NW of Cilli) – Trbovlje (German Trifail, approx. 20 km SW of Cilli) and Kamnik (German Stein, approx. 20 km N of Laibach). In July 1942 the battalion was in Veldes, where it became ***I./Panzer-Regiment 19***.

Reserve-Polizei-Bataillon 73 was established in autumn 1939 and transferred to Lublin in the *Generalgouvernement*. It was disbanded there in 1940.

Reserve-Polizei-Bataillon 74 (FPNr. 07 708) was formed in Augsburg at the beginning of 1940, and from June to October 1940 was stationed in Alsace (Strasbourg). It was subsequently transferred to Munich, and at the beginning of 1941 to the *Generalgouvernement*—in March 1941 it was attached to the commander of *Ordnungspolizei* in Cracow. In the summer of 1941 the battalion was sent to the Senior SS and Police Commander "Russia North," and in 1942 it became ***II./Polizei-Regiment 17***.

Wehrkreis VIII (Breslau)

Polizei-Bataillon 81 (FPNr. 16 695) was created at the end of September 1939 through the renaming of *Polizei-Bataillon IV/1* (garrison Beuthen) and was attached to *Polizei-Regiment "Warschau."* From 1940 until its disbandment in 1942 the battalion was stationed in Beuthen (Silesia), and then in Olmütz and Brünn in the "Protectorate of Bohemia and Moravia."

Reserve-Polizei-Bataillon 82 (FPNr. 37 330) was established in Kattowitz at the end of September 1939, and in the spring of 1940 it took part in the rounding up and imprisonment of Polish intellectuals (teachers, officials, doctors, etc.). In December 1940, in the Trzebina area (approx. 20 km NE of Auschwitz), the battalion participated in the deportation of Polish forced laborers to Germany and the guarding of Jewish ghettoes, including the one in Chrzanow (approx. 30 km NE of Auschwitz). In April 1941 it was attached to the Inspector of *Ordnungspolizei* Breslau, and in August, as part of *Polizei-Regiment "Süd,"* to the *454. Sicherungs-Division* in the Zhitomir region. In August 1941 it shot male members of the local Jewish population. In September 1941 the battalion was employed to track down Red Army stragglers. The battalion initially proceeded to Briansk via Kiev and then to Tula, approximately 280 km away. Sent to *Korück 532* at the end of 1941, the battalion was frequently employed in the Maloye Polpins area with *Polizei-Bataillon 309*. From 1 to 10 March 1942 the unit took part in "Operation Anton" in the Zhukovka – Staraya Lavshina area near Briansk. There were skirmishes with partisans near Kolovka on 2 April 1942, in which 15 partisans were shot and eight houses burned down. From mid-July 1942 the battalion was deployed in the Gremyach area (approx. 120 km SW of Briansk). There it became ***I./Polizei-Regiment 6***.

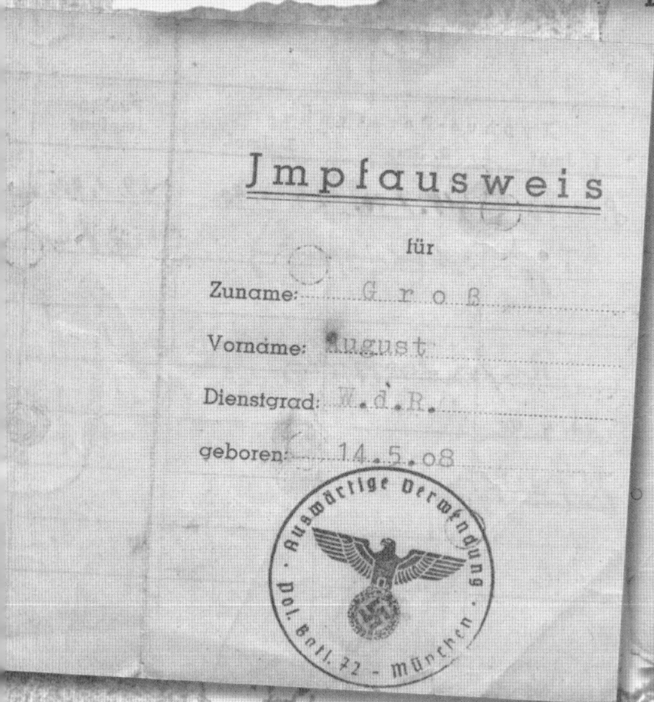

Jmpfausweis

für

Zuname: Groß

Vorname: August

Dienstgrad: W.d.R.

geboren: 14.5.08

Auswärtige Verwendung Pol. Batl. 72 - München

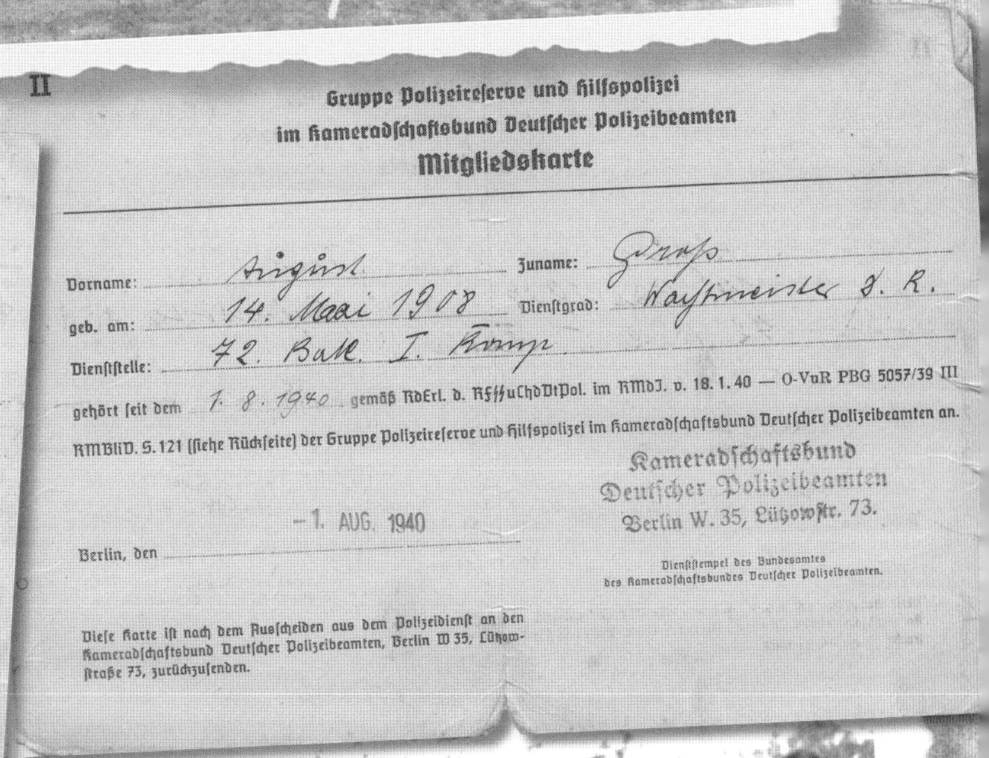

II

Gruppe Polizeireserve und Hilfspolizei
im Kameradschaftsbund Deutscher Polizeibeamten

Mitgliedskarte

Vorname: August Zuname: Groß

geb. am: 14. Mai 1908 Dienstgrad: Waffenmeister d. R.

Dienststelle: 72. Batl. I. Komp.

gehört seit dem 1. 8. 1940 gemäß RdErl. d. RFSSuChdDtPol. im RMdJ. v. 18. 1. 40 — O-VuR PBG 5057/39 III RMBliV. S. 121 (siehe Rückseite) der Gruppe Polizeireserve und Hilfspolizei im Kameradschaftsbund Deutscher Polizeibeamten an.

Berlin, den -1. AUG. 1940

Kameradschaftsbund Deutscher Polizeibeamten Berlin W. 35, Lützowstr. 73.

Dienststempel des Bundesamtes des Kameradschaftsbundes Deutscher Polizeibeamten.

Diese Karte ist nach dem Ausscheiden aus dem Polizeidienst an den Kameradschaftsbund Deutscher Polizeibeamten, Berlin W 35, Lützowstraße 73, zurückzusenden.

Police reservists and auxiliary police officials could join the Social Club of German Police Officials. Membership provided insurance in the event of incapacity or death due to accident or combat. The insurance benefit for a man killed in action was 500 RM, for accidental death 1,500 RM, and for invalids up to 2,250 RM.

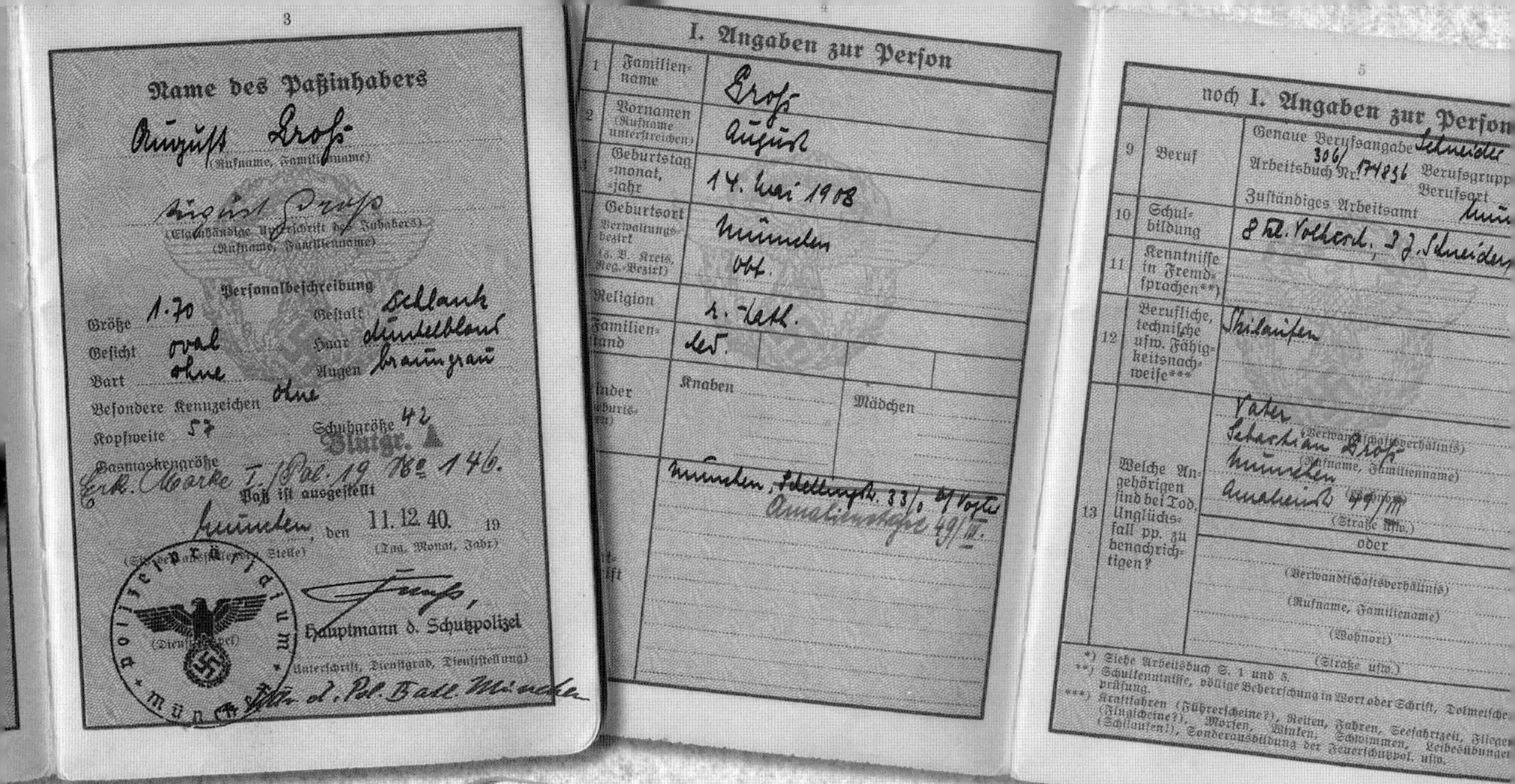

3

Name des Paßinhabers

August Groß

(Rufname, Familienname)

August Groß

(Eigenhändige Unterschrift des Inhabers) (Rufname, Familienname)

Personalbeschreibung

Größe 1.70 Gestalt schlank

Gesicht oval Haar dunkelblond

Bart ohne Augen braungrau

Besondere Kennzeichen ohne

Kopfweite 57 Schuhgröße 42

Blutgr. A

Gasmaskengröße

Erk. Marke I./Pol. 19 Nr. 146.

Paß ist ausgestellt

München, den 11.12.40. 19

(Ausstellende Stelle) (Tag, Monat, Jahr)

Hauptmann d. Schutzpolizei

Unterschrift, Dienstgrad, Dienststellung

Führer d. Pol. Batl. München

4

I. Angaben zur Person

1	Familienname	Groß
2	Vornamen (Rufname unterstreichen)	August
3	Geburtstag -monat, -jahr	14. Mai 1908
4	Geburtsort Verwaltungsbezirk (z. B. Kreis, Reg.-Bezirk)	München Obb.
	Religion	r. kath.
	Familienstand	led.
	Kinder	Knaben / Mädchen
	Anschrift	München, Schellingstr. 33/0 b/ Vogl; Amalienstraße 49/III

5

noch I. Angaben zur Person

9	Beruf	Genaue Berufsangabe Schneider; Arbeitsbuch Nr. 306/174836; Berufsgruppe; Berufsort; Zuständiges Arbeitsamt Mün
10	Schulbildung	8 Kl. Volksch., 3 J. Schneider
11	Kenntnisse in Fremdsprachen**)	
12	Berufliche, technische usw. Fähigkeitsnachweise***	Skilaufen
13	Welche Angehörigen sind bei Tod, Unglücksfall pp. zu benachrichtigen?	Vater (Verwandtschaftsverhältnis); Sebastian Groß (Rufname, Familienname); München (Wohnort); Amalienstr. 49/III (Straße usw.); oder; (Verwandtschaftsverhältnis); (Rufname, Familienname); (Wohnort); (Straße usw.)

*) Siehe Arbeitsbuch S. 1 und 5.
**) Schulkenntnisse, völlige Beherrschung in Wort oder Schrift, Dolmetscherprüfung.
***) Kraftfahren (Führerscheine?), Reiten, Fahren, Seefahrzeit, Flieger (Zeugnisse?), Morsen, Winken, Schwimmen, Leibesübungen (Skilaufen!), Sonderausbildung der Feuerschutzpol. usw.

August Groß joined the Munich Police Reserve on 1/9/1939, and from 5/10/39 to 16/1/43 served in Polizei-Bataillon 72. Transferred to the 17. SS-Panzergrenadier-Division "Götz von Berlichingen," on 19/3/45 he was captured by the Americans.

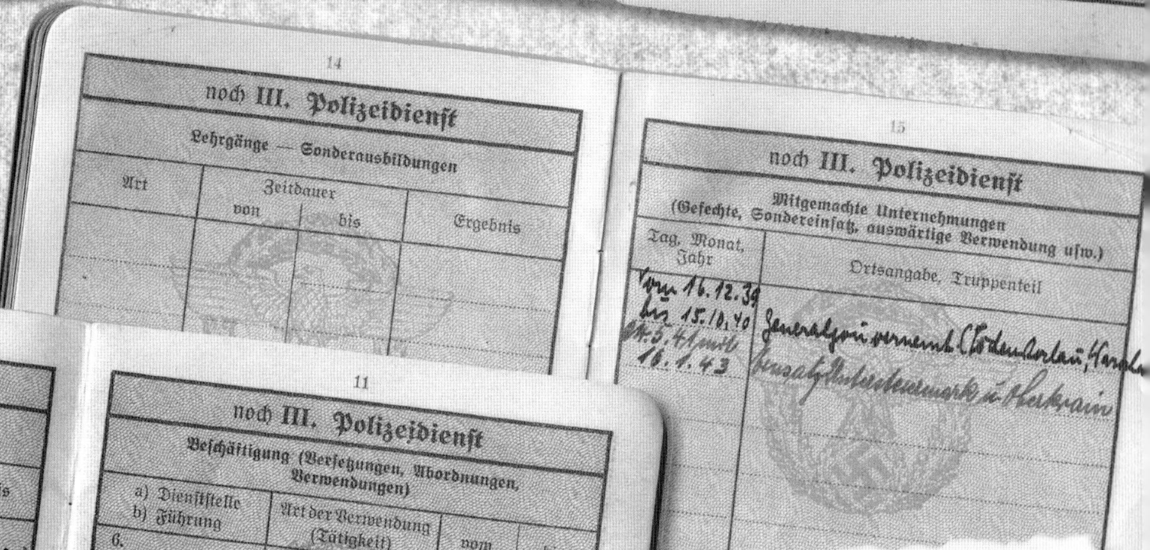

14

noch III. Polizeidienst

Lehrgänge — Sonderausbildungen

Art	Zeitdauer von	bis	Ergebnis

15

noch III. Polizeidienst

Mitgemachte Unternehmungen (Gefechte, Sondereinsatz, auswärtige Verwendung usw.)

Tag, Monat, Jahr	Ortsangabe, Truppenteil
vom 16.12.39 bis 15.10.40	Generalgouvernement (Lodenarlau, Krakau)
ab 5.41 mit 16.1.43	Ersatzeinheit Ostmark u. Ukraine

10

noch III. Polizeidienst

Beschäftigung (Versetzungen, Abordnungen, Verwendungen)

a) Dienststelle b) Führung	Art der Verwendung (Tätigkeit)	vom	bis
Pol.-Verw. Münch. Pol. 72	Truppendienst	1.9.39.	4.10.39.
Pol.-Verw. München Pol.-Batl. "Mü" (Süd) gut	abgeordnet zum Pol.-Batl. 72 Truppendienst	5.10.39	16.1.43

11

noch III. Polizeidienst

Beschäftigung (Versetzungen, Abordnungen, Verwendungen)

a) Dienststelle b) Führung	Art der Verwendung (Tätigkeit)	vom	bis
6. a) b)			
7. a) b)			
8. a) b)			
9. a) b)			
10. a) b)			

Reserve-Polizei-Bataillon 83 was established in Gleiwitz in autumn 1939, and in October 1941 was still attached to the commander of the *Ordnungspolizei* in Breslau. Transferred to the *Generalgouvernement*, it became ***I./Polizei-Regiment 24*** in Lvov in July 1942.

Reserve-Polizei-Bataillon 84 (FPNr. 35 103 and 35 206) was established in Beuhen in early 1940 using ethnic Germans from Silesia, and from April 1941 it was attached to the commander of the *Ordnungspolizei* in Prague. There it served as *Polizei-Bataillon "Holleschau,"* part of *Polizei-Regiment "Mähren."* In January 1942 the battalion was under the commander of the *Ordnungspolizei* in Cracow, and at the end of April 1942 it was airlifted to Krasnogvardeysk. As part of the *SS-Polizei-Division*, it saw action in Lyuban and at the Volkhov. In mid-June 1942 the battalion was relieved and transferred to Vyritsa. On 21 June 1942 the unit was disbanded and its remnants[52] incorporated into the *SS-Polizei-Division*.

Reserve-Polizei-Bataillon 85 (FPNr. 12 047) was established in Kattowitz in spring 1940 and was deployed in the *Generalgouvernement* until the beginning of 1942. Attached to *Polizei-Regiment "Mitte,"* the battalion moved into the Smolensk area. In July 1942 it was briefly transferred back to Kattowitz and was renamed ***II./Polizei-Regiment 13***.

Wehrkreis IX (Kassel)

Polizei-Bataillon 91 (FPNr. 33 747 and 13 683) was created in Poland at the end of September 1939 from *Polizei-Bataillon IV/6* and was attached to *Polizei-Regiment "Warschau."* In November 1940, 360 Jews were shot in Ostrov (approx. 80 km NE of Warsaw) in reprisal for an act of arson. Transferred to Norway in spring 1940, the battalion was stationed in Narvik until February 1941 and guarded the Swedish-Norwegian border. It was transferred back to Germany in preparation for the Russian campaign and later relieved a battalion of *Polizei-Regiment "Mitte."* Deployed in the Krynki area (approx. 40 km NE of Bialystok), it took part in the shooting of Jews in the local ghetto. In July 1942, in the Briansk – Chotimsk area in the *221. Sicherungs-Division*'s sector, it became ***I./Polizei-Regiment 8***.

Polizei-Bataillon 92 (FPNr. 00 869) was created in Poland in 1939 from *Polizei-Bataillon I/1* but was disbanded in 1940.

Reserve-Polizei-Bataillon 93 was established in Frankfurt/Main in autumn 1939 and was deployed in the Netherlands from June to December 1940. Sent back to Germany at the end of September 1941, it was detached to Radovjica (German Radmannsdorf, approx. 40 km NW of Laibach), in the Upper Krain. There was an execution of partisans (suspected) during operations in the Veldes area. From December 1941 to 12 January 1942 the battalion took part in a large-scale anti-partisan operation in Slovenia, together with *Polizei-Bataillone 44, 171, 181, 325*, and *Landesschützen-Bataillone 322* and *857*. In April 1942 the battalion was deployed to the border between the German and Italian zones of occupation in the Upper Krain. In June 1942 it was renamed ***III./Polizei-Regiment 24***.

Wehrkreis X (Hamburg)

Reserve-Polizei-Bataillon 101 (FPNr. 24 062) was created from *Polizei-Bataillon* I/2 in Poland at the end of September 1939 and was deployed in the Kielce area. Its duties there included searching for Polish Army stragglers, securing abandoned war materiel, and guarding a POW camp. The battalion returned to Hamburg in mid-December 1939 and relinquished about 100 of its career policemen for the formation of new units. They were replaced by reservists called up in autumn 1939. After renewed training, in May 1940 the battalion was transferred to the Warthe District. First deployed in Posen, from June 1940 it was active in Litzmannstadt and took part in resettlement actions. On 28 November 1940 the battalion assumed responsibility for guarding the Litzmannstadt ghetto. The battalion returned to Hamburg in May 1941 and was reorganized once more. All enlisted ranks who had been recruited before the war were assigned to other battalions being formed in the *Wehrkreis* and were replaced by new reservists. Beginning in October 1941, elements of the battalion took part in the deportation of Hamburg's Jews and gypsies. In June 1942 the unit was transferred back to the *Generalgouvernement*. It was sent to the Bilgoraj area (approx. 80 km S of Lublin) and attached to *Polizei-Regiment "Lublin."* In June 1942, now renamed ***III./Polizei-Regiment 25***, the battalion was transferred into the Radzyn – Lukow area (approx. 70 km N of Lublin). During the course of *Aktion "Reinhard,"* the battalion participated in the shooting of Jews in Jozefow (approx. 60 km SW of Lublin) on 13 July 1942 and near Lomazy (approx. 80 km NE of Lublin) on 19 August.

Reserve-Polizei-Bataillon 102 (FPNr. 27065 + 46 749) was created at the end of September 1939 in Poland through the renaming of *Polizei-Bataillon II/2*. In April 1941, after being employed in the Lubartow (approx. 25 km N of Lublin) – Kasnik (approx. 50 km SW of Lublin) area, the battalion was attached to the commander of *Ordnungspolizei* in Hamburg for reorganization. On 10 March 1942 *Reserve-Polizei-Bataillon 102* reinforced *Polizei-Kampfgruppe "Jeckeln"* in front of Leningrad, and there in July was renamed ***II./Polizei-Regiment 16***.

Polizei-Bataillon 103 (FPNr. 30 225) was created in Poland at the end of September 1939 through the renaming of *Polizei-Bataillon III/2* and was stationed in Posen. In May 1940 it was transferred back to Hamburg for reorganization. The battalion was renamed ***I./Polizei-Regiment 12*** in July 1942.

Polizei-Bataillon 104 was established in autumn 1939, and in January 1940 was transferred to Lublin. In the summer of 1940 it was in Zamosc. Ordered back to Hamburg, in July 1942 it became ***II./Polizei-Regiment 12***.

Reserve-Polizei-Bataillon 105 (FPNr. 38 739) was established in Bremen at the end of September 1939. It was stationed in Oslo from June 1940 to February 1941 and was subsequently ordered back to Bremen. After the start of the war against Russia, in July 1941 the battalion was attached to the *207. Sicherungs-Division* as part of *Polizei-Regiment "Nord"* and deployed to northern Russia. In February 142 it saw front line action in the Lyuban – Mostki area (west of the Volkhov) as part of *Kampfgruppe "Böhme."* In May 1942 it was transferred to the Netherlands. There the battalion was quartered in Westerbork, and its duties included guarding transports taking Jews to Auschwitz. In July 1942 in Hamburg the battalion became ***III./Polizei-Regiment 12***.

Polizei-Bataillon 106 was established in Neumünster in autumn 1939 for service in the *Generalgouvernement* and was deployed to Jaslo (approx. 120 km SE of Cracow). It was disbanded in 1940 during the reorganization of *Wehrkreis X*'s police battalions.

Wehrkreis XI (Hannover)

Reserve-Polizei-Bataillon 111 (FPNr. 10 742) was established in September 1939. In December it was transferred to Kielce, where it was attached to *Polizei-Regiment "Radom."* Its duties included the guarding of installations, patrols, and legal executions. In October 1940 the battalion was ordered back to Hallendorf (Salzgitter), and in January 1942 was sent back into the *Generalgouvernement* to Rzszow (Reichshof). Subsequent to this it was attached to *Polizei-Regiment "Krakau."* In May 1942 the battalion relieved a battalion of *Polizei-Regiment "Nord."* In July 1942 it was renamed ***II./Polizei-Regiment 8***.

Reserve-Polizei-Bataillon 112 (FPNr. 04 097) was established in Magdeburg in September 1939, and at the beginning of 1941 was transferred to Tilburg, in the Netherlands. It was pulled out of the Netherlands for the eastern campaign and later relieved a battalion in *Polizei-Regiment "Nord."* In July 1942 it became ***II./Polizei-Regiment 9***.

Wehrkreis XII (Coblenz)

Reserve-Polizei-Bataillon 121 (FPNr. 24 126) was established in September 1939, and at the beginning of 1941 was transferred to the Diedenhofen area in Lorraine. Under the commander of the *Ordnungspolizei* in Saarbrücken in June 1942, one month later the battalion was sent to *Polizei-Kampfgruppe "Jeckeln"* in the Leningrad siege line. There, in July 1942, it was renamed ***IV./Polizei-Regiment 16***.

Reserve-Polizei-Bataillon 122 (FPNr. 11 136) was established in Mannheim in autumn 1939, and in June 1940, during the campaign in the west, it was transferred to the recaptured area of Metz (Lorraine). After the invasion of Russia it was sent to the Senior SS and Police Commander "Russia Center" and there became ***II./Polizei-Regiment 14*** in July 1942.

Reserve-Polizei-Bataillon 123 was established in Wiesbaden in autumn 1939 and transferred to the *Generalgouvernement*. At the beginning of 1941 it was ordered to Luxemburg, and in summer 1941 to the Cilli – Krsko (German Gurkfeld) area of Slovenia. It was ordered to Hallendorf (Salzgitter) in autumn 1941, and in June 1942 the battalion was sent to Norway. In July 1942, in the Narvik area, it became ***III./Polizei-Regiment 7***.

Wehrkreis XIII (Nuremberg)

Reserve-Polizei-Bataillon 13 (FPNr. 38 064) was established in Wurzburg in autumn 1939, and at the beginning of 1940 was transferred to Norway. At the end of 1940 the battalion was ordered to Nuremberg and, in the summer of 1941, joined the Russian campaign with companies attached to *Polizei-Regiment "Mitte."* In summer 1941 the *1. Kompanie* was in Grodno, the *2. Kompanie* in Hölzel, and the *3. Kompanie* in Kalvarija and Vilnius. For a time the *3. Kompanie* was attached to *Einsatzkommando 7a* and took part in the executions of Jews and communists in Latvia. In August 1941 the battalion was sent to the *403. Sicherungs-Division* in the Smolensk area, and that autumn was located in the Nevel – Polotsk – Velikiye Luki area. In December, after the start of the Russian winter offensive, the battalion was attached to the *290. Infanterie-Division* and sent to the front in the Kaluga area. It was virtually destroyed in the fighting in early 1942 and was disbanded on 20 June. The surviving elements of the battalion were used to form *Polizei-Panzer-Kompanien* (armored police companies) of the *Polizei-Regimenter "Nord," "Mitte," "Süd,"* and *"z.b.V."*

Reserve-Polizei-Bataillon 132 (FPNr. 14 121) was established in autumn 1939 and deployed in *Wehrkreis XXI* (Warthe District). In April 1941 it was still attached to the commander of the *Ordnungspolizei* in Posen. Later, during the eastern campaign, it relieved a battalion of *Polizei-Regiment "Nord."* In July 1942 it became ***III./Polizei-Regiment 9***.

Reserve-Polizei-Bataillon 133 was established in autumn 1939. After parts of the Western Ukraine were incorporated into the *Generalgouvernement* as the District of Galicia on 1 August 1941 the battalion was stationed in the area of Delatyn – Kolomea (Kolomyia) – Stanislavov (Stanislau). There it took part in the execution of several thousand Jews. In spring 1942 the units of *Polizei-Regiment "Radom"* were used in the depopulation of the Zamosc area (*Generalplan "Ost"*) and the shipping out of the Jewish elements—mainly to Belzec. In Lvov in July 1942 the battalion became ***II./Polizei-Regiment 24***.

Reserve-Polizei-Bataillon 134 was established in Wurzburg in autumn 1939, and for a time was stationed in the "Protectorate of Bohemia and Moravia." Transferred to the *Generalgouvernement*, during the eastern campaign it relieved a battalion of *Polizei-Regiment "Mitte."* In Lvov in July 1942 it became ***II./Polizei-Regiment 8***.

Wehrkreis XVII (Vienna)

Polizei-Bataillon 171 (FPNr. 11 307) was created by the commander of the *Ordnungspolizei* in Litzmannstadt through the renaming of *Polizei-Bataillon III/3*. Initially attached to *Polizei-Regiment "Radom,"* it was subsequently transferred to Karlsbad, in the Sudetenland. In August 1941 the battalion was transferred to the Kamnik area (German Stein, approx. 24 km NE of Laibach) of Slovenia, where it immediately took part in an operation in the mountains southwest of Radovlljica (German Radmannsdorf). From December 1941 to 12 January 1942, the battalion took part in a large-scale operation against partisans in Slovenia along with *Polizei-Bataillone 44, 93, 181*, and *325*, plus *Landesschütze-Bataillone 322* and *857*. In July 1942 it supported an Italian anti-partisan action in the Horjul area near Laibach. In Veldes in July 1942 the battalion became ***II./Polizei-Regiment 19***.

Reserve-Polizei-Bataillon 172 was established in autumn 1939, and in February 1941 was used to form *Polizei-Bataillon 318*.

Wehrkreis XVIII (Salzburg)

Reserve-Polizei-Bataillon 181 (FPNr. 24 921) was established in autumn 1939, and in December was attached to *Polizei-Regiment "Radom"* in the *Generalgouvernement*. It was transferred to the Upper Krain in April 1941, helping resettle "undesirable and unreliable" elements of the Slovenian population. In August 1941 the battalion participated in an operation in the mountains southwest of Radovlljica (German Radmannsdorf). From December 1941 to 12 January 1942, from the quartering area near Kamnik, the battalion took part in a large-scale operation against bandits in Slovenia along with *Polizei-Bataillone 44*, *93*, *171*, and *325*, plus *Landesschütze-Bataillone 322* and *857*. In July 1942 it supported an Italian anti-partisan action in the Horjul area near Laibach. In Veldes in July 1942 the battalion became ***III./Polizei-Regiment 19***.

Battalions Not Associated with a *Wehrkreis*

Polizei-Bataillon 251 (FPNr. 40 059) was created from *Polizei-Ausbildungs-Bataillon "Deggingen"* in Stuttgart in autumn 1940. In April 1941 it was transferred to Trondheim (Norway), where it was deployed along the nearby Swedish-Norwegian border as *III./Polizei-Regiment "Nord-Norwegen."* In July 1942 it became ***I./Polizei-Regiment 26***.

Polizei-Bataillon 252 (FPNr. 42 144) was established in Wiesbaden in autumn 1940, and in the summer of 1941 it was transferred to *Polizei-Regiment "Süd-Norwegen"* in Norway. In July 1942 it became ***I./Polizei-Regiment 27***.

Polizei-Bataillon 253 (FPNr. 44 077) was formed from *Polizei-Ausbildungs-Bataillon "Fürstenfeldbruck"* in 1940, and in 1941 was sent to *Polizei-Regiment "Süd-Norwegen."* In July 1942 it became ***II./Polizei-Regiment 27***.

Polizei-Bataillon 254 (FPNr. 46 931) was established in Königsberg in 1940, and that autumn was prepared for deployment to the Netherlands. The battalion was subsequently transferred to Norway in 1941, and at the end of the year was integrated into the *SS-Polizei-Division* as a replacement unit.

Polizei-Bataillon 255 (FPNr. 44 334) was established in Brüx in 1940, and in December was transferred to Trondheim (Norway). Initially employed as *I./Polizei-Regiment "Nord-Norwegen,"* in July 1942 in Trondheim it became ***II./Polizei-Regiment 26***.

Polizei-Bataillon 256 (FPNr. 40 562) was created from *Polizei-Ausbildungs-Bataillon "Wien"* in 1940, and that December was transferred to Trondheim (Norway). Initially employed as *II./Polizei-Regiment "Nord-Norwegen,"* in July 1942 in Trondheim it became ***III./Polizei-Regiment 26***.

Polizei-Bataillon 301 (F 09 159) was established in 1940 from the *Polizei-Ausbildungs-Kompanien Bochum*, *Dortmund* and *Recklinghausen*. It was transferred to the *Generalgouvernement* in the summer of 1940, and in October 1940 formed *Polizei-Bataillon "Warschau I"* of the *Polizei-Regiment "Warschau."* Its duties included guarding camps for Polish POWs. Sent to *Polizei-Regiment "Mitte"* in the summer of 1941, in July 1942 it finally became ***III./Polizei-Regiment 13***.

Polizei-Bataillon 302 (FPNr. 46 393 and 17 228) was established in Munich in 1940, and in September was assigned to Norway. On 21 April 1942 the battalion was relieved and sent back to Germany, where it was initially designated *Polizei-Gebirgsjäger-Bataillon 302* (police mountain infantry battalion). In July 1942 it became ***I./Polizei-Gebirgsjäger-Regiment 18*** and was stationed in the Upper Krain.

Polizei-Bataillon 303 (FPNr. 38 101) was established in Bremen in 1940, and in October was attached to *Polizei-Regiment "Krakau"* as *Polizei-Bataillon "Tarnow."* Spring

1941 found it in the Jaslo area. Assigned to *Polizei-Regiment "Süd"* during the eastern campaign, on 19 September 1941 the battalion took part in the execution of about 18,000 Jews in Zhitomir. From 29 September to 5 October 1941 elements of the battalion were used in the mass executions at Babi Yar, in which about 33,000 Jews are believed to have been shot to death. In July 1942 it finally became ***II./Polizei-Regiment 10***.

Polizei-Bataillon 304 (FPNr. 46 177) was established in Chemnitz in 1940, and in November was employed in the *Generalgouvernement* as *Polizei-Bataillon "Warschau II"* in the *Polizei-Regiment "Warschau."* There it participated in the shooting of Jews. It was attached to *Polizei-Regiment z.b.V.* for the eastern campaign, and in September 1941 took part in the executions of approximately 5,300 Jews in Starokonstantinov, Vinnitsa, Kirovograd, Uman, and Kiev under the command of *Einsatzgruppe "D."* At the end of March 1942 the battalion was ordered from the Ukraine to White Russia, where it took part in a major anti-partisan operation in the Bobruisk area that concluded on 4 April. In July 1942 it became ***I./Polizei-Regiment 11***.

Polizei-Bataillon 305 (FPNr. 20 080) was created in Hamburg in September 1940 from *Polizei-Ausbildungs-Bataillon "Itzehoe."* In December 1940, as *Polizei-Bataillon "Kielce,"* it was attached to *Polizei-Regiment "Radom"* in the *Generalgouvernement* and was used to guard the Kielce ghetto. On 20 February 1942 the battalion was flown to Krasnogvardeysk, and from there was sent to *Polizei-Kampfgruppe "Jeckeln"* in the Leningrad siege line. In July 1942 it was initially supposed to become ***I./Polizei-Regiment 15***, but a short time later it was named ***III./Polizei-Regiment 16***.

Polizei-Bataillon 306 (FPNr. 21 241) was established at Frankfurt/Main in the late summer of 1940, and at the beginning of October was attached to *Polizei-Regiment "Lublin"* as *Polizei-Bataillon "Lublin."* Assigned to the Biala Podlaska – Zamosc – Krasnik area, its duties included "*combating black-marketeering*." From the summer of 1941 its role was expanded to include the guarding of POW camps for Soviet prisoners. During this period there were executions of Poles, Jews, and Red Army soldiers. From 21 to 28 September alone, as many as 6,000 members of the Red Army were executed under the so-called "commissar order." In mid-February 1942 the battalion was airlifted to *Polizei-Kampfgruppe "Jeckeln"* in northern Russia, and in July 1942 it was renamed ***II./Polizei-Regiment 15***.

Polizei-Bataillon 307 (FPNr. 43 985) was created from *Polizei-Ausbildungs-Bataillon "Lübeck"* in 1940, and was initially employed in the *Generalgouvernement* as *Polizei-Bataillon "Warschau III"* of *Polizei-Regiment "Warschau."* In the summer of 1941 it was attached to *Polizei-Regiment "Mitte"* and took part in operations to secure the supply lines with the *162.* and *252. Infanterie-Division*. When the Red Army was able to break out of the Vyazma pocket, elements of the battalion were used to seal off the breakthrough. Other elements were attached to *Einsatzgruppe "B"* and took part in the shooting of thousands of Jews at Brest-Litovsk, Baranowice, and Starobin. In October 1941 the units of the battalion were deployed in Mogilev, Smolensk, and Bobruisk, where they executed Jews and partisans (suspected). From December 1941 to the end of February 1942 the battalion took part in the battle for Kaluga (approx. 300 km E of Smolensk) as part of the *4. Armee*. Briefly employed as part of a battle group near Beresina, in April 1942 it was transferred back to the *Generalgouvernement*. The battalion headquarters and the *1. Kompanie* were in Reichshof (Rzeszow), the *2. Kompanie* in Przemsyl, and the *3. Kompanie* in Tarnow. In July 1942 in Cracow the battalion became ***I./Polizei-Regiment 23***.

Polizei-Bataillon 308 (FPNr. 26 310) was established in Duisburg in 1940, and in October was sent to *Polizei-Regiment "Warschau"* in Warsaw, where its duties included guarding the Warsaw ghetto. The *1. Kompanie* was temporarily seconded to the SD (*Sicherheitsdienst*) for executions in the *Stalags* (POW camps). Finally, it formed *Polizei-Bataillon "Biala Podlaska"* in *Polizei-Regiment "Lublin."* Sent to *Polizei-Regiment "Mitte,"* it saw action at the front near Yuchnov in the winter of 1941/42. The battalion was virtually wiped out in the fighting, and what remained was divided among *Polizei-Bataillone 307* and *32*. In March 1942 the battalion was disbanded.

Polizei-Bataillon 309 (FPNr. 45 785) was created from *Polizei-Ausbildungs-Bataillon "A"* in Cologne in September 1940. It was transferred to Poland at the end of September, where it became *Polizei-Bataillon "Radom"* of *Polizei-Regiment "Radom."* The battalion was employed in Pionki in January 1941 and in Ostrolenka (approx. 100 km NE of Warsaw) in May as part of the *221. Sicherungs-Division*. On 27 June 1941, at the start of the Russian campaign, hundreds of Jews were shot in Bialystok. The battalion then moved via Slutsk, Bobruisk, Smolensk, and Shlobin to Gomel. The battalion was in the Briansk area in spring 1942. At the beginning of March it took part in "Operation Anton," and at the end of March "Operation Jobst." Ordered back to Cologne at the end of April 1942, in July it was transferred to Norway as ***I./Polizei-Regiment 7***.

Polizei-Bataillon 310 (F 22 665) was created from *Polizei-Ausbildungs-Bataillon "Oranienburg"* in Berlin in October 1940, and as *Polizei-Bataillon "Tschenstochau* was transferred to *Polizei-Regiment "Radom"* in the *Generalgouvernement."* Assignment to *Polizei-Kampfgruppe "Jeckeln"* in the Leningrad siege line followed in mid-February 1942. The battalion was in Dvinsk in July 1942 and there became ***III./Polizei-Regiment 15***.

Polizei-Bataillon 311 (FPNr. 14 502) was established in Jesau in 1940, and in October formed *Polizei-Bataillon "Krakau I,"* part of *Polizei-Regiment "Krakau"* in the *Generalgouvernement.* In July 1941 the battalion moved to Dnepropetrovsk as part of *Polizei-Regiment "Süd,"* and in October 1941 it took part in the shootings of several thousand Jews. From December 1941 to the end of January 1942 the battalion was attached to the *444. Sicherungs-Division* in the Pavlograd area. During the Soviet winter offensive, on 10 February 1942 the battalion relieved elements of *Infanterie-Regiment 525* of the *298. Infanterie-Division* in the Lozovaya area (approx. 100 km S of Kharkov). Attached to that division, at the end of February 1942 the battalion was near Ivanovka. In mid-June 1942 the battalion was near Taganrog with elements of the *SS-Panzergrenadier-Division "Leibstandarte-SS Adolf Hitler,"* and in July 1942 it became ***II./Polizei-Regiment 6***.

Polizei-Bataillon 312 (FPNr. 44 123 and 18 146) was established in Innsbruck in spring 1940. Transferred to Norway in September 1940, it was employed as a ski battalion at the Arctic Circle. It was relieved at the end of April 1942, and in July of that year—since renamed *Polizei-Gebirgsjäger-Bataillon 312*—it became ***II./Polizei-Gebirgsjäger-Regiment 18***.

Polizei-Bataillon 313 (FPNr. 20 758) was established in Stettin in 1940, and as *Polizei-Bataillon "Zamosc"* was attached to *Polizei-Regiment "Lublin"* in the *Generalgouvernement.* During the eastern campaign, in January 1942 it marched via Brest-Litovsk and Bobruisk to *Heeresgruppe Mitte's* hard-pressed front and was attached to the *268. Infanterie-Division.* After serving at the front, in July 1942 the battalion was in Wismar and there became ***III./Polizei-Regiment 14***.

Polizei-Bataillon 314 (FPNr. 37 049) was established in Vienna in October 1940, and as *Polizei-Bataillon "Reichshof"* was attached to *Polizei-Regiment "Krakau"* in the *Generalgouvernement.* Attached to *Polizei-Regiment "Süd"* in the summer of 1941, the battalion participated in mass executions in the Kovel area. In September 1941 it assisted *Einsatzkommando 6* in shootings in Vinnitsa and Dnepropetrovsk. The same was repeated in Kharkov in November 1941 and January 1942. In July 1942 the battalion was renamed ***III./Polizei-Regiment 10***.

Polizei-Bataillon 315 (FPNr. 45 718) was formed in Halle in 1940 using Sudeten-German volunteers, and was transferred to the "Protectorate of Bohemia and Moravia" as *Polizei-Bataillon "Brünn"* of *Polizei-Regiment "Mähren."* In the autumn of 1941 it was attached to *Polizei-Regiment "z.b.V."* and participated in mass executions in Rovno. From 26 March to 6 April 1942 the battalion took part in an anti-partisan operation by the *707. Infanterie-Division* in the Oktyabrski and Kopakevichi area of White Russia. In July 1942 it became ***II./Polizei-Regiment 11***.

Polizei-Bataillon 316 (FPNr. 44 173) was established in Recklinghausen in May 1940, and in February 1941, as *Polizei-Bataillon "Tabor,"* was attached to *Polizei-Regiment "Böhmen"* in the "Protectorate of Bohemia and Moravia." At the beginning of June 1941 it was transferred to Radom, where it formed *I./Polizei-Regiment "Mitte."* In cooperation with *Einsatzgruppe "B,"* the battalion participated in numerous mass executions in Bialystok Slonim, Baranowice, Slutsk, Mogilev, and Bobruisk in the period until December 1941. It subsequently served at the front with *Polizei-Regiment "Mitte,"* and in spring 1942 was ordered to its garrison in Bottrop to rest and reequip. In July 1942 it was transferred to Paris as ***I./Polizei-Regiment 4***.

Polizei-Bataillon 317 (FPNr. 39 745) was created from *Polizei-Ausbildungs-Bataillon "Oberhausen"* in Wuppertal in 1940. It was subsequently attached to *Polizei-Regiment "Böhmen"* in the "Protectorate of Bohemia and Moravia" as *Polizei-Bataillon "Pardubitz."* It was transferred to the *Generalgouvernement* in April 1941 and attached to *Polizei-Regiment "Mitte."* Actions followed in Bobruisk and Smolensk as part of the *286. Sicherungs-Division.* In the winter of 1941/42 the battalion was placed under the Senior SS and Police Commander "Russia Center." In July 1942 it was transferred back to its garrison in Wuppertal. There it became ***II./Polizei-Regiment 7***.

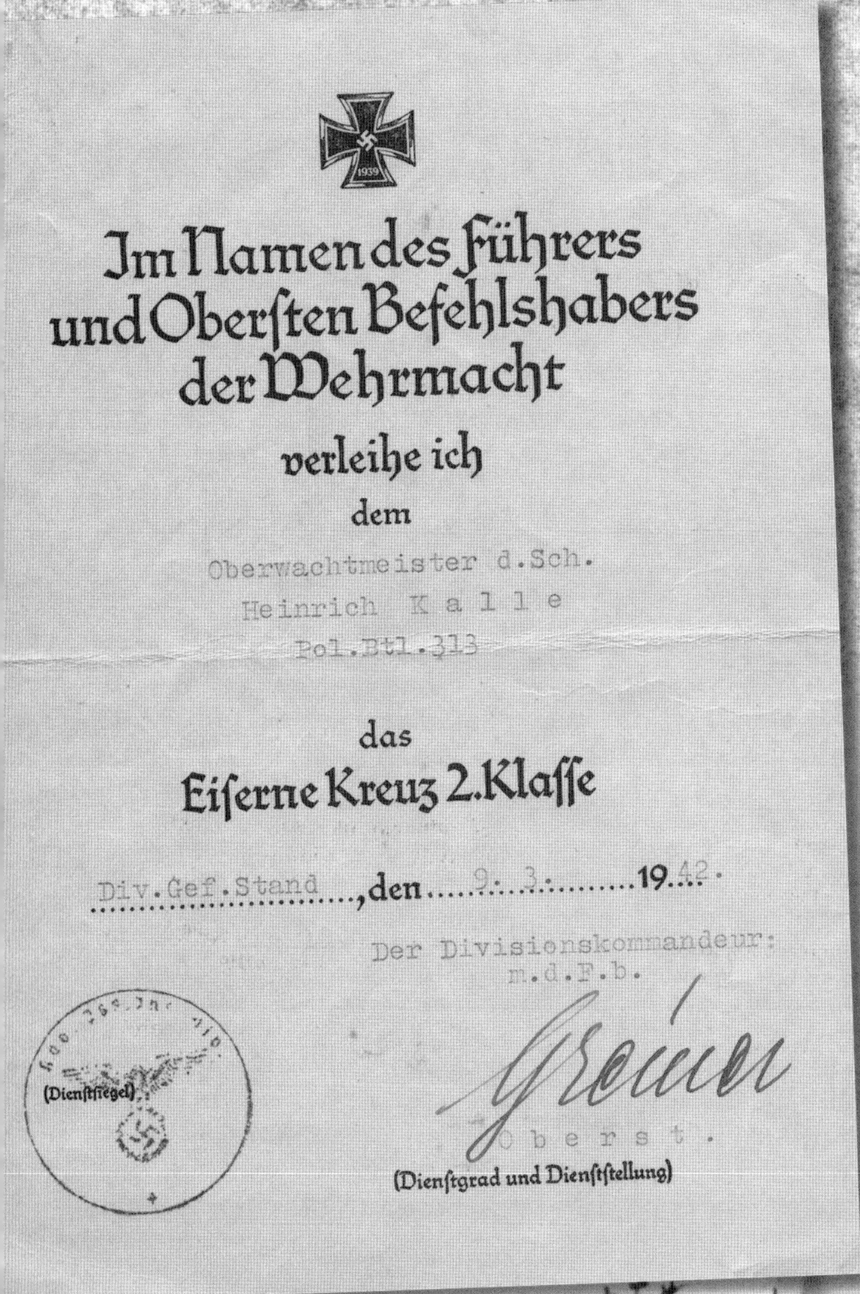
Im Namen des Führers und Obersten Befehlshabers der Wehrmacht

verleihe ich

dem

Oberwachtmeister d.Sch.
Heinrich Kalle
Pol.Btl.313

das

Eiserne Kreuz 2.Klasse

Div.Gef.Stand, den 9. 3. 1942.

Der Divisionskommandeur:
m.d.F.b.

(Dienstsiegel)

Oberst.

(Dienstgrad und Dienststellung)

IM NAMEN DES FÜHRERS UND OBERSTEN BEFEHLSHABERS DER WEHRMACHT

IST DEM

Oberwachtm.d.Schutzpol.
Heinrich Kalle
Pol.Batl.313

AM 15. August 1942

DIE MEDAILLE WINTERSCHLACHT IM OSTEN 1941/42 (OSTMEDAILLE)

VERLIEHEN WORDEN.

Der Höhere SS- u. Pol.-Führer Rußland-Mitte

SS-Gruppenführer u.
Generalleutnant der Polizei

For acts of bravery in combat, in the spring of 1942 Oberwachtmeister Kalle was awarded the Iron Cross, Second Class by the commander of the 269. Infanterie-Division and the Eastern Front Medal by the Senior SS and Police Commander "Russia Center."

Left: Certificate for the Awarding of the Croatian Medal of Bravery in Bronze

U IME HRVATSKOGA NARODA

POGLAVNIK

NEZAVISNE DRŽAVE HRVATSKE

PODJELJUJE SVOJOM ODREDBOM

BROJ 16929-HR-1943.

ZUGWACHTM.

FELDPOST 30764 A

KALLE HEINRICH

BRONČANU

KOLAJNU POGLAVNIKA

ANTE PAVELIĆA

ZA HRABROST

DANO U GLAVNOM GRADU ZAGREBU 23. STUDENOGA 1943.

MINISTAR I ZAPOVJEDNIK

ORUŽANIH SNAGA

ZRAKOPLOVNI GENERAL:

Navratil

NEZAVISNA DRŽAVA HRVATSKA · POGLAVNIK

On 3/5/1942 Major der Schupo Bernhard Griese, commander of Polizei-Bataillon 323, was awarded the Knight's Cross of the Iron Cross.

BESITZZEUGNIS

Dem Zugwachtmeister der Schutzpolizei
(Dienstgrad)

Heinrich Kalle
(Vor- und Familienname)

I./ϟϟ Pol.-Rgt.14
(Truppenteil)

verleihe ich das

INFANTERIE-STURMABZEICHEN

in

Silber

Dienststelle · (Stempel) · Feldpostnummer 04...6

Rgt.Gef.Stand, den 9.4.1944
(Ort und Datum)

Griese
(Unterschrift)

Oberst der Schutzpolizei
und Regiments-Kommandeur.
(Dienstgrad und Dienststellung)

Südost-Druck Cilli

Zugwachtmeister der Schupo Kalle was awarded the Infantry Assault badge in Silver by Oberst der Schupo Griese for three days of offensive combat in Slovenia.

Polizei-Bataillon 318 (FPNr. 37 632) was formed in Vienna in 1940 through the renaming of *Reserve-Polizei-Bataillon 172* and was attached to *Polizei-Regiment "Mähren"* in the "Protectorate of Bohemia and Moravia" as *Polizei-Bataillon "Iglau."* In the summer of 1941 it relieved a battalion of *Polizei-Regiment "Süd"* and in July 1942 became ***III./Polizei-Regiment 6***.

Polizei-Bataillon 319 (FPNr. 40 493) was established in Cologne in 1940, and in the "Protectorate of Bohemia and Moravia" it formed *Polizei-Bataillon "Prag,"* part of *Polizei-Regiment "Böhmen."* In June 1941 it was attached to *Polizei-Regiment "Nord,"* and companies were deployed independently with the *207.*, *281.*, and *285. Sicherungs-Division*. In December 1941 the battalion saw front line action with the *81. Infanterie-Division* near Raschutscha on Lake Ilmen. In April 1942 the battalion and the other battalions of *Polizei-Regiment "Nord"* saw action at Staraya Russa—attached to the *18. Infanterie-Division*. It was transferred to Oslo, Norway, in July 1942, and there became ***I./Polizei-Regiment 27***.

Polizei-Bataillon 320 (FPNr. 46 591) was established in Berlin in spring 1940, and in the "Protectorate of Bohemia and Moravia" it formed *Polizei-Bataillon "Jungbunzlau,"* part of *Polizei-Regiment "Böhmen."* After the end of the campaign in the Balkans, in mid-April 1941 the battalion was temporarily transferred to the Cilli area of Slovenia. At the end of May it moved to the Jaslo area in the *Generalgouvernement* and made preparations for the coming invasion of the Soviet Union. There, together with elements of the *1. SS-Infanterie-Brigade*, it took part in the execution of several hundred Jews in Starokonstantinov on 20 August 1941. At the end of the month the battalion sealed off the Kamenets Podolsk area for the execution of probably 23,600 Jews by the Headquarters Company of the Senior SS and Police Commander "Russia South." In association with *Einsatzkommando 5*, in November it participated in the shooting of more than 10,000 Jews in Rovno. December 1941 brought action at the front near Taganrog. In spring 1942 the battalion became part of *Polizei-Regiment "z.b.V.,"* and in July in the Taganrog area was renamed ***III./Polizei-Regiment 11***.

Polizei-Bataillon 321 (FPNr. 41 064) was established in Breslau in 1940, and in the "Protectorate of Bohemia and Moravia" it formed *Polizei-Bataillon "Olmütz,"* part of *Polizei-Regiment "Mähren."* Transferred to the *Generalgouvernement*, it functioned as *Polizei-Bataillon "Krakau II"* within *Polizei-Regiment "Krakau."* During the Russian campaign, in the summer of 1941 it was attached to *Polizei-Regiment "Nord"* and deployed in the sector of *Heeresgruppe "Nord."* In July 1942 the battalion was ordered to the Halden area in Norway and was renamed ***II./Polizei-Regiment 27***.

Polizei-Bataillon 322 (FPNr. 44 762) was created from *Polizei-Ausbildungs-Bataillon "Kagran"* in Vienna in 1940. At the beginning of June 1941 it was attached to *Polizei-Regiment "Mitte"* as a so-called *Radfahr-Bataillon* (bicycle battalion) and transferred to the Warsaw area. In July 1941, under the *221. Sicherungs-Division*, the battalion took part in mass executions of Jews in Bialystok. In August 1941 it participated in similar actions in Bialowiecze, Pinsk, and Minsk under the commander of the *Ordnungspolizei* in White Ruthenia, From September to November 1941 the battalion took part in mass executions in Mogilev and Minsk with *Einsatzkommando 8*. It was subsequently tasked with securing railway lines in the Roslavl – Yanivo – Smolensk – Vitebsk area. For this purpose, about 45 strong points were set up at road and rail bridges, as well as in train stations and businesses, each manned by seven men. Battalion personnel also guarded a POW camp. The battalion was in Smolensk in January 1942, and until May it guarded lines of transportation between Smolensk, Orsha, and Vitebsk. In July 1942 it was transferred to Belgrade (Serbia) as ***II./Polizei-Regiment 5***.

Polizei-Bataillon 323 (FPNr. 43 315) was established in Tilsit in 1940, and in the summer of 1941 it marched into the Kovno area. Its duties there included guarding the local ghetto. In December 1941 it saw action against a large force of Red Army parachute troops in the Orsha area. Battalion commander Major Griese was decorated with the Knight's Cross of the Iron Cross at that time. The battalion was stationed in Yelnya in March 1942 and was subsequently transferred, first to Tilsit and then to Paris as ***II./Polizei-Regiment 4***.

Polizei-Bataillon 324 was established in Stuttgart in 1940 and provided replacements for the *SS-Polizei-Division*.

Polizei-Bataillon 325 (FPNr. 19 754) was established in Dresden in 1940, and in December was transferred to the Upper Krain. From 27 December 1941 to 12 January 1942 it participated in a large-scale anti-partisan operation in Slovenia between Laibach and Krain together with other units, including *Polizei-Bataillone 44*, *93*, *171*, and *181*. At the end of April 1942, as *Polizei-Gebirgsjäger-Bataillon 325* it moved to Garmisch and there in July 1942 became ***III./Polizei-Gebirgsjäger-Regiment 18***.

When not on active duty against the partisans, the units spent time improving their quarters, improving relationships with the local population, or seeing to the well being of the men.

The *SS-Polizei-Regimenter*

At the beginning of 1939 two police regimental headquarters, *"Böhmen"* and *"Mähren,"* were established in the "Protectorate of Bohemia and Moravia." In the autumn of that year the headquarters for the *Polizei-Regimenter "Warschau," "Radom," "Krakau,"* and *"Lublin"* were established in the *Generalgouvernement*. The regimental headquarters *"Nord-Norwegen"* and *"Süd-Norwegen"* followed in Norway in 1941, along with the formation of *Polizei-Regimenter "Nord," "Mitte," "Süd,"* and *"z.b.V."* for the coming campaign against the Soviet Union. All of these formations were strictly regimental headquarters that were administratively responsible for frequently changing battalions often deployed far from one another.

On 9 July 1942 Himmler also ordered the concentration of all police battalions[54] in a total of 28 police regiments *"to ensure the standardized and effective command of the police and reserve police battalions."* Initially this did nothing to alter existing tactical attachments and was probably intended to demonstrate internally and externally the strength of the *Ordnungspolizei* elements deployed outside the Reich.[55]

In a decree dated 24 February 1943, Himmler awarded these police regiments the prefix "SS-" *"in recognition of their particularly brave and successful operations."* Consequently the units were designated *"SS-Polizei-Regimenter."* This step should, however, be seen against the background that Himmler, in his capacity as *Reichsführer-SS* and Chief of German Police, was striving to merge the SS and the police, and that these 28 regiments would probably be incorporated into the *Waffen-SS* at a later date. This link between the *Waffen-SS* and the police was also depicted in an extremely propagandistic fashion in the final comments in the contemporary publication from 1942, of which mention was previously made:[56]

"From this book, many parents are learning for the first time of the limitless range of duties of the German police, thereby becoming convinced that service in it is true service with and for the people, and so many young men will now perhaps make the decision to place their entire strength and being at the disposal of the German people and therefore volunteer for service in the Waffen-SS or the German Police."

After the heavy German losses in early 1943, an order issued on 29 March created the so-called *Polizei-Schützen-Regimenter*, in which the 1st battalion consisted of members of the German Police and the 2nd and 3rd battalions volunteers from Eastern Europe. The formation of police regiments made up of men from South Tyrol also began in 1943.

What follows is a chronological listing of the *SS-Polizei-Regimenter* with capsule histories of their employment until disbandment or the end of the war. In contrast to the army, there was little regional homogeneity in the police regiments. For example, Saxons, Bavarians, and Rhinelanders served side by side in *SS-Polizei-Regiment 17*. The individual battalions were still frequently deployed far from one another, carrying out the same *Ordnungspolizei* duties as before in the same way as independent battalions. This included manning police precincts in cities and districts, patrol duty, guard duty, and active participation in anti-partisan warfare as part of independent anti-partisan operations by the *Wehrmacht* or the Senior SS and Police Commanders in the occupied territories. As well, the remnants of 15 SS police regiments saw action at the front from the summer of 1944 until the end of the war.

SS-Polizei-Regiment 1

The regimental headquarters was established in Berlin in July 1942 for *Polizei-Bataillone 2*, *3*, and *10*. The battalions were deployed separately, however, far from each other:

I. Bataillon with the Senior SS and Police Commander "Russia North"
II. Bataillon with the *Sicherheitspolizei* in the east
III. Bataillon in the Upper Krain in the Laibach – Kramberg (Kranj) – Stein (Kamnik) area

From 13 July until August 1942 the *III. Bataillon* took part in "Operation Enzian" in the Laibach security zone, and in November was committed in a major operation in the Franz (Vransko) area.

In spring 1943, the *I.* and *III. Bataillon* were transferred to the Marseille area[57] in France for the reformation of *Polizei-Regiment 14*, which had been decimated on the Eastern Front. In June 1943 the *II. Bataillon*, stationed in the sector of the Senior SS and Police Commander "Russia Center and White Ruthenia," became *I./Polizei-Schützen-Regiment 36*.

Feldpostnummern:	
I./SS-Polizei-Regiment 1	40 848
II./SS-Polizei-Regiment 1	15 119
III./SS-Polizei-Regiment 1	10 124

After almost 1½ years, in August 1944 a new *SS-Polizei-Regiment 1* was created using personnel seconded by:

II./SS-Polizei-Regiment 12
II./SS-Polizei-Regiment 20
III./SS-Polizei-Regiment 21

In October 1944, however, *II.* and *III. Bataillon* were used in the reestablishment of *SS-Polizei-Regiment 6*, leaving the regiment with just the *I. Bataillon*. A new *II. Bataillon* was formed in Budapest using available members of the *Ordnungspolizei* and ethnic Germans, and the regiment was transferred to the Lausitz before Budapest was encircled by the Red Army in December 1944. There it was initially attached to *Divisionsstab 608 z.b.V.* The regiment was then disbanded on 12 March 1945. What was left of the unit was absorbed by the newly-established *SS-Polizei-Regiment 29* of *Polizei-Brigade "Wirth"*—the later *35. SS-Polizei-Division*.[58]

Feldpostnummern:	
Stab (Headquarters)	13 188
I./SS-Polizei-Regiment 1	02 647
II./SS-Polizei-Regiment 1	08 811
III./SS-Polizei-Regiment 1	04 879

SS-Polizei-Regiment 2

The regimental headquarters was established in Tilsit in July 1942 for *Polizei-Bataillone 11*, *13*, and *22* and sent to the Senior SS and Police Commander "Russia Center" in Polotsk. In addition to its daily duties, such as patrolling, the regiment took part in the following actions:

20/07 – 07/08/42 "Operation Adler" in the triangle formed by the Mogilev – Beresino – Bobruisk – Mogilev road
01/08 – 05/08/42 "Operation Nordpol II" in the area north of Smolensk
00/11 – 00/11/42 "Operation Wisent"
00/12 – 00/12/42 "Operation Hamburg" in the Slonim area
18/01 – 27/01/43 "Operation Erntefest I" in the area NE of Slutsk
16/02 – 26/02/43 "Operation Hornung" in the Morocz – Milewicze area in the Pripyat Marshes as part of *Kampfgruppe* *"Ost."* Under the command of the C.O. of *Polizei-Regiment 2*, it consisted of:

Polizei-Regiment 2
Bataillon "Radjanoff"
Bataillon "Borissow" of the *1. SS Infanterie-Brigade*
Panzer-Kompanie/Polizei-Gebirgsjäger-Regiment 18

08/04 – 13/04/43 "Operation Lenz-Nord" in the Borisov – Smolevichi – Lahoysk – Sembin area
17/04 – 24/04/43 "Operation Zauberflöte" in the White-Russian capital of Minsk – sealing off of the Jewish ghetto
28/04 – 10/05/43 "Operations Draufgänger I and II" in the Molodechno and Manila – Rudnya Forest areas
22/05 – 21/06/43 "Operation Cottbus" to destroy the partisan republic in the area around Palik Lake between Beresino and Borisov. It is believed that approximately 10,000 partisans and partisan helpers and sympathizers were killed.
29/06 – 07/07/43 "Operation Günter" in the Manila – Rudnya Forest area
07/07 – 05/08/43 "Operation Hermann" in the Nalibocki Forest
01/11 – 04/11/43 "Operation Heinrich" to destroy the Rosony partisan Republic in the area Polotsk – Krasnopolye – Pustoshka – Idritsa – Sebezh. Deployed north of Polotsk, the regiment formed part of *Kampfgruppe "von Gottberg,"* which was made up of the following units:

SS-Polizei-Regiment 2
SS-Polizei-Regiment 13 (less *II. Bataillon* in Smolensk)
SS-Polizei-Regiment 24 (less *III. Bataillon*)

16/04 – 12/05/44 "Operation Frühlingsfest" in the Ushatshi area, with:

SS-Polizei-Regiment 24 and *26*
III./Polizei-Schützen-Regiment 31
I./Polizei-Schützen-Regiment 36

22/05 – 20/06/44 "Operation Kormoran" in the area north of the Minsk – Borisov rail line against partisan units that escaped "Operation Frühlingsfest"
00/06 – 00/07/44 Action in the Nalibocki Forest (west of Minsk) as part of *Polizei-Kampfgruppe* "von Gottberg." Retreat in the direction of Stolpce.
11/07/44 Together with *Polizei-Regiment*er *17*, *22*, and *31* in the area 20 km west of Lida
14/07/44 Together with *Polizei-Regiment*er *17*, *22*, *31*, and *36* in the area 20 km east of Grodno
17/07/44 Part of *Korpsgruppe "von Gottberg"* in Grodno
26/07/44 After yet another renaming, now part of *Korps-Abteilung "von Gottberg"* west of Lipetsk
08/08 – 21/09/44 Action as part of *Polizei-Brigade "Anhalt"* with:

SS-Polizei-Regiment 2 (new)
SS-Polizei-Regiment 4 (*I.* and *II. Bataillon*)
SS-Polizei-Regiment 17
I./SS-Polizei-Regiment 17
I./Polizei-Schützen-Regiment 34

22/09 – 06/10/44	Action as part of *Gruppe "Oberst Danz"* with *VI. Armee-Korps* (*4. Armee*)
07/10 – 12/10/44	Action as part of *Gruppe "Oberst Hannibal"*

The regiment was subsequently ordered to Brandenburg/Havel, reformed, and sent to the *XIV. SS-Armee-Korps* on the Upper Rhine. In January 1945 it was transferred to the Lausitz and attached to *Divisionsstab 608 z.b.V.* On 12 March 1945 the regiment was disbanded. What was left of the unit was absorbed by the newly-established *SS-Polizei-Regiment 30* of *Polizei-Brigade "Wirth"*—the later *35. SS-Polizei-Division*.[60]

Feldpostnummern:

Stab	02 112
I./SS-Polizei-Regiment 2	07 338
II./SS-Polizei-Regiment 2	09 571
III./SS-Polizei-Regiment 2	47 348

SS-Polizei-Regiment 3

The regiment was established from *Polizei-Bataillone 66*, *68*, and *105* in July 1942, and was sent to the Senior SS and Police Commander "Netherlands." The headquarters and *I. Bataillon* were based in Tilburg, the *II. Bataillon* in Amsterdam, and the *III. Bataillon* in The Hague.

In January 1943 *I./Polizei-Regiment 3* was renamed *III./Polizei-Regiment 5* and sent to Serbia, leaving just the *II.* and *III. Bataillon* in the Netherlands.

The regiment was sometimes called *SS-Polizei-Regiment "Böhmer"* after its commanding officer. In September 1944 individual companies took part in the fighting in the North Brabant ("Operation Market Garden"). In autumn 1944 the regiment was again strengthened to three battalions and attached to *Polizei-Brigade "Nordwest"* for the imminent defensive battles. The brigade was organized as follows:

SS-Polizei-Regiment "Nordwest 1" (former *SS-Polizei-Regiment* 3)
SS-Polizei-Regiment "Nordwest 2" (formed from *Polizei-Waffenschule III*)
SS-Polizei-Regiment "Nordwest 3"
SS-Polizei-Artillerie-Abteilung "Nordwest"
SS-Polizei-Nachrichten-Kompanie 22 (signals company)

Deployed in "Fortress Netherlands," on 9 May 1945 the regiment surrendered to the British.

Feldpostnummern:

Stab	58 140
I./SS-Polizei-Regiment 3	08 023
II./SS-Polizei-Regiment 3	59 091
III./SS-Polizei-Regiment 3	38 739

SS-Polizei-Regiment 4

The regiment was established in July 1942 from *Polizei-Bataillone 316, 322*, and elements of *Reserve-Polizei-Bataillon 62* and placed under the Senior SS and Police Commander "France" in Paris. In June 1943 the regiment was transferred to the *Generalgouvernement* where, in addition to daily duties such as patrolling, it took part in the following actions:

27/06 – 11/07/43	"Operation Werewolf I and II" in the Zamosc – Bilgoraj area
01/08 – 10/08/43	"Operation Weichsel III" in Wohlhynia together with: *Wolgatatarischen Infanterie-Bataillon 825* (Volga Tatars) *Kosaken-Kavallerie-Abteilung 102* (Cossack cavalry) elements of *SS-Polizei-Regimenter 12, 13*, and *26*
30/07 – 25/08/43	"Operation Karpaten" in the Carpathians SW of Stanislau with: elements of the *154.* and *174. Reserve-Division* *Gendarmerie-Bataillon 1 (mot.)* elements of *Polizei-Regiment 13*
05/05 – 16/05/44	"Operation Maigewitter" in the Lublin area (Parczew – Krasnik) with elements of: *5. SS-Panzer-Division "Wiking"* *SS-Polizei-Regiment 25*
08/6 – 25/06/44	"Operation Sturmwind I and II" in the area 70 km S of Lublin between Janow – Bilgoraj against an estimated 5,000 partisans, with: elements of the *154.* and *174. Reserve-Division* *213. Sicherungs-Division* *Landesschützen-Regiment 115* *Landesschützen-Bataillone 994* and *995* *Gendarmerie-Bataillon 1 (mot.)* *Kalmücken-Kavallerie-Korps* (Kalmuk cavalry) elements of the Hungarian 5th Reserve Division
08/06 -23/06/44	"Operation Vagabund" in the area NE of Lublin (Radzyn – Parczew – Wlodawa – Cholm) with: elements of *Polizei-Schützen-Regiment 32* elements of *SS-Polizei-Regiment 25* *Landesschützen-Bataillone 991* and *992*
00/06 – 00/07/44	Movement of the first elements into the Minsk area, approx. 500 km away. Attached to *Polizei-Kampfgruppe "von Gottberg"* and took part in "Operation Kormoran" in the area north of the line Minsk – Borisov
08/08 – 21/09/44	Actions as part of *Polizei-Brigade "Anhalt"* in the area Grodno – Bialystok –East Prussian border with: *SS-Polizei-Regiment 2* *SS-Polizei-Regiment 4* (*I.* and *III. Bataillon*) *SS-Polizei-Regiment 17* *I./SS-Polizei-Regiment 17* *I./Polizei-Schützen-Regiment 34*
22/09 – 06/10/44	Action as part of the *Gruppe "Oberst Danz"* with *VI. Armee-Korps* (*4. Armee*)
07/10 – 09/03/45	Action as art of *Gruppe "Hannibal"* initially in the Grayevo area. End of January 1945 retreat via Lyck, Arys, and Milken into the area SE of Lötzen.
10/03/45	Disbandment of the regiment and incorporation of the remnants into *Polizei-Schützen-Regiment 31.*

Feldpostnummern

Stab	57 316
I./SS-Polizei-Regiment 4	48 274
II./SS-Polizei-Regiment 4	43 315
III./SS-Polizei-Regiment 4	11 853

SS-Polizei-Regiment 5

The regiment was established in Serbia in July 1942 from *Polizei-Bataillone 64, 322*, and a newly-formed *III. Bataillon*[62] made up of ethnic Germans from the Banat. The regiment was placed under the commander of *Ordnungspolizei* in Belgrade. It took part in the following actions, with the battalions usually deployed individually:

28/06/42	"Operation Enzian" in Slovenia
04/01/43	operation against partisans in Mitrovica (Kapaonik Mountains) together with:
	Bulgarian 24th Division
	Serbian Volunteer Corps
00/04/43	"Operations Adam" and "Bajcetina-Gledic"
00/07/43	"Operation Morgenluft"
10/08 – 18/08/43	"Operation Stiefelknecht" in the Jastrebac Mountains NW of Nis
19/08/43	transfer from Kragujevac (approx. 50 km NW of Nis) to Arandelovac (approx. 50 km S of Belgrade)
00/09/43	Action SW of Krusevac and NW of Prokuplje. Area between Mitrovica and Krusevac. The three battalions were under the Senior SS and Police Commander "Serbia" and stationed in Topola, Kragujevac, and Krusevac.
03/10 – 08/10/43	"Operation Maiskolben" in the area between Valjevo and Cacak together with:
	Bulgarian 24th Division
	Serbian Volunteer Corps
10/10 – 20/10/43	"Operation Krumm" in the Cacak – Uzice – Bajina Basta on the Drina, to engage partisans who had fled to East Bosnia.
31/10 – 05/11/43	"Operation Hammelbraten" west of Uzice (S of Cacak)
00/11 – 00/12/43	billeted in Topola and Pozega
16/02 – 05/03/44	"Operation Treibjagd" in the Arandelovac area with:
	III./4. Regiment "Brandenburg"
	Serbian Volunteer Corps
	Bulgarian 70th Infantry Regiment
19/03 – 12/05/44	"Operation Margarethe" (occupation of Hungary) as part of *XXII. Gebirgs-Korps*:
	Kampfgruppe "Hildebrandt"
	Grenadier-Regiment 92 (mot.)
	III./4. Regiment "Brandenburg"
	Panzer-Abteilung 202
	Sturmgeschütz-Brigade 201
	Brüko B 658 (mot.)
	SS-Polizei-Regiment 5
	II./Flak-Regiment 25 (mot.)
13/05/44	transferred via Essig back to Serbia to the Cacak – Usce – Kraljevo area
18/06 – 03/07/44	"Operation Endlich" as part of *XXI. Gebirgs-Korps* in the Albanian-Montenegrin border region together with elements of the *21. Waffen-Gebirgsdivision der SS "Skanderbeg"*
00/06/44	"Operation Trumpf" in the area of the western Morava Mountains together with the Bulgarian 27th Division
6/07 – 28/07/44	"Operation Draufgänger" in the Berane area (Montenegro) with:
	21. Waffen-Gebirgsdivision der SS "Skanderbeg"
	SS-Freiwilligen-Gebirgsjäger-Regiment 14
05/08 – 22/08/44	"Operation Rübezahl" in the area SE of Sarajevo together with:
	7. SS-Freiwilligen-Gebirgs-Division "Prinz Eugen"
	13. Waffen-Gebirgsdivision der SS "Handschar"
	21. Waffen-Gebirgsdivision der SS "Skanderbeg"

Because of the regiment's tense situation, a few days later it was sent to the *LXIX. Armee-Korps* in the Valjevo area, and at the beginning of October 1944 it was transferred into the area south of Belgrade. Until mid-October the regiment took part in the

Many ethnic Germans from the former Austria-Hungary—most of whom had served in the First World War—were called up by the police. Often they were equipped in part with Austrian equipment and weapons (here Mannlicher rifles).

at times fierce defensive fighting there, and by the beginning of November it withdrew into the area south of Sid by way of Mitrovica and Semlin. It was attached to *Kampfgruppe z.b.V. "Stephan,"* which consisted mainly of the remnants of shattered German units from the Belgrade area.

Operating as part of *XXXIV. Armee-Korps* or *Korpsgruppe "Kübler,"* by mid-December the regiment reached the area northwest of Vinkovci. By the beginning of April 1945 the unit had moved to the Drau, and at the end of the month it marched through Legrad toward the old Reich border with Austria, where it surrendered to the western Allies.

Feldpostnummern

Stab	27 085
I./Polizei-Regiment 5	22 732
II./Polizei-Regiment 5	48 819
III./Polizei-Regiment 5	21 591

SS-Polizei-Regiment 6

The regimental headquarters was established in July 1942 for *Polizei-Bataillone 82*, *311*, and *318* by *Korück 103** (*Heeresgruppe "Süd"*) and assigned to the Kiev area (*Korück* = commander army rear area). At first the battalions were still deployed separately within *Polizei-Regiment "Süd"* attached to the three army security divisions:

Polizei-Bataillon 82	with	*454. Sicherungs-Division*
Polizei-Bataillon 311	with	*444. Sicherungs-Division*
Polizei-Bataillon 318	with	*213. Sicherungs-Division*

Feldpostnummern

Stab	48 270
I./SS-Polizei-Regiment 6	37 330
II./SS-Polizei-Regiment 6	14 502
III./SS-Polizei-Regiment 6	37 632

In response to the Soviet winter offensive on the Don, in mid-December 1941 the *I.* and *II. Bataillon* were ordered to the front, and within a few days both units were almost completely destroyed south of Voronezh near Ivanovka, at the small Don bend. What was left of the regiment—including the *III. Bataillon* still with the *213. Sicherungs-Division*—were transferred to Adlershof (West Prussia) and disbanded there.

In October 1944 the Hungarian Regent Admiral von Horthy planned to take Hungary out of the war. Among the many response measures taken by the Germans was the reformation of *SS-Polizei-Regiment 6* in Hungary. *II.* and *III./SS-Polizei-Regiment 1* became the new regiment's 1st and 2nd battalions. The 3rd and 4th battalions were formed using ethnic German recruits. On 29 January 1945 *Heeresgruppe "Süd"* requested that the four battalions be released to man a quiet sector in the *2. Panzer-Armee*'s sector. In March-April 1945 up to three battalions were at the front with the *XXII. Gebirgs-Korps* (first attached to *Gruppe "Steyrer,"* then the *16. SS-Panzergrenadier-Division*). At the end of April the regiment was part of *Korpsgruppe "Rösener"* in the Marburg – Dravograd area, where it was captured.

Feldpostnummern

Stab	23 378
I./SS-Polizei-Regiment 6	08 811
II./SS-Polizei-Regiment 6	04 879
III./SS-Polizei-Regiment 6	19 111
IV./SS-Polizei-Regiment 6	16 792

SS-Polizei-Regiment 7

The regiment was established in *Wehrkreis VI* in July 1942 from *Polizei-Bataillone 123*, *309*, and *317*. In January 1943 it was transferred to the following areas of Norway:

Stab and *I. Bataillon*	Trondheim
II. Bataillon	Spillum
III. Bataillon	Narvik

The regiment remained in the *Reichskommissariat* for the Occupied Norwegian Territories until the end of the war, when it surrendered to the British.

Feldpostnummern

Stab	00 093
I/SS-Polizei-Regiment 7	04 869
II/SS-Polizei-Regiment 7	03 338
III./SS-Polizei-Regiment 7	02 416

SS-Polizei-Regiment 8

The regimental headquarters was established by *Korück 102* (*Heeresgruppe "Mitte"*) in July 1942 for *Polizei-Bataillone 91*, *111*, and *134*. At first the battalions were still deployed separately within *Polizei-Regiment "Mitte,"* attached to the three army security divisions:[64]

Polizei-Bataillon 91	with	*221. Sicherungs-Division*
Polizei-Bataillon 111	with	*403. Sicherungs-Division*
Polizei-Bataillon 134	with	*286. Sicherungs-Division*

Feldpostnummern

Stab	48 012
I./SS-Polizei-Regiment 8	13 683
I/SS-Polizei-Regiment 8	10 742
III./SS-Polizei-Regiment 8	14 268

In August 1942 the battalions were in Gomel, and in September they moved into the Ostrov – Velikiye Luki, an area almost 200 kilometers across. After the start of the Soviet winter offensive, in December 1942 the regiment saw action on the Don front. During the retreat to the Donets, the regiment was virtually wiped out south of Voronezh and was subsequently disbanded. In the spring of 1943 the remnants became the *I. Bataillon* of the newly-formed *Polizei-Schützen-Regiment 38*.

In October 1944 *Polizei-Schützen-Regiment 38* was itself disbanded. The unit's remaining members, bolstered by Hungarian and Slovakian personnel, were used to reestablish *SS-Polizei-Regiment 8*. *I./Polizei-Schützen-Regiment 38* formed the *II. Bataillon*, while Hungarians and Slovakians made up the *I.*, *III.* and *IV. Bataillone*. Establishment of the last two units was not completed, however. By the end of the month elements of the regiment were already in action at the front north of Paks, on the Danube, in the *LXXII. Armee-Korps*' sector. On 13 November 1944 the regiment was in Dunavöldvar, and at the beginning of December it was attached to the *271. Volksgrenadier-Division*. What was left of the regiment was withdrawn from action in January 1945, transferred to the "Protectorate of Bohemia and Moravia" for reorganization, and finally sent to *Heeresgruppe "Weichsel."* Still with just three battalions, together with the newly-formed *Polizei-Regiment 50* it formed the *1. Polizei-Jäger-Brigade*.

The regiment was then attached to *Division 610 z.b.V.* in the Wilhelmshöhe area southwest of Stettin. At the beginning of April 1945 the division was organized as follows:

I./Polizei-Regiment 50
I./SS-Polizei-Regiment 8 (Hungary)
II./SS-Polizei-Regiment 8
10./SS-Polizei-Regiment 8
2 *Volkssturm* battalions
2 construction pioneer companies

On 20 April 1945 the Soviet 65th Army crossed the Oder south of Stettin and established a bridgehead near Wilhelmshöhe in *SS-Polizei-Regiment 8*'s sector. On 21 April 1945 the *3. Panzer-Armee* recorded in its war diary:

"Due to the failure of Polizei-Brigade 1, the enemy gained footholds east and north of Pargow and expanded his bridgehead on both sides of the autobahn through attacks with air and artillery support in the direction of Kolbitzow, Hohenzahden, and Kurow."

While the fighting strength and morale of many *Wehrmacht* units had already fallen by this time, *SS-Polizei-Regiment 8* demonstrated that it was no longer fit for operations, not least because of its mixed composition of ethnic Germans, Hungarians, and Slovakians. Failures of leadership and the poor performance of the attached police units resulted in the commanding general of the *Oder-Korps*, *SS-Obergruppenführer und General der Polizei* von dem Bach, being relieved of his command. The regiment was in a state of disintegration, and from the end of April 1945 had to be viewed as destroyed.

Feldpostnummern

Stab	66 334
I./SS-Polizei-Regiment 8	64 106
II./SS-Polizei-Regiment 8	67 448
III./SS-Polizei-Regiment 8	65 318

SS-Polizei-Regiment 9

The regimental headquarters was established in July 1942 by *Korück 101* (*Heeresgruppe "Nord"*) for *Polizei-Bataillone 61*, *112*, and *132* of *Polizei-Regiment "Nord"* and billeted in Ostrov. Initially the battalions were still deployed separately within *Polizei-Regiment "Nord,"* attached to the three army security divisions:[65]

Polizei-Bataillon 112 with *207. Sicherungs-Division*
Polizei-Bataillon 132 with *281. Sicherungs-Division*
Polizei-Bataillon 61 with *285. Sicherungs-Division*

The regiment took part in the following actions—usually a single battalion separated from the rest of the regiment:

September 1942	*I./Polizei-Regiment* 9 km SE of Krasnogvardeysk *III./Polizei-Regiment* 9 in Mogilev
24/02 – 20/03/43	"Operation Winterzauber" on the Latvian-Russian border
25/10 – 15/11/43	"Operation Heinrich" in the area between Nevel and the Latvian border as part of *Polizei-Kampfgruppe "Jeckeln"*: *Sicherungs-Regiment 113* with attached *III./SS-Polizei-Regiment 9* *Sicherungs-Regiment 773 with attached* *Schutzmannschafts-Bataillon 319* *Polizei-Regiment 1 "Riga"*
00/11/43	*I.* and *II./SS-Polizei-Regiment 9* in action as part of *Sperrverband Oberst von Wagner* (blocking unit) (*132. Infanterie-Division*) in the area north of Lepel.

04/07 – 00/08/44	Action in the Vydziai (Russian Vidze, approx. 60 km S of Dvinsk) between the *215. Infanterie-Division* and *PzAOK 3* as part of *Polizei-Kampfgruppe "Jeckeln"*: *SS-Polizei-Regiment 9* *Polizei-Kampfgruppe "Krukenberg"*[66] *Polizei-Kampfgruppe "Knappe"*[67] *Polizei-Kampfgruppe "Osis"*[68]

Polizei-Regiment 9 was destroyed in the fighting, and the remnants of the *I.* and *III. Bataillon* were merged into *III./SS-Polizei-Regiment 16.* In mid-August 1944 what was left of the *II. Bataillon* was attached to the SS and Police Commander "Bozen." In January 1945 the *Polizei-Regiment "Alpenvorland"* of the SS and Police Commander "Bozen" was renamed *SS-Polizei-Regiment 9.*

Feldpostnummern

Stab	48 526
I./SS-Polizei-Regiment 9	06 545
II./SS-Polizei-Regiment 9	04 097
III./SS-Polizei-Regiment 9	15 121

SS-Polizei-Regiment 10

The unit was established through the renaming of *Polizei-Regiment "Süd"* with *Polizei-Bataillone 45*, *303*, and *314*. Elements of the regiment took part in the following actions:

Summer 1942	Harvest protection in the Ukraine (Nikolayev)
Autumn 1942	Anti-partisan operation in the Pripyat – Rokitno marshes, the so-called "Wet Triangle"
16/02 – 26/02/43	"Operation Hornung" in the Morocz – Milewicze area
09/05 – 10/06/43	"Operation Weichsel I" as part of *Polizei-Kampfgruppe "Schimana"*[69] in the area between marshes in the southwest – the Dniepr in the east, and the Mozyr – Gomel rail line in the north.
18/06 – 24/06/43	"Operation Weichsel II" in the Ovruch – Mozyr – Petrikov – Olevsk area as part of *Polizei-Kampfgruppe "Schimana."*
00/06 – 30/06/43	"Operation Seydlitz" in the Olevsk – Perga – Slavechno area[70]

On 24 December 1943 the Soviet 1st Ukrainian Front again attacked the *4. Panzer-Armee* on the Kiev – Zhitomir road. On 10 January 1944, by order of *SS-Obergruppenführer* Prützmann, Senior SS and Police Commander "Ukraine and Russia South," the German police forces in that area were combined to form a battle group and placed under the *Wehrmacht* Commander "Ukraine" for combat operations in and around Rovno. The police units initially fought in

isolation, but were subsequently reinforced as other police forces arrived. Fighting alongside elements of the *454. Sicherungs-Division*, the best the police units could do was delay the enemy's movements slightly. On 15 January 1944 *Polizei-Kampfgruppe Prützmann* had under its command:[71]

Abteilung "Koellner"		
Stab/SS-Polizei-Regiment 10	FPNr.	36 524
I./SS-Polizei-Regiment 10 (3 companies)		37 718
SS-Polizei-Reiter-Abteilung I		45 231
2./Polizei-Schützen-Regiment 35		03 963
2./Gendarmerie-Hauptmannschaft Charkow (1 platoon)		
1 anti-tank platoon of *SS-Polizei-Regiment 11*		04 562
Abteilung "Gewehr"		
Stab/SS-Polizei-Regiment 11		44 870
III./SS-Polizei-Regiment 10 (3 companies)		37 049
II./SS-Polizei-Regiment 11 (3 companies)		45 718
III./SS-Polizei-Regiment 11		46 591
1 company of *Polizei-Schützen-Regiment 35*		

At the end of March 1944 *SS-Gruppenführer und Generalleutnant der Polizei* Karl Brenner assumed command of the battle group, which was positioned in the area southeast of Dubno (about 50 km NE of Brody). On 5 May, *SS-Polizei-Regimenter 10* and *11* under the command of *Oberst der Schutzpolizei* Koellner were attached to the *361. Infanterie-Division* (*4. Panzer-Armee*) in the main line of resistance near Brody. On 8 July 1944 the battle group was relieved by *Sicherungs-Regiment 360* and all elements were moved to the Yablonka – Krasny area. Not long after this, near Brody, the Red Army encircled elements of the *XIII. Armee-Korps*—including the *361. Infanterie-Division*.

On 21 June 1944 orders were issued for the regiment to proceed to Italy, and at the end of July *SS-Polizei-Regiment 10*, including *Polizei-Nachrichten-Kompanie 121*, was sent to the *Befehlshaber der Ordnungspolizei Triest* in Görz. At first the battalions were rested and brought up to strength in the following areas:

I. Bataillon Senosetsch (approx. 20 km NE of Trieste)
II. Bataillon Zoll (approx. 28 km SE of Görz)
III. Bataillon Görz

Ultimately the battalions took part in the following actions (usually committed separately):

27/09 – 29/09/44	"Operation Klagenfurt" in the Zapatocco – Calle – Hill 720/872 – Taironis – Masarolis – Monte Forchis – Monte Picat – Valle – Costelunga area.
08/10 – 22/10/44	"Operation Wildläufer" in the Tolmezzo – Paluzza – Villa – Santina area
28/11 – 01/12/44	Action in the S. Lucia – Chiapovano – Auzza area
19/12 – 23/12/44	"Operation Adler" in the Görz – Sambasso – Vipacco (Wippach) area with: 1st Regiment of the Serbian Volunteer Corps *III./SS-Polizei-Regiment 10*

	III./SS-Polizei-Regiment 15
	Italian Bersaglieri Battalion "Mussolini"
January 1945	Actions in the Baccia Valley in the Görz Region[72]
March 1945	Actions near Idriza (approx. 30 km NE of Görz) and in the Trieste area
End of April 1945	The regiment marched via Tarvis into the Villach area. Together with other retreating elements of the *10. Armee* and the *LXXXXVII. Armee-Korps*, at the beginning of May 1945 it was ordered back into the Gemona area to establish a defense position. It then went into Allied captivity as part of *SS-Kampfgruppe "Harmel."*

Feldpostnummern

Stab	36 524
I./SS-Polizei-Regiment 10	37 718
II./SS-Polizei-Regiment 10	38 101
III./SS-Polizei-Regiment 10	37 049

SS-Polizei-Regiment 11

The regiment was formed in July 1942 from *Polizei-Bataillone 304*, *315*, and *320* of the former *Polizei-Regiment z.b.V.* in southern Russia, and was deployed in the area east of Dnepropetrovsk. In addition to the usual patrol and guard duties, the battalions also took part in the following actions, often separated from one another:

Summer 1942	Harvest protection in the Ukraine
Autumn 1942	Anti-partisan operations in the Pripyat – Rokitno marshes, the so-called "Wet Triangle"
16/02 – 26/02/43	"Operation Hornung" in the Morocz – Milewcze area
09/05 – 10/06/43	"Operation Weichsel I" as part of *Polizei-Kampfgruppe "Schimana"* in the area between Pripyat in the southwest – the Dniepr in the east, and the Mozyr – Gomel railway line in the north
18/06 – 24/06/43	"Operation Weichsel II" in the Ovruch – Mozyr – Petrikov – Olevsk area as part of *Polizei-Kampfgruppe "Schimana."*
25/06 – 27/07/43	"Operation Seydlitz" in the Olevsk – Perga – Slavechno area
01/08 – 26/10/43	Action in the Shepetovka area (approx. 150 km S of Olevsk)
27/10 – 20/11/43	"Operation Oslo"
10/01 – 26/03/44	Front line action as part of *Kampfgruppe "Prützmann"*[73]
27/03 – 30/04/44	Action in *Polizei-Kampfgruppe "Brenner"*
01/05 – 08/06/44	Action as part of the 361. *Infanterie-Division* in the Brody area
09/06 – 12/06/44	Transfer into the Yablonka – Krasny area
24/07 – 04/09/44	Transfer into the Andrzejowo area (approx. 20 km E of Ostrov) and action as part of the *214. Infanterie-Division* of the *LVI. Panzer-Korps*

The *II.* and *III. Bataillon* were disbanded in November 1944, and their remaining assets reinforced the *I. Bataillon*, which was employed in the *Generalgouvernement* until December 1944. This battalion was then also disbanded near Chelmno.

Feldpostnummern

Stab	44 870
I./SS-Polizei-Regiment 11	46 177
II./SS-Polizei-Regiment 11	45 718
III./SS-Polizei-Regiment 11	46 591

SS-Polizei-Regiment 12

The regimental headquarters was established in Hamburg in July1942 for *Polizei-Bataillone 103*, *104*, and *105* and transferred to the Netherlands. In April 1943 the *I. Bataillon* was sent away to assist in the formation of *Polizei-Schützen-Regiment* 31. That summer the *II. Bataillon* was sent to the *Generalgouvernement*, where it took part in the following actions:

01/08 – 10/08/43 "Operation Weichsel III" in Wolhynia along with:

Wolgatatarischen Infanterie-Bataillon 825 (Volga Tatars)
Kosaken-Kavallerie-Abteilung 102 (Cossack cavalry)
SS-Polizei-Regimenter 4, *13*, and *26*

In April 1944 the unit was transferred to Hungary, and there in August 1944 formed *I./SS-Polizei-Regiment* 1.

The *III. Bataillon* left the Netherlands in October 1943. It was transferred to northern Italy to bolster the German forces there and was placed under the Senior SS and Police Commander "Verona." It took part in the following actions:

01/07 – 07/07/44 "Operation Wallenstein I" in the Emilia – Romagna area under the command of the Flak Commander Italy, together with:

Festungs-Brigade 135
Flak-Regiment 131
Guardia Nazionale Repubblicana

18/07 – 29/07/44 "Operation Wallenstein II" in the Parma – Piacenza – La Spezia area with the same command relationship

00/01 – 00/05/44 Action in Campiglia Marittima in Tuscany

Feldpostnummern

I./SS-Polizei-Regiment 12	no number assigned
II./SS-Polizei-Regiment 12	02 647
III./SS-Polizei-Regiment 12	38 739

During operations the German units frequently lived off the land. Here members of a police unit are "requisitioning" chickens. Interestingly, this police unit is equipped with the modern VW Kübelwagen.

SS-Polizei-Regiment 13

The regimental headquarters was established in July 1942 in Minsk for *Polizei-Bataillone 6, 85*, and *301 of Polizei-Regiment "Mitte"* in central Russia. The battalions, which usually operated independently, took part in the following actions:

18/01 – 27/01/43	"Operation Erntefest I" in the area west of Cherven – Ossipovichi to the Minsk – Slutsk road
28/01 – 09/02/43	"Operation Erntefest II" in the area between Minsk and Slutsk
08/02 – 26/02/43	"Operation Hornung as part of "*Kampfgruppe West*" in the Morocz – Milewicze area in the Pripyat Marshes
01/04 – 04/04/43	"Operation Lenz-Süd" as part of *Einsatzstab "Schimana"* in the Borisov – Sloboda – Smoleviche – Borisov area (less *III. Bataillon*)
08/04 – 13/04/43	"Operation Lenz-Nord" in the Borisov – Smolevichi – Lahoysk – Sembin area
17/04 – 24/04/43	"Operation Zauberflöte" in metropolitan Minsk
27/06 – 11/07/43	"Operation Werwolf I and II" in the Zamosc – Bilgoraj Area (*Generalgouvernement*)
01/08 – 10/08/43	"Operation Weichsel III" in Wohlhynia together with: *Wolgatatarischen Infanterie-Bataillon 825* (Volga Tatars) *Kosaken-Kavallerie-Abteilung 102* (Cossack cavalry) elements of *SS-Polizei-Regimenter 4, 12*, and *26*
30/07 – 25/08/43	"Operation Karpaten" in the Carpathians with: elements of the *154.* and *174. Reserve-Division* *Gendarmerie-Bataillon 1 (mot.)* elements of *Polizei-Regiment 4*
17/08 – 29/08/43	"Operation Greif" in the Vitebsk – Orsha area together with *SS-Polizei-Regiment 14.*
01/11 – 04/11/43	"Operation Heinrich" to destroy the Rosony partisan republic in the area Polotsk – Krasnopolye – Pustoshka – Idritsa – Sebezh. Deployed north of Polotsk, the regiment formed part of *Kampfgruppe "von Gottberg,"*[74] which was made up of the following units: *SS-Polizei-Regiment 2* *SS-Polizei-Regiment 13* (less *II. Bataillon* in Smolensk) *SS-Polizei-Regiment 24* (less *III. Bataillon*)

Because of losses, *III. Bataillon* was disbanded in early 1944 and its remaining assets divided among the other two battalions. In April 1944, the *I.* and *II. Bataillone* were transferred from White Russia to Klagenfurt and placed under the Senior SS and Police Commander "Alpenland" in *Wehrkreis XVIII*. They subsequently took part in actions against partisans between Bleiburg (approx. 35 km E of Klagenfurt) and Solcava (German Sulzbach, approx. 20 km SW of Bleiburg). In mid-December 1944 the regiment participated in an anti-partisan operation with *SS-Polizei-Regiment 28* and the *Lehr-Regiment "Brandenburg"* in the Gornja Savinja area. At the beginning of April 1945 the railway line around Bled (in German Veldes, approx. 30 km S of Villach) was guarded. On 9 April 1945 the regiment moved into the Vorau (approx. 45 km NE of Graz) – Mönichwald area and was attached to *III. Panzer-Korps* (*6. Armee*). Its orders were to hold the area northwest of the Lafnitz together with *Volkssturm* and mountain pioneers of *Sperrverband "Motschmann"* (blocking unit). Costly fighting at the front from 10 April 1945 showed that, like most of the deployed alert and replacement units, the regiment was incapable of stopping the Soviet advance. At the end of April elements of the *I. Bataillon* were again employed against partisans, for example in Eisenkoppel (approx. 20 km SW of Bleiburg).[75] When the war ended the unit surrendered to the western Allies in the Villach area.

Feldpostnummern

Stab	42 307
I./SS-Polizei-Regiment 13	03 316
II./SS-Polizei-Regiment 13	12 047
III./SS-Polizei-Regiment 13	08 159

SS-Polizei-Regiment 14

The regiment was formed in southern Russia in July 1942 from *Polizei-Bataillone 51*, *122*, and *313*, and was deployed in the Kharkov area. The units were initially assigned the following *Feldpostnummern*:

Stab	00 078
I./SS-Polizei-Regiment 14	09 414
II./SS-Polizei-Regiment 14	11 136
III./SS-Polizei-Regiment 14	28 758

In addition to the usual police functions, the regiment also took part in the following actions:

00/06 – 00/06/42	"Operation Potsdam"
19/07 – 12/08/42	20/07 – 07/08/42 "Operation Adler" in the triangle formed by the Mogilev – Beresino – Bobruisk road
14/08 – 26/08/42	"Operation Greif" west and east of the Vitebsk – Orsha road.
02/09 – 07/09/42	"Operation Nordsee" in the area east of Stary Bykhov – South of Mogilev
00/09 – 00/09/42	"Operation Dabusha"
23/09 – 26/09/42	Operation northwest of Kolishenko
04/10 – 09/10/42	"Operation Regatta" in the area south of Gorki and Rekotka
12/10 – 20/10/42	"Operation Karlsbad" north of the Beresino – Chervin road together with: *1. SS-Infanterie-Brigade*, *SS-Sonderkommando "Dirlewanger"*
20/11 – 26/11/42	"Operation Nürnberg" in the area east of Lake Bonin

After the start of the Soviet winter offensive in the sector held by *Heeresgruppe "Süd,"* which led to the defeat at Stalingrad, on 27 November 1942 *Polizei-Regiment 14* was transferred to the Basavka area on the Don. On 15 December it was attached to the *385. Infanterie-Division* near Ivanovka in the area of the hard-pressed and badly battered Italian 8th Army. Largely because of poor tactical decisions, the regiment was decimated in a few days of fierce fighting. It was subsequently combined with the remnants of *I./Polizei-Regiment 6* to form *Kampfgruppe "Grimm."* After the remnants of *Polizei-Regiment 15* arrived *Kampfgruppe "Josten"* was formed in Kupyansk. The regiment was subsequently pulled out of action and sent back to Mogilev. In March 1943, what remained of the regiment was transferred from Alexandriya to Berdichev, and finally to France for reformation. There it was assigned to *Armeegruppe "Felber"* on the Mediterranean Coast front.[76] In the Marseille area the remnants of *Polizei-Regiment 14* formed the new *II. Bataillon*, while *SS-Polizei-Regiment 1* provided the *I.* and *III. Bataillon*. The new *Feldpostnummern* were:

Stab	04 486
I./SS-Polizei-Regiment 14	30 764
II./SS-Polizei-Regiment 14	57 461
III./SS-Polizei-Regiment 14	10 124

The battalions remained on the south coast of France until mid-July 1943, helping evacuate and seal off the port quarter of Marseille, which was destroyed. According to the OKW War Diary, on 16 July 1943 *Polizei-Regiment "Griese" ("Marseille")* was supposed to be transferred to Syrmia for three weeks, as the forces of the *Reichsführer-SS* were no longer sufficient to destroy the bandits appearing in Upper Krain and Lower Styria. In reaction to the change of government in Italy, on 29 July 1943 the regiment—now assigned the number 14—was placed at the disposal of the

Members of SS-Polizei-Regiment 14 during the unit's deployment to northern Italy and Slovenia in the winter of 1943-44.

Oberbefehlshaber "Südost" (CIC Southeast) to guard the border crossings between Croatia and Italy. On 15 August 1943 the regiment was placed under the *Generalkommando III. (germanisches) SS-Panzer-Korps* within the *2. Panzer-Armee*. Nothing came of a planned three-week deployment, and instead the regiment took part in the following actions:

12/10 – 10/11/43	"Operation Wolkenbruch" in the Delnice (approx. 30 km NE of Fiume) – Kocevje (German Gottschee, approx. 50 km NE of Fiume) area, together with: *Infanterie-Regiment 132* and *314* *SS-Polizei-Regiment 19* *SS-Karstwehr-Bataillon* *Gebirgsjäger-Regiment 901* elements of the *71. Infanterie-Division*
02/01 – 14/01/44	"Operation Ostsee" in the Diabla Gora area, together with: *Gendarmerie-Bataillon 1 (mot.)* *Landesschützen-Bataillon 619* *Feldgendarmerie-Zug 62*
00/01/44	Guarding of railway lines around Novo Mesto (German Rudolfswerth, approx. 60 km SE of Laibach)
16/03/44	Combat with partisans near Sentjernej
00/01/44	Fighting near Crnomelj (German Tschernembl, approx. 80 km SE of Laibach)
02/02/45	Partisan attack in the Stranice area (approx. 29 km NE of Cilli)

In March 1945 *SS-Polizei-Regiment 14* received orders to join the *SS-Polizei-Division* on the Eastern Front. For this deployment one battalion was disbanded, resulting in the formation of two stronger battalions. The regiment was taken into the *Waffen-SS* on 6 April 1945 and renamed *SS-Polizei-Grenadier-Regiment 91*. The regiment was destroyed in fighting at Lübben on 22/23 April 1945.[78]

SS-Polizei-Regiment 15

The regiment was formed from *Polizei-Bataillone 305*, *306*, and *310* in July 1942 within *Polizei-Kampfgruppe "Jeckeln"* in northern Russia. It was initially assigned the following *Feldpostnummern*:

Stab	24 745
I./SS-Polizei-Regiment 15	20 080
II./SS-Polizei-Regiment 15	21 241
III./SS-Polizei-Regiment 15	22 665

While the *I. Bataillon* was renamed *III./SS-Polizei-Regiment 16* in northern Russia, *II.* and *III./SS-Polizei-Regiment* were ordered transferred to the Senior SS and Police Commander "Russia South." The regiment was supposed to be brought back up to three battalions there through the addition of *II./SS-Polizei-Regiment 28*.[79] Until the beginning of December 1942 the two battalions were deployed in the Rokitno marshes southeast of Pinsk to prevent White Ruthenian and Wohlhynian partisan groups from linking up along the Pripyat. During this time elements of the regiment were deployed in the area Brest Litovsk – Oltusz (approx. 50 km SE of Brest Litovsk) – Leczna (approx. 22 km east of Lublin) – Zablocie (approx. 50 km NW of Kovel), and in the Kartuska Bereza (approx. 90 km NW of Pinsk) area. There they took part in numerous executions of Polish and Soviet Jews and civilians—for allegedly "*lending aid*" to the partisans. At the end of October 1942 elements of the regiment helped liquidate the ghetto in Pinsk.

After the start of the Soviet winter offensive in the sector held by *Heeresgruppe "Süd,"* at the beginning of December 1942 the regiment was put aboard trains in Pinsk and sent via Gomel, Konotop, Kharkov, and Kupyansk to Valuyki on the Oskol (approx. 125 km NE of Kharkov). From there the two battalions marched through Alexeyevka to Tatarino. They were subsequently deployed with the 2nd Hungarian Army along the Don south of Voronezh. On 18 December 1942 the regiment was attached to *SS-Kampfgruppe "Fegelein"* with the *XXIV. Panzer-Korps* and sent toward the Don Bend. It took up quarters in Mikhailovka. The regiment was subsequently all but wiped out in January 1943 in the fighting for Taly Goloya between the Don and Donets Rivers. What was left was combined with the remnants of the equally decimated *SS-Polizei-Regiment 14* to form *Kampfgruppe "Josten."* In March 1943 the remnants of the regiment were transferred from Alexandriya to Berdichev and finally ordered to Norway for reformation. As of 29 March 1943 the *I. Bataillon* was in Sarpsborg, the *II. Bataillon* in Mysen, and the *III. Bataillon* in Bergen.

Scarcely four months later, on 26 August 1943 the regiment was ordered to northern Italy. Under the SS and Police Commander "Northern Italy-West," the *I. Bataillon* took up quarters in Turin, the *II. Bataillon* in Milan, and the *III. Bataillon* in Trieste.

The battalions took part in the following actions, usually separate from one another:

22/03 – 21/04/44 "Operation Sperber" in the Turin area, together with:
Italian SS Battalion "Debica"[80]
05/09 – 05/10/44 "Operation Strassbourg" in the Val Grande area (east of Ornovasso), together with:
Waffen-Grenadier-Brigade der SS (italienische Nr. 1)[81]

Under the Supreme SS and Police Commander "Italy," when the war ended the regiment marched to Austria and surrendered to British forces there.

Feldpostnummern

Stab	58 985
I./SS-Polizei-Regiment 15	44 077
II./SS-Polizei-Regiment 15	59 243
III./SS-Polizei-Regiment 15	33 345

SS-Polizei-Regiment 16

The regimental headquarters was formed in July 1942 to command four police battalions: *Polizei-Bataillone 56, 102, 121,* and *305* within *Polizei-Kampfgruppe "Jeckeln"* in northern Russia. The *I. Bataillon* was soon withdrawn, rested in Tilsit, and effective 5 February 1943 renamed *I./SS-Polizei-Regiment 3*. The regiment then consisted of three battalions, generally in keeping with the authorized strengths. The individual battalions took part in the following actions:

Summer 1942 Action in *Polizei-Kampfgruppe "Jeckeln"* in front of Leningrad
15/11 – 30/04/43 Attached to the *2. SS-Infanterie-Brigade (mot.)* as part of the so-called *Gruppe "SS-Polizei-Ost,"* together with:
Freiwilligen-Legion "Flandern"
I./Freiwilligen-Legion "Niederlande"
25/10 – 15/11/43 "Operation Heinrich" as part of *Polizei-Kampfgruppe "Jeckeln"* near Nevel with *VIII. AK.*
26/11/43 Action with the *132. Infanterie-Division* in the area of Lake Nesherdo (approx. 50 km NE of Polotsk on the border between Russia and White Russia)
20/12 – 30/12/43 "Operation Otto" under the Senior SS and Police Commander "Ostland and Russia North" in the Rudnya (approx. 10 km SE of Sebezh) – Borkovichi (approx. 30 km NW of Polotsk) area
00/04/44 Guarding of the ghetto in Vilnius

Decimated in action (at the front), in mid-July 1944—probably in anticipation of the expected Soviet summer offensive—an order was issued for the Commander of *Ordnungspolizei* Riga to bring *SS-Polizei-Regiment 16* back up to strength as quickly as possible. What remained of the regiment formed the *I.* and *II. Bataillone*, while the remnants

Hauptwachtmeister der Schupo Herbert Wollnitz was wounded in the Courland on 22/2/1945.

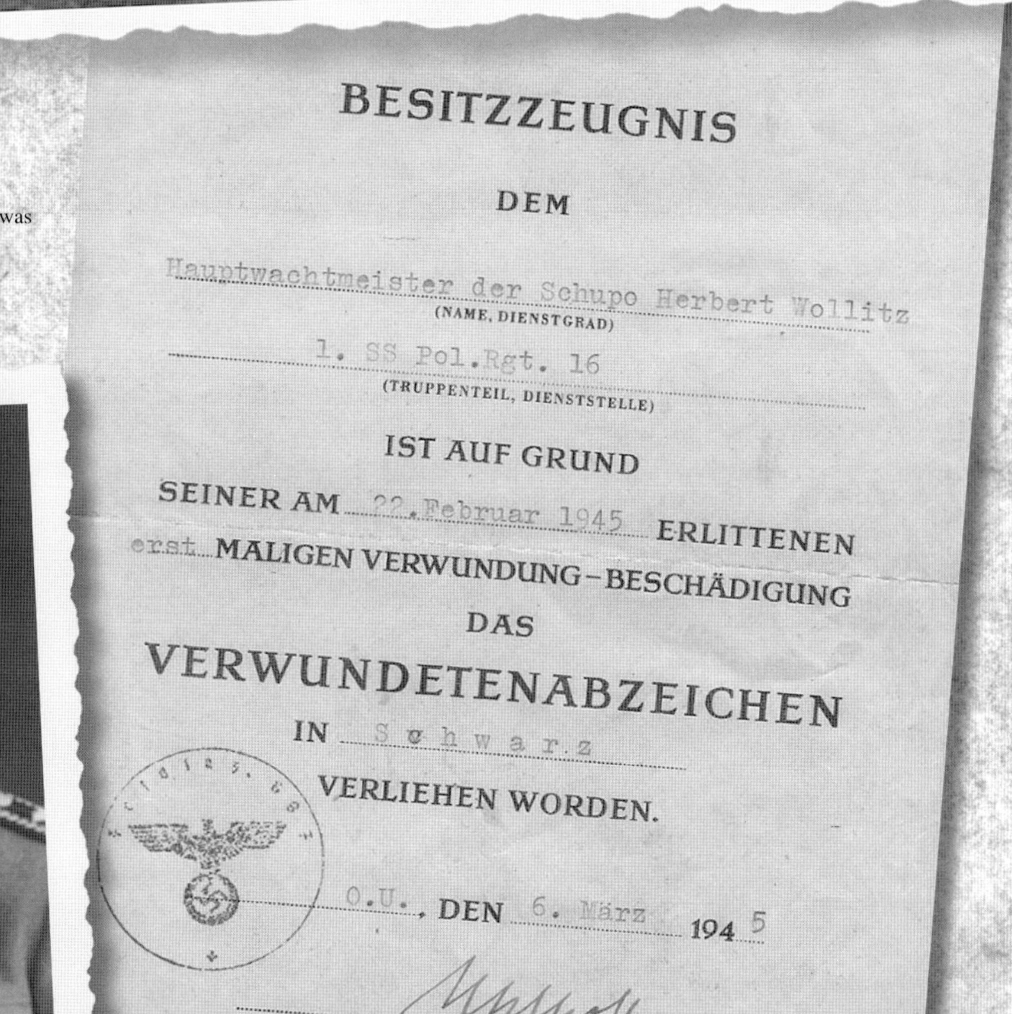

BESITZZEUGNIS

DEM

Hauptwachtmeister der Schupo Herbert Wollitz
(NAME, DIENSTGRAD)

1. SS Pol.Rgt. 16
(TRUPPENTEIL, DIENSTSTELLE)

IST AUF GRUND

SEINER AM 22.Februar 1945 ERLITTENEN
erst MALIGEN VERWUNDUNG – BESCHÄDIGUNG
DAS

VERWUNDETENABZEICHEN

IN Schwarz

VERLIEHEN WORDEN.

O.U., DEN 6. März 1945

(UNTERSCHRIFT)
Oberstabsarzt u.Chefarzt
Feldlazarett (mot) 607
(DIENSTGRAD UND DIENSTSTELLE)

of *I.* and *III./SS-Polizei-Regiment 9* formed the *III. Bataillon.* From the end of July until August 1944 the regiment again saw action at the front with the *132. Infanterie-Division* in the Dvinsk (Dünaberg) area. Attached to *Kampfgruppe "Werther,"* it retreated to Riga, and in October 1944 was placed under the Commander of *Ordnungspolizei* "Ostland" in Libau. Until the end of the war it was mainly engaged in battling partisans in the Courland Pocket.

Feldpostnummern

Stab	25 657
I./SS-Polizei-Regiment 16	23 418
II./SS-Polizei-Regiment 16	46 749
III./SS-Polizei-Regiment 16	20 080
IV./SS-Polizei-Regiment 16	24 126

SS-Polizei-Regiment 17

The regiment was established in northern Russia in July 1942 with *Polizei-Bataillone 42, 69,* and *74.* Soon afterward, the *III. Bataillon* became *I./Polizei-Schützen-Regiment 32* and was replaced by *I./SS-Polizei-Regiment 28* from Norway. In addition to the daily guard duties the regiment participated in the following actions:

27/10 – 29/10/43	"Operation Memel" against Polish partisans in the Starachowice area (approx. 35 km S of Radom), together with: *Gendarmerie-Bataillon 1 (mot.)*; *Polizei-Wach-Bataillon 3*
16/01 – 07/05/44	Action in Kovel as part of Gruppe "von dem Bach"
00/06 – 00/07/44	Action in the area of the Nalibocki Forest (W of Minsk) as part of *Polizei-Kampfgruppe "von Gottberg."* Retreat in the direction of Stolpce.
05/07/44	Retreat as part of *Polizei-Kampfgruppe "von Gottberg"* with the *VI. Armee-Korps* via Lida – Grodno into the Augustov area.[82]
11/07/44	In the area 20 km W of Lida with *Polizei-Regimenter 2, 22,* and *31*
14/07/44	In the area 20 km E of Grodno with *Polizei-Regimenter 2, 22, 31,* and *36*
25/07 – 07/08/44	Reorganization of the regiment at the "Kuznica" training camp (approx. 20 km S of Grodno)
08/08 – 21/09/44	*I./SS-Polizei-Regiment 17*, reinforced by *I./Polizei-Schützen-Regiment 34*, attached to *Polizei-Brigade "Anhalt"* in the Grodno – Bialystok – East Prussian border area, together with *SS-Polizei-Regimenter 2* and *4* (*I.* and *III. Bataillone*)
22/09 – 06/10/44	Action as part of *Polizei-Kampfgruppe "Oberst Danz"* with *VI. Armee-Korps (4. Armee)*
07/10 – 12/10/44	Action as part of *Polizei-Kampfgruppe "Hannibal"*
00/11/44	Transfer to the Slovenska Bistrica area (approx. 20 km NE of Cilli) in Slovenia and participation in an operation in the mountains north of Sostanj (German Schöstein, approx. 20 km NW of Cilli)
30/03 – 09/05/45	Transfer to Kranj (German Kramburg).[83] The regiment was ultimately attached to *Kampfgruppe "von Seeler"* and with it marched through the Loibl Pass and across the Drau together with *SS-Polizei-Regimenter 19* and *28.* It surrendered to the British north of Ferlach on 9 May 1945.

Feldpostnummern

Stab	26 764
I./SS-Polizei-Regiment 17	03 634
II./SS-Polizei-Regiment 17	07 703
III./SS-Polizei-Regiment 17	40 937

SS-Polizei-Gebirgsjäger-Regiment 18

The formation of a *SS-Polizei-Gebirgsjäger-Regiment* began in the Garmisch-Partenkirchen – Mittenwald area in response to an order issued on 23 May 1942. *Polizei-Bataillone 302*, *312*, and *325* were brought together for this purpose. In July 1942 the regiment was given the number "18." Initially deployed in the Upper Krain, the regiment took part in the following actions:

00/07/42	"Operation Enzian" in the Horjol area (approx. 15 km W Laibach)
03/08 – 05/08/42	Fighting in the Blega massif (approx. 30 km NW of Laibach)
10/08 – 14/08/42	Fighting on the Jelovica Plateau (approx. 40 km NW of Laibach)
19/08 – 21/08/42	Fighting on the Krvavec (25 km N of Laibach)
08/09 – 09/09/42	Fighting on the Jelovica Plateau (approx. 40 km NW of Laibach)
13/09 – 14/09/42	Fighting in the Herzogwald

At the beginning of 1943 the regiment was transferred to the *20. Gebirgs-Armee* in Finland. Attached to *SS-Gebirgs-Division "Nord,"* it was deployed in the southern sector of the so-called "Gudrun Position" in the area northeast of Kiestinki on the division's right flank. There was no serious fighting there, and in early July 1943 Himmler requested its transfer to the Balkans. The OKW subsequently advised that the regiment was expected to arrive in the Amfissa area (approx. 20 km W of Liakoura) of Greece in mid-August 1943. Initially deployed on security duties on the mainland, at the beginning of June 1944 the regiment was moved to Megalopolis, and for about a month it was under the direct command of the "Leader of the Defense of the Peloponnese" (C.O. of the *117. Jäger-Division*). In addition to defending against a feared Allied invasion of the Peloponnese, the regiment took part in the following actions:

06/06 – 20/06/44	"Operation Natter" in a battle group of the *117. Jäger-Division* in the Tripolis – Sparta area
25/06 – 05/07/44	"Operation Adler," the largest operation on the Peloponnese, with: elements of the *117. Jäger-Division* *Aufklärungs-Abteilung 116* *Aufklärungs-Abteilung 83* *Luftwaffen-Jäger-Regiment 22* Greek volunteer units

On 5 July 1944 the regiment was transferred back to the mainland in the Tripolis – Sparta area and proceeded via Corinth to Athens and Lamia. There elements of the division took part in the following actions:

05/08 – 26/08/44	"Operation Kreuzotter" with the *104. Jäger-Division* west of Amfissa in the Karoutia area
15/09/44	After the retreat from Greece the bulk of the regiment was in Pozarvac
03/10 – 23/10/44	Attached to *Panzergrenadier-Division "Brandenburg"* within *Generalkommando "Müller,"* it took part in the fighting for Belgrade
25/10 – 01/12/44	Retreat into the Erdevik area as part of *Kampfgruppe "Lindemann"*
03/12 – 14/02/45	Action as part of the *118. Jäger-Division* (*XXIV. A.K.*) between Valpovo and Osiek (German Esseg)
15/02 – 31/03/45	Positions in the Sopje area (approx. 80 km NW of Essig) on the Drau
01/04 – 09/05/45	March into the Koprivnica – Varasdin area and attached to *Kampfgruppe "Fischer"* within the *XV. Kosaken-Kavallerie-Korps*. Retreat through Marburg to Austria.

Feldpostnummern

Stab	12 085
I./SS-Polizei-Gebirgsjäger-Regiment 18	17 228
II./SS-Polizei-Gebirgsjäger-Regiment 18	18 146
III./SS-Polizei-Gebirgsjäger-Regiment 18	19 754

Wilhelm Hütten joined the police as a Wachtmeister with no prior service on 1/3/41. He subsequently joined Polizei-Ausbildungs-Bataillon Eilenburg II for training, which lasted from 15/3 – 15/8/1941.

Training subjects included:

- weapons training
- civil air defense
- ideological instruction, which by circular order became mandatory in the Ordnungspolizei on 15/4/1937
- police law
- traffic law

As a rule, training for members of police battalions lasted six months. As it was assumed in the beginning that the Ordnungspolizei would not be engaged in regular combat duties, guidelines for improvised operational training for action in the east were not issued until 1942. Nevertheless, because of the age of its personnel and gaps in training the police battalions and regiments were not nearly as capable as those of the army.

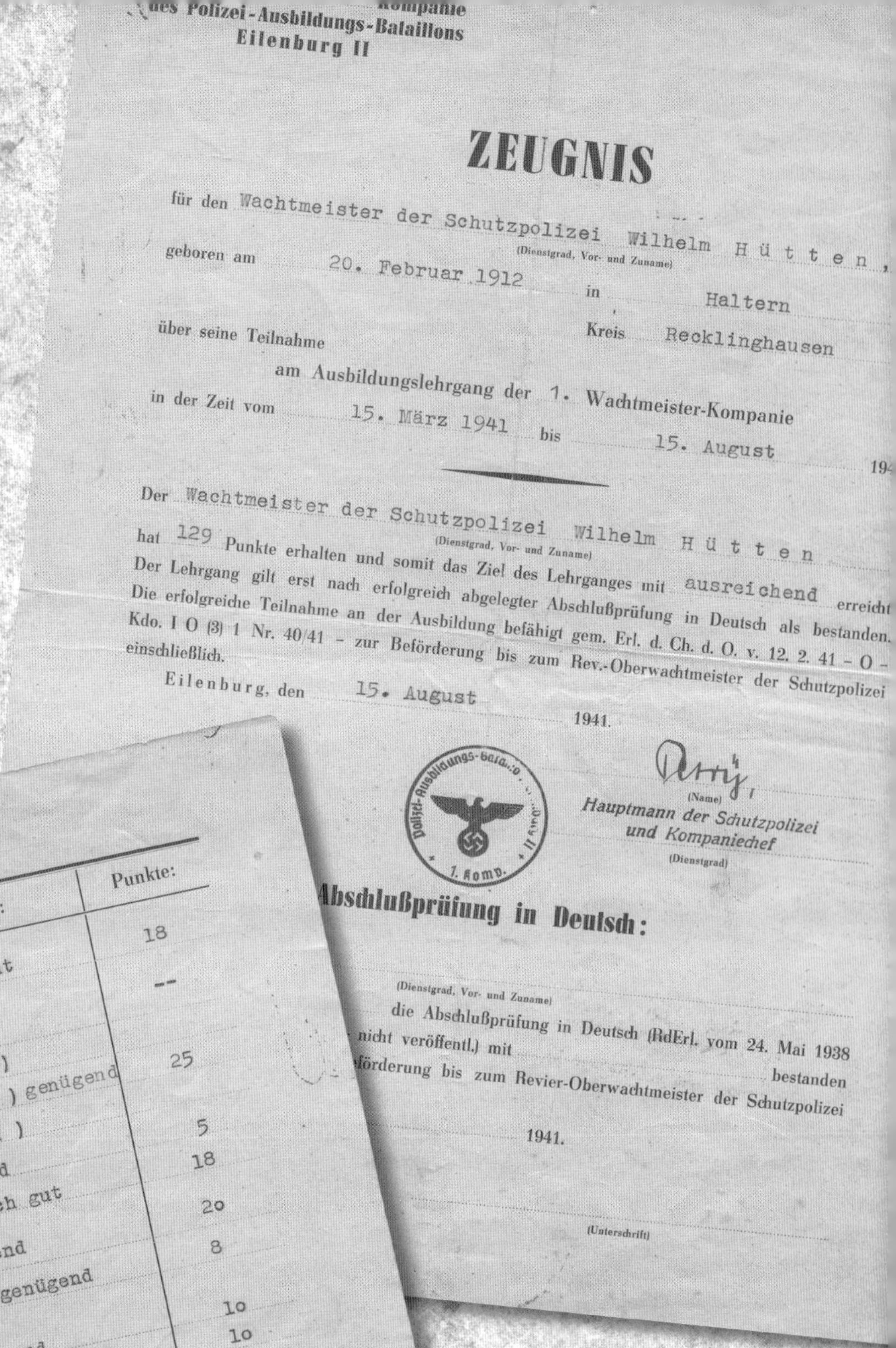

Kompanie
des Polizei-Ausbildungs-Bataillons
Eilenburg II

ZEUGNIS

für den Wachtmeister der Schutzpolizei Wilhelm Hütten,
(Dienstgrad, Vor- und Zuname)
geboren am 20. Februar 1912 in Haltern
Kreis Recklinghausen
über seine Teilnahme
am Ausbildungslehrgang der 1. Wachtmeister-Kompanie
in der Zeit vom 15. März 1941 bis 15. August 19

Der Wachtmeister der Schutzpolizei Wilhelm Hütten
(Dienstgrad, Vor- und Zuname)
hat 129 Punkte erhalten und somit das Ziel des Lehrganges mit ausreichend erreicht.
Der Lehrgang gilt erst nach erfolgreich abgelegter Abschlußprüfung in Deutsch als bestanden.
Die erfolgreiche Teilnahme an der Ausbildung befähigt gem. Erl. d. Ch. d. O. v. 12. 2. 41 – O – Kdo. I O (3) 1 Nr. 40/41 – zur Beförderung bis zum Rev.-Oberwachtmeister der Schutzpolizei einschließlich.

Eilenburg, den 15. August 1941.

Polizei-Ausbildungs-Bataillon Eilenburg II, 1. Komp.

(Name)
Hauptmann der Schutzpolizei und Kompaniechef
(Dienstgrad)

Abschlußprüfung in Deutsch:

(Dienstgrad, Vor- und Zuname)
die Abschlußprüfung in Deutsch (RdErl. vom 24. Mai 1938 nicht veröffentl.) mit bestanden
förderung bis zum Revier-Oberwachtmeister der Schutzpolizei
1941.
(Unterschrift)

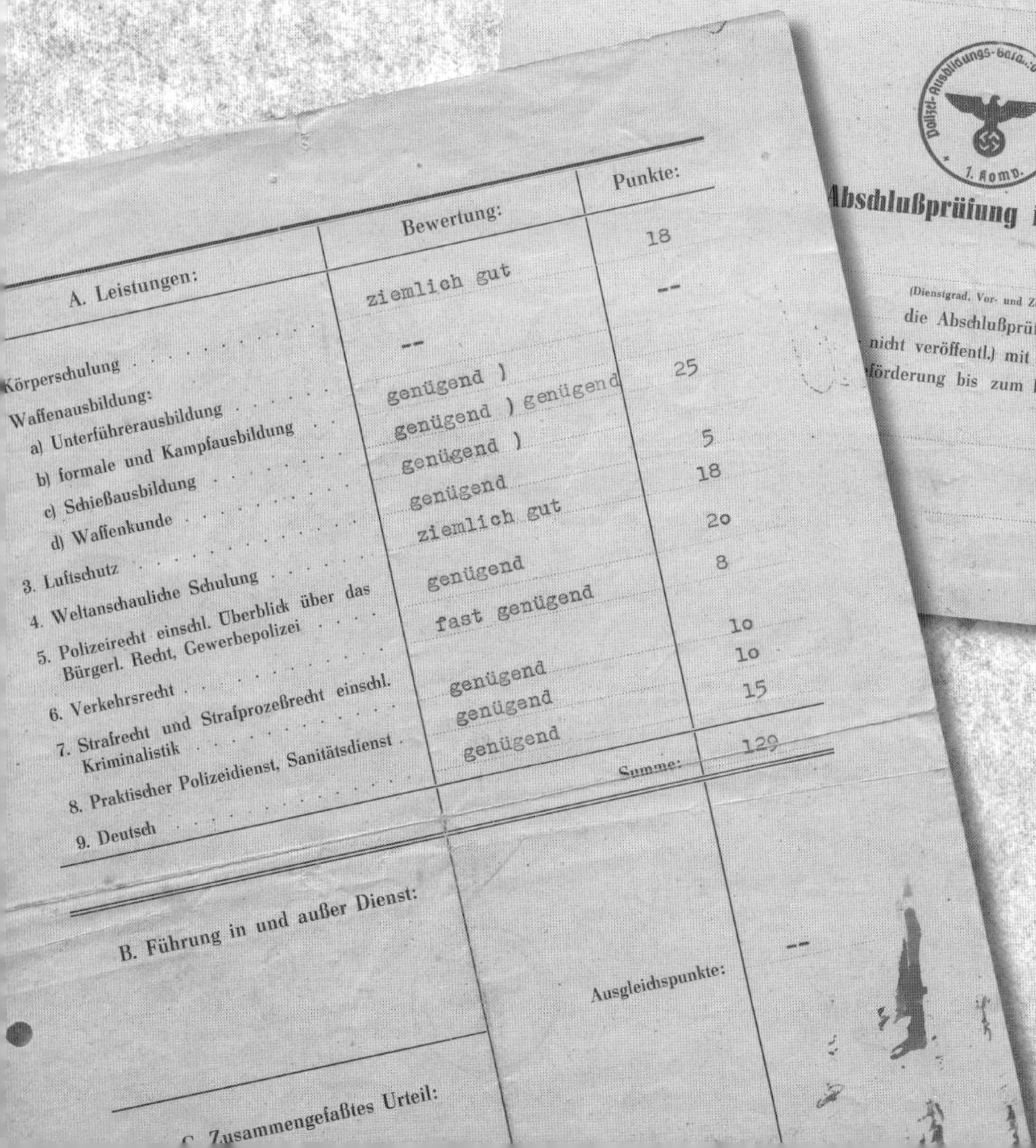

A. Leistungen:	Bewertung:	Punkte:
Körperschulung	ziemlich gut	18
Waffenausbildung:	--	--
a) Unterführerausbildung	genügend)	25
b) formale und Kampfausbildung	genügend) genügend	
c) Schießausbildung	genügend)	
d) Waffenkunde	genügend	5
3. Luftschutz	ziemlich gut	18
4. Weltanschauliche Schulung	genügend	20
5. Polizeirecht einschl. Überblick über das Bürgerl. Recht, Gewerbepolizei	fast genügend	8
6. Verkehrsrecht	genügend	10
7. Strafrecht und Strafprozeßrecht einschl. Kriminalistik	genügend	10
8. Praktischer Polizeidienst, Sanitätsdienst	genügend	15
9. Deutsch	Summe:	129

B. Führung in und außer Dienst:

Ausgleichspunkte: --

C. Zusammengefaßtes Urteil:

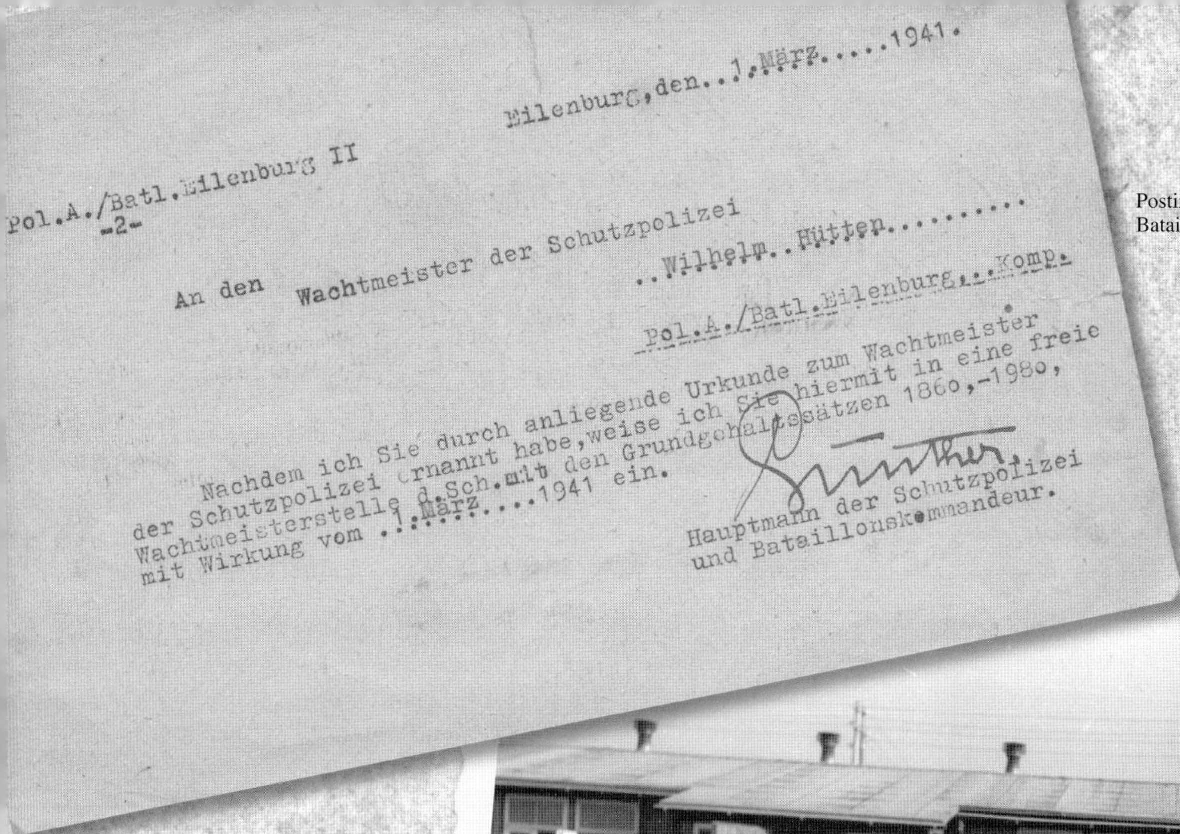

Eilenburg, den...1.März.....1941.

Pol.A./Batl.Eilenburg II
-2-

An den Wachtmeister der Schutzpolizei
..Wilhelm..Hütten.........
Pol.A./Batl.Eilenburg...Komp.

Nachdem ich Sie durch anliegende Urkunde zum Wachtmeister der Schutzpolizei ernannt habe, weise ich Sie hiermit in eine freie Wachtmeisterstelle d.Sch.mit den Grundgehaltssätzen 1860,-1980, mit Wirkung vom ..1.März.....1941 ein.

Günther
Hauptmann der Schutzpolizei
und Bataillonskommandeur.

Posting order issued by Polizei-Ausbildungs-Bataillon Eilenburg II, dated 1/3/41.

Inspection by the police training battalion's commanding officer.

After completion of training followed operational assignments.

St.Qu., den 9.11.1943

SS-Pol.Geb.Jäg.Rgt.18

An den

Obw.d.Sch. Wilhelm H ü t t e n , III.Btl.

Hiermit weise ich Sie in eine freie Rev.-Obw.-Stelle der Gruppe A 8 c 2 der Reichsbesoldungsordnung mit Wirkung vom 1.11.1943 ein.

Obstlt.u.Rgts.-Kdr.

Members of SS-Polizei-Gebirgsjäger-Regiment 18.

SS-Polizei-Regiment 19

The regiment was formed in Veldes in July 1942 from *Polizei-Bataillone 72*, *171*, and *181* for the Senior SS and Police Commander "Alpenland," and was deployed primarily in the Kamnik (German Stein) area. In addition to the usual police duties such as site protection and patrolling, elements of the regiment took part in the following actions:

29/09/42	Operation in the Trbovlje (German Trifail, approx. 20 km SW of Cilli) – Prebold (German Pragwald, approx. 15 km NW of Cilli)
00/01/43	Combing of the mountains near Kropa (German Kropp, approx. 80 km W of Cilli)
25/02/43	Action near Marija Reka near Pragwald
19/09/43	Disarming of Italian troops
12/10 – 10/11/43	"Operation Wolkenbruch" in the Delnice (approx. 30 km NE of Fiume) – Kocevje (German Gottschee, approx. 50 km NE of Fiume) area, together with: *Infanterie-Regiment 132* and *314* *SS-Polizei-Regiment 14* *SS-Karstwehr-Bataillon* *Gebirgsjäger-Regiment 901* elements of the *71. Infanterie-Division*
00/05/44	Transfer into the Mont Mouchet area (Départements Cantal – Haute-Loire – Loziere) of France
00/06/44	Transfer into the Paris area following the Allied invasion in Normandy
05/06/44	Action in the so-called "Free Republic of Vercors" together with: *157. Reserve-Division* *I./Sicherungs-Regiment 200* 3 *Ost-Bataillone*
15/08/44	After the Allied invasion of southern France, transfer into the Grenoble area to guard the formation area of the *16. Volksgrenadier-Division*.[84]

On 3 September 1944 Himmler ordered that the regiment was to guard Marshall Petain and his administration in Belfort. During the course of the Allied advance, in mid-September 1944 elements of the regiment were sent to *Kampfgruppe "Ottenbacher"*[85] (*LXIV. Armee-Korps*) in the Langres area (65 km N of Dijon). Then, at the end of September, the regiment was attached to the *LXVI. Armee-Korps*. In October 1944 the regiment was in the Bruyeres area (50 km NW of Colmar) in Alsace as part of the *16. Volksgrenadier-Division* fighting against American troops.

At the beginning of March 1945 the regiment was transferred to the Cilli area in Slovenia. Ultimately it was attached to *Kampfgruppe "von Seeler."* Together with *Polizei-Regimenter 17* and *28* the regiment marched through the Loibl Pass and across the Drau, and on 9 May 1945 it surrendered to the British north of Ferlach.

Feldpostnummern

Stab	56 526
I./SS-Polizei-Regiment 19	57 205
II./SS-Polizei-Regiment 19	59 731
III./SS-Polizei-Regiment 19	58 498

Members of SS-Polizei-Regiment 19 in Slovenia. The obsolete weapons (e.g., MG 08/15) and old vehicles (e.g. Ford AA) are typical for units of the Ordnungspolizei deployed in "secondary theaters."

SS-Polizei-Regiment 20

The regiment was created in July 1942 through the renaming of *Polizei-Regiment "Böhmen"*—which included *Polizei-Bataillone 316* and *320*. In April 1943, *I. Bataillon* from Prague became *I./Polizei-Schützen-Regiment 33* and was replaced by *Polizei-Ausbildungs-Bataillon "Klagenfurt."* In October 1943 this new *I./SS-Polizei-Regiment 20* moved to the Rome area as an independent battalion. In June 1944 it was assigned to Emilia (northern Italy), and in September to Biella (approx. 90 km W of Milan). It took part in the following actions:

29/03 – 07/04/44	Operations near Perugia (approx. 135 km N of Rome, with: alert units of *Platzkommandantur "Rieti"* (approx. 60 km NE of Rome) *II./3. Regiment "Brandenburg"* *Panzer-Aufklärungs-Abteilung 103* *Panzer-Aufklärungs-Abteilung 190* *Panzer-Abteilung 190*
07/04 – 17/04/44	"Operation Monte Tancia" (approx. 50 km NE of Rome)
12/04 – 13/04/44	"Operation Osterei" in the same area
24/06 – 26/06/44	Action together with *Flak-Regiment 131* and elements of the *1. Fallschirmjäger-Division* near Marzabotto (SW of Bologna)
00/10 – 00/11/44	"Operation Avanti" in the Lago Maggiore area against the Ossola partisan republic (approx. 90 km NW of Milan), together with: *Marinekommando 80* elements of *SS-Polizei-Regiment 15*

Finally, until the end of the war the battalion was attached to the Senior SS and Police Commander (Upper Italy West).

In March 1944 the *II. Bataillon* was transferred from Kolin to Hungary to serve as an occupation unit, and in August 1944 formed the new *I./SS-Polizei-Regiment 1*.

The *III. Bataillon* and the regimental headquarters remained in Klattau (Bohemia) until the end of the war.

Feldpostnummern

I./SS-Polizei-Regiment 20	01 662
II./SS-Polizei-Regiment 20	08 811
III./SS-Polizei-Regiment 20	in the Protectorate, no *Feldpostnummer*

SS-Polizei-Regiment 21

The regiment was created in July 1942 through the renaming of *Polizei-Regiment "Mähren."* In April 1943 the *I. Bataillon* in Brünn became *I./Polizei-Schützen-Regiment 34*, and only later was the unit nominally rebuilt from various police companies stationed in the "Protectorate of Bohemia and Moravia." The regimental headquarters and the newly-formed *I. Bataillon* remained in Brünn, and in April 1945, together with the *II. Bataillon* from Iglau, they were mobilized for front line action against the Red Army in the Beskiden. In March 1944 the *III. Bataillon* moved from Mährisch-Ostrau to Hungary as an occupation unit. There it became *III./SS-Polizei-Regiment 1* in August 1944.

Feldpostnummern

Stab	40 973
I./SS-Polizei-Regiment 21	43 750
II./SS-Polizei-Regiment 21	44 618
III./SS-Polizei-Regiment 21	04 879

SS-Polizei-Regiment 22

The regiment was established in July 1942 from the regimental headquarters of the *Polizei-Regiment "Warschau," Polizei-Bataillone 41* and *53*, and a new *III. Bataillon* created from police companies stationed in the *Generalgouvernement*. From mid-April to the end of May 1943 the regiment took part in the liquidation of the Warsaw ghetto. "Operation Erntefest" began in November 1943 and saw Jews from the labor camps at Trawniki and Poniatowo taken to Maidanek (Lublin concentration camp) and shot. In June 1944 the regiment was assembled in Warsaw and sent to *Polizei-Kampfgruppe "von Gottberg"* in *Heeresgruppe "Mitte."* The regiment was almost completely wiped out in the fighting in the area of the Nalibocki Forest (west of Minsk). The remnants were attached to *SS-Polizei-Regiment 2* on 12 July 1944, and on 21 December the regiment was disbanded.

Feldpostnummern

Stab	56 739
I./SS-Polizei-Regiment 22	58 244
II./SS-Polizei-Regiment 22	57 181
III./SS-Polizei-Regiment 22	39 947

SS-Polizei-Regiment 23

The regiment was created in July 1942 from the regimental headquarters of *Polizei-Regiment "Krakau," Polizei-Bataillon 307*, and numerous individual police companies stationed in the *Generalgouvernement*. It took part in the following actions, mainly in separate units:

25/08 – 03/09/42	"Operation Sumpffieber", together with the *1. SS-Infanterie-Brigade (mot.)* in the Baranovichi area
00/11/42	"Operation Tannenbaum"
24/12/42	"Operation Ristow" in the Pripyat Marshes near Lusino
05/01 – 14/01/43	"Operation Franz" in the area southeast of Cherven
01/04 – 04/04/43	"Operation Lenz-Süd" as part of *Einsatzstab "Schimana"* in the Borisov – Sloboda – Smoleviche – Borisov area
08/04 – 13/04/43	"Operation Lenz-Nord" in the Borisov – Smolevichi – Lahoysk – Sembin area
17/04 – 24/04/43	"Operation Zauberflöte" in the White-Russian capital of Minsk
25/06 – 27/07/43	"Operation Seydlitz" in the Ovruch – Mozyr area
01/11 – 04/11/43	"Operation Heinrich" in the Rosony area
06/11 – 07/11/43	"Operation Ulanen" in the Dabrovka – Yaroslav area, together with:
	Polizei-Schützen-Regiment 32
	Landesschützen-Bataillon 405
00/11 – 00/04/44	Action at the front in the Polotsk area
16/04 – 12/05/44	"Operation Frühlingsfest" in the Ushatshi area
26/06 – 14/07/44	Action at the front near Orsha, Borisov, and Minsk
15/07 – 21/07/44	"Operation Wirbelsturm" in the Parczew area with:
	Landesschützen-Bataillone 310, 619, 887, 888, 990, 991, and *992*
	Transfer to Kattowitz for rest and refit
	Disbandment of *II. Bataillon* in November 1944
18/01 – 00/03/45	*I. Bataillon* in action at the front near Bendsburg – Sossnowitz – Hindenburg – Gleiwitz

The regiment, whose *III. Bataillon* had long been employed to guard the labor camp at Auschwitz, was disbanded in March 1945.

Feldpostnummern

Stab	59 030
I./SS-Polizei-Regiment 23	20 822
II./SS-Polizei-Regiment 23	57 506
III./SS-Polizei-Regiment 23	58 416

Opposite, in the center: the SS and Police Commander in the Warsaw District, SS-Brigadeführer Stroop, during the liquidation of the Warsaw Ghetto in May

Im

Namen des Führers

ernenne ich

unter Berufung in das Beamtenverhältnis

den

Johannes Vogelsang

zum Polizei-Wachtmeister

Ich vollziehe diese Urkunde in der Erwartung, daß der Ernannte getreu seinem Diensteide seine Amtspflichten gewissenhaft erfüllt und das Vertrauen rechtfertigt, das ihm durch diese Ernennung bewiesen wird. Zugleich darf er des besonderen Schutzes des Führers sicher sein.

Heidenheim (Brenz), den 25. Juni 1940

Für den Reichsminister des Innern

Major d. Sch.
und
Kommandeur des Ausbildungsbataillons

For his actions during the liquidation of the Warsaw Ghetto in April-May 1943, Oberwachtmeister Vogelsang was awarded the War Merit Cross, Second Class with Swords by the SS and Police Commander in the Warsaw District.

IM NAMEN DES FÜHRERS
UND OBERSTEN BEFEHLSHABERS
DER WEHRMACHT
VERLEIHE ICH
DEM

Oberwachtmeister d. Schutzpolizei
Johannes Vogelsang
II./SS- Polizei Regiment 22

DAS
KRIEGSVERDIENSTKREUZ
2. KLASSE
MIT SCHWERTERN

Warschau, DEN 15.Juni 1943

GENERALGOUVERNEMENT (DIENSTSIEGEL) DER SS- UND POLIZEIFÜHRER IM DISTRIKT WARSCHAU

Der SS- u. Polizeiführ
im Distrikt Warscha

SS- Brigadeführer u.
Generalmajor d. Polize
(DIENSTGRAD UND DIENSTSTELLUNG)

SS-Polizei-Regiment 24

The regiment was established in Lemberg (Lvov) in July 1942 from the regimental headquarters of *Polizei-Regiment "Radom"* and *Polizei-Bataillone 83*, *93*, and 133, with the *III. Bataillon* separate from the others in Upper Krain. In September 1942 the *I.* and *II. Bataillon* were employed in the *Generalgouvernement* to move several thousand Jews to the "Belzec" camp. In mid-October 1942 the regimental headquarters, together with *I.* and *II. Bataillon*, moved to the Lahoysk area (approx. 40 km NE of Minsk) in White Russia and took part in the following actions:

07/01 – 14/01/43	"Operation Franz" as part of *Polizei-Kampfgruppe "von Gottberg"* in the area between Minsk and Beresina
05/02 – 10/02/43	"Operation Albert" in the Uzda area together with:
	II./Polizei-Regiment 14
	Sicherungs-Bataillon 555
00/03/43	Action at the front near Briansk as part of the *2. Panzer-Armee*
01/11 – 11/11/43	"Operation Heinrich" in the Polotsk area as part of *Polizei-Kampfgruppe "von Gottberg"*
26/03 – 16/04/44	"Operation Regenschauer" attached to PzAOK 4
16/04 – 12/05/44	"Operation Frühlingsfest" in the Ushatshi area
22/05 – 20/06/44	"Operation Kormoran" in the Molodechno area with:
	SS-Polizei-Regiment 2 and *13*
	221. Sicherungs-Division
	391. Feldausbildungs-Division
22/06 – 08/07/44	Retreat from Molodechno to Lido as part of *Kampfgruppe "von Gottberg"*

On 12 July 1944 the remnants of the two battalions were attached to *SS-Polizei-Regiment 2*. Orders were issued for the battalions to be reformed in the Kattowitz – Hindenburg area in November 1944. In spring 1945, together with *I./SS-Polizei-Regiment 23*, they were attached to *Kampfgruppe "Aug"*[86] and saw action in the Schwanowitz – Brieg area in Upper Silesia.

III./SS-Polizei-Regiment 24, which was deployed apart from the other two battalions, took part in the following actions in the Upper Krain:

00/08 – 00/09/42	"Operation Enzian" west of Laibach
00/09/42	Action in the area east of Kamnik
11/11/42	Action in the Vransko area (German Franz, approx. 20 km W of Cilli)
00/01/43	Transfer to France for the formation of *Polizei-Regiment "Griese"* in Marseille

Feldpostnummern

Stab	58 830
I./SS-Polizei-Regiment 24	13 639
II./SS-Polizei-Regiment 24	22 086
III./SS-Polizei-Regiment 24	03 963

SS-Polizei-Regiment 25

The regiment was formed in Lublin in July 1942 from the regimental headquarters of *Polizei-Regiment "Lublin"* and *Polizei-Bataillonen 65 "Cholm," 67*, and *101*. In addition to the usual duties of a police unit in the *Generalgouvernement*, elements of the regiment took part in the following actions:

22/11 – 00/07/43 Formation of a special purpose police battalion for the resettlements in the Zamosc area.[87]
02/02 – 11/02/43 "Operation Attila" in the Zamosc – Bilgoraj area together with:
Landesschützen-Bataillon 582
Gendarmerie-Bataillon 1
22/04 – 24/04/43 "Operation Ostersegen" in the Parczew – Ostrow (approx. 40 km NE of Lublin) area together with:
Landesschützen-Bataillon 268
Polizei-Schützen-Regiment 32
Schutzmannschafts-Bataillon 203
02/06 – 04/06/43 "Operation Nachpfingsten" with:
Polizei-Schützen-Regiment 32
Schutzmannschafts-Bataillon 203
27/06 – 11/07/43 "Operation Werewolf I and II" in the Zamosc – Bilgoraj area together with:
SS-Polizei-Regimenter 4, 13, 26 and *32*
Infanterie-Bataillon 790 (turk.)
14/10/43 Putting down of the uprising in the Sobibor camp
19/10 – 28/10/43 "Operation Gebrüll" in the Diabla Gora with:
Schutzmannschafts-Bataillon 206
Landesschützen-Bataillonen 994 and *995*
00/11/43 "Operation Erntefest"[88]
04/01 – 10/01/44 "Operation Wintersport" in the Opole Lubelskie together with:
Landesschützen-Bataillone 992
09/04 – 27/04/44 "Operation Immergrün" in the Chelmno – Krasnytav area together with:
Polizei-Schützen-Regiment 32
Landesschützen-Bataillone 991
05/05 – 16/05/44 "Operation Maigewitter" in the Lublin (Parczew – Krasnik) area together with elements of:
5. SS-Panzer-Division "Wiking"
SS-Polizei-Regiment 4
08/06 – 23/06/44 "Operation Vagabund" in the Radzyn Podlaski – Wlodawa – Cholm – Parczew together with:
Polizei-Schützen-Regiment 32
SS-Polizei-Regiment 4
Landesschützen-Bataillonen 991 and *992*

The I./*SS-Polizei-Regiment* 25 was transferred into the Cilli – Laibach area in March 1944 and took part in the following actions:

14/05 – 25/05/44 "Operation Anton I" in the Kamnik – Celje – Sostanj – Crna – Slovenjgradec area with:
SS-Polizei-Regimenter 13 and *14*
Landesschützen-Regiment 18
Gebirgsjäger-Regiment 134
elements of the Styrian *Wehrmannschaft*
15/02/45 Transfer to Novo Mesto

In May 1945 the battalion marched out of the Rudolfswerth area through Zidani to Cilli, where on 14 May 1945 it surrendered to British forces.

Feldpostnummern

Stab	57 607
I./SS-Polizei-Regiment 25	38 608
II./SS-Polizei-Regiment 25	59 596
III./SS-Polizei-Regiment 25	56 048

SS-Polizei-Regiment 26

At the end of July 1942 *Polizei-Regiment "Nord-Norwegen,"* consisting of *Polizei-Bataillone 251, 255,* and *256*, was renamed *Polizei-Regiment 26.* At the beginning of May 1943 it was moved to *Wehrkreis XX* (Danzig – West Prussia) and reorganized for employment in the east. At the end of the month a total of just under 700 young police members from the Dortmund and Fichtenwalde garrisons joined the regiment. The battalions took part in the following actions, initially in the *Generalgouvernement*:

19/06 – 06/07/43	Employment in the Tomaszow area (*Generalgouvernement*)
27/06 – 11/07/43	"Operation Werewolf I and II" in the Zamosc – Bilgoraj area
08/07 – 25/07/43	Employment in the Lutsk – Kovel area (Ukraine)
26/07 – 11/08/43	Employment in the Stanislau – Hungarian border area
01/08 – 10/08/43	"Operation Weichsel III" in Wohlhynia
16/08 – 20/08/43	Liquidation of the ghettos in Bialystok and Glebokie and the deportation of approx. 10,000 Jews to Treblinka
00/09/43	Action in the Zamosc area against the so-called Kolpak Brigade
25/10 – 15/11/43	"Operation Heinrich" between Nevel and the Latvian border
20/12 – 31/12/43	"Operation Otto" in the Rudnya – Klyastitsy – Tserkovische – Borkovichi – Martinovo – Strelki – Chernovoki – Stoki area. Advancing from the area on both sides of Zebezh, the regiment was to advance south to the Dvinsk – Polotsk rail line.
16/01 – 10/02/44	Deployed with the *263. Infanterie-Division* (*16. Armee*) as part of *Polizei-Kampfgruppe "Jeckeln"*
14/02 – 07/03/44	Deployed with the *83. Infanterie-Division* (*16. Armee*) as part of *Polizei-Kampfgruppe "Jeckeln"*
16/04 – 12/05/44	"Operation Frühlingsfest" in the Ushatshi area

In July 1944, as part of *Polizei-Kampfgruppe "Jeckeln,"* the regiment was almost wiped out during the German retreat. The remnants were temporarily attached to *SS-Polizei-Regiment 2*. The men were finally withdrawn from action and transferred to Italy for the establishment of *Polizei-Regiment "Brixen." SS-Polizei-Regiment 26* was subsequently disbanded in November 1944.

Feldpostnummern

Stab	18 706
I./SS-Polizei-Regiment 26	40 059
II./SS-Polizei-Regiment 26	44 334
III./SS-Polizei-Regiment 26	40 562

SS-Polizei-Regiment 27

At the end of July 1942 in Oslo *Polizei-Regiment "Süd-Norwegen,"* consisting of *Polizei-Bataillonen 9, 44, 319*, and *321*, was renamed *Polizei-Regiment 27.* The regiment was stationed in Norway until the end of the war.

Feldpostnummern	
Stab	42 241
I./SS-Polizei-Regiment 27	40 493 in Bergen
II./SS-Polizei-Regiment 27	41 064 in Halden
III./SS-Polizei-Regiment 27	32 850 in Kongsvinger
IV./SS-Polizei-Regiment 27	33 345 in Oslo

SS-Polizei-Regiment 28 "Todt"

The regiment was established in November 1942 as a protective unit for elements of the *Organisation Todt* working in the occupied territories. The regiment consisted of *Polizei-Bataillone 33, 62*, and *69*. Like those in most police regiments, the battalions were deployed apart from one another, with *I. Bataillon* in Brest (France), *II. Bataillon* in Riga (Latvia), and *III. Bataillon* in Poltava (Ukraine).

In March 1943 the entire regiment was assembled in Arnhem, and in August was transferred to Marseille (southern France). On 14 December it was moved into the Vichy and Dijon-Lyons area. In February 1944 the regiment marched into the Krainj – Kamnik area of Upper Krain and took part in the following actions:

11/04 – 28/04/44	Action east of Kamnik with *Landesschützen-Regiment 184.*
15/08/44	Action in the Laibach area with the *Lehr-Regiment "Brandenburg"*
20/10 – 25/12/44	Action in the area of the Kamnik – Kamniska Bistrica rail line together with: *Lehr-Regiment "Brandenburg"* 1 Cossack unit *SS-Polizei-Regiment 13* and *25* *Landesschützen-Regiment 18*

After continuous employment in the protection areas, as part of the command of the Commanding General of Rear Army Area "E" the regiment marched in the direction of Austria. On 26 April 1945 the Commanding General of Rear Army Area "E" reported that *SS-Polizei-Regiment 28* was deployed in the line Göttenitz – Gottschee to the Gurk River. Ultimately the regiment was attached to *Kampfgruppe "von Seeler,"* and with it marched through the Loibl Pass and across the Drau, together with *Polizei-Regimenter 17* and *19*. On 9 May 1945 the regiment surrendered to British forces north of Ferlach.

Feldpostnummern	
Stab	30 337
I./SS-Polizei-Regiment 28	40 113
II./SS-Polizei-Regiment 28	40 937
III./SS-Polizei-Regiment 28	48 252

SS-Polizei-Regiment 29

On 16 March 1945 *SS-Polizei-Regiment 1*, which had moved from Hungary to Germany, was renamed *SS-Polizei-Regiment 29* during the organizational establishment of *Polizei-Brigade "Wirth"* (later *35. Polizei-Grenadier-Division*). On 6 April 1945 the regiment was north of Guben. On that day it was incorporated into the *Waffen-SS* and renamed *SS-Polizei-Grenadier-Regiment 89.* The regiment was destroyed while attempting to break out of the Halbe Pocket near Baruth.

Feldpostnummern	
Stab	39 346
I./SS-Polizei-Regiment 29	64 215
II./SS-Polizei-Regiment 29	66 285
III./SS-Polizei-Regiment 29	64 742

SS-Polizei-Regiment 30

On 16 March 1945 *SS-Polizei-Regiment 2*, which had been transferred from *Heeresgruppe "Oberrhein"* (Army Group Upper Rhine) to the Eastern Front, was renamed *SS-Polizei-Regiment 30* during the organizational establishment of *Polizei-Brigade "Wirth"* (later *35. Polizei-Grenadier-Division*). On 6 April 1945 the regiment was north of Guben. On that day it was incorporated into the *Waffen-SS* and renamed *SS-Polizei-Grenadier-Regiment 90*. The regiment was destroyed while attempting to break out of the Halbe Pocket near Baruth.

Feldpostnummern

Stab	65 942
I./SS-Polizei-Regiment 30	35 916
II./SS-Polizei-Regiment 30	37 510

Polizei-Schützen-Regiment 31

The regiment was established on 21 April 1943 for duty in central Russia. *I./SS-Polizei-Regiment 12* became the new unit's *I. Bataillon*, while the 2nd and 3rd battalions were made up of Ukrainian *Schutzmannschaften*. The regiment took part in the following actions:

24/05 – 30/06/43	"Operation Cottbus" in the Lake Palik area
07/07 – 05/08/43	"Operation Hermann" in the Nalibocki Forest area
16/04 – 12/05/43	"Operation Frühlingsfest" in the Ushatshi area with: *SS-Polizei-Regiment 24* and *26* *SS-Sonder-Bataillon "Dirlewanger"* *I./Polizei-Schützen-Regiment 36*
22/05 – 27/06/44	"Operation Kormoran" in the area north of the Minsk – Borisov rail line against partisan units that escaped "Operation Frühlingsfest"
05/07/44	Retreat as part of *Kampfgruppe* "Metz" together with: elements of the *170. Infanterie-Division* elements of the *221. Sicherungs-Division*
08/07/44	Retreat to Lida as part of *Polizei-Kampfgruppe "von Gottberg,"* together with: *SS-Polizei-Regiment 17* *Polizei-Schützen*-Regiment 36
14/07/44	Retreat into the area 20 km E of Grodno as part of *Polizei-Kampfgruppe "von Gottberg,"* together with: *SS-Polizei-Regimenter 2, 17*, and *22* *Polizei-Schützen-Regiment 36*
17/07 – 12/10/44	Attached to *Polizei-Brigade "Anhalt"* within the *VI. Armee-Korps* and retreat to positions along the Bobr River (approx. 40 km W of Grodno) near the East Prussian border.
13/10 – 25/01/44	The regiment's commanding officer, *Oberst der Schupo* Hannibal, assumes command of the brigade. In November 1944 it is attached to the *XXVII. Armee-Korps* (*4. Armee*) in the same area.
26/01/45	Beginning of the retreat through Lyck, Arys, Milken into the area southeast of Lötzen.
21/02/45	Positions near Grünwalde (approx. 6 km S Landsberg) – Dixen – Neukrug
18/03/45	After absorbing the remnants of *SS-Polizei-Regiment 4*, the regiment is attached to the 349. *Volksgrenadier-Division* in the Heiligenbeil area. There the regiment is wiped out in the so-called Heiligenbeil Pocket.

Feldpostnummern

Stab	56 204
I./Polizei-Schützen-Regiment 31	57 546
II./Polizei-Schützen-Regiment 31	58 888
III./Polizei-Schützen-Regiment 31	57 015

At the end of July 1940, 38-year-old Paul Rieckmann joined the Hamburg Schutzpolizei as an auxiliary police official. In July 1942 he was assigned to the 2nd Company of Polizei-Regiment 12, which had just been established in Hamburg. In April 1943 the unit's 1st Battalion formed the German core of Polizei-Schützen-Regiment 31.

— 1 —

Dienstausweis

Nr. 13531

Paul Rieckmann
(Name des Inhabers)

Polizeiwachtmeister d. Res.
(Dienstgrad)

DIN A 7d (74×105 mm). Vordr. R.Pol. Nr.

...nhabers:

(DIN A 9, 37×52 mm)

Paul Rieckmann
(Eigenhändige Unterschrift des Inhabers)

— 2 —

Hamburg, am 22.7.1940

Inhaber dieses Ausweises

Paul Rieckmann
(Vor- und Zuname)

geboren am 30.4.02 in Wilhelmsburg

ist Hilfspolizeibeamter der

Schutzpolizei Hamburg

Er ist berechtigt, Waffen zu tragen.

Der Kommandeur:
Im Auftrage

Ergänzu...
ausweis...

1944

1945

Major der Schutzpolizei

Oberwachtmeister Rieckmann joined Polizei-Schützen-Regiment 31 on 25/1/1944. The unit's 2nd and 3rd battalions were made up of Ukrainian Schutzmannschaften. He took part in a number of operations, including "Cottbus," Hermann," and "Kormoran."

...mmungen auf Seiten 35/36 des Buches beachten!
...u den einzelnen Teilen des Buches weitere Blätter erforder-
...len, sind sie hinter Seite 36 einzuheften und mit Seitenzahlen
...hen. Am Schlusse des zu ergänzenden Teiles ist auf die neue
...ungsseitenzahl hinzuweisen.)

Soldbuch

für den Obw. Paul Rieckmann
(Dienstgrad, Amtsbezeichnung)
Besoldungsgruppe: (für Aktive)
Vergütungsgruppe: A 8 c 3 (Ein. Res.) (für Pol.-Res.)

(Datum — neuer Dienstgrad)	
ab	Besold.-Gr. / Vergüt.-Gr.
ab	Besold.-Gr. / Vergüt.-Gr.
ab	Besold.-Gr. / Vergüt.-Gr.
ab	Besold.-Gr. / Vergüt.-Gr.
ab	Besold.-Gr. / Vergüt.-Gr.

Paul Rieckmann
(Vor- und Zuname)
Paul Rieckmann
(Vor- und Zuname vom Buchinhaber, eigenhändig geschrieben)
geboren am 30. April 1902 in Hbg.-Wilhelmsburg
(Ort, Kreis, Verwaltungsbezirk)
Erkennungsmarke: 2./Pol. 72 - 78 -
Din, A 6 H (32) 105x148 mm
Vordruck RPol. Nr. 431

3

Religion ev. luth. Stand, Beruf Holzplatzarbeiter
Größe 1,67 Gestalt schlank
Gesicht oval Haar blond
Bart keinen Augen blau
Besondere Kennzeichen (z. B. Brillenträger)
Schuhgröße 42 Kopfweite 55
Gasmaskengröße 2 Blutgruppe A
Die Richtigkeit der vorstehenden, nicht umrandeten Angaben, der eigenhändigen Unterschrift des Buchinhabers, der Eintragungen zu Lfd. Nr. ...... bis ...... auf S. 7 und der Lfd. Nr. ...... bis ...... auf S. 8 ~~sowie der umrandeten Angaben auf S. 9 „Gebührnisse"~~ bescheinigt
Ort Hamburg
oder OU., den 25. Januar 1944
(Dienststelle)
SW-Abschnitt-B-
(Bezeichnung der Pol.-Einheit)
(Eigenhändige Unterschrift des Führers der vorstehenden Pol.-Einheit)
Major der Schutzpolizei
Abschnitts-Kommandeur
(dessen Dienstgrad u. Dienststellung)

Der Polizeiabschnitt Hamburg – Schutzpolizei-Abschnitt

6

Zuständige Heimatbehörde
Planstelle des Buchinhabers
stelle bei Pol.-Reservisten)
*) Hamburg
ab
ab
ab
ab
Zuständige Ersatz-Einheit:
*) Pol.-Waffenschule I, Dresden-Hellerau
(Datum)
ab
ab
ab
ab
Zuständige Einsatzpolizeieinheit:
*) 5./Pol. Schtz. Rgt. 31
(Datum)

Bescheinigungen über Änderungen und Ergänzungen
...oweit nicht schon auf S. 3 oder 4 des Buches eingetragen.
Die Änderung und die Seite des Buches, auf der sie angebracht ...wurden, sind anzugeben; Datum, Unterschrift, Dienstgrad, Dienst-...stelle und Dienstsiegel sind unter jeder Bescheinigung anzubringen.

Seite: 8. Unternehmen Cottbus
Unternehmen Hermann
Leutnant u. Komp.-Führer
Dienststelle Feldpostnummer – Briefstempel

Seite 8: „Unternehmen Kormoran"
Rückzugskämpfe bei Lida
O.U., den 3.10.1944
SS-Hauptsturmführer u.
Hauptmann
Polizei-Schützen-Regiment

Polizei-Schützen-Regiment 32

The regiment was established in Bialystok on 21 April 1943 for use in the *Generalgouvernement*. *III./SS-Polizei-Regiment 17* became the regiment's *I. Bataillon*, while Ukrainian *Schutzmannschaften* formed the 2nd and 3rd battalions. Elements of the regiment took part in the following actions:

22/04 – 24/04/43	"Operation Ostersegen" in the Parczew – Ostrow (approx. 40 km NE of Lublin) area together with: *Landesschützen-Bataillon 268* *SS-Polizei-Regiment 25* *Schutzmannschafts-Bataillon 203*
23/06 – 04/07/43	"Operation Nachpfingsten" with: *SS-Polizei-Regiment 25* *Schutzmannschafts-Bataillon 203*
27/06 – 11/07/43	"Operation Werewolf I and II" in the Zamosc – Bilgoraj area together with: *SS-Polizei-Regimenter 4, 13, 25* and *26* *Infanterie-Bataillon 790 (turk.)*
06/11 – 07/11/43	"Operation Ulanen" in the Dabrovka – Yaroslav area, together with: *Polizei-Schützen-Regiment 23* *Landesschützen-Bataillon 405*
19/12 – 21/12/43	"Operation Sonnenschein" in the Dabrowka – Bilgoraj area, together with: *Landesschützen-Bataillon 405*
09/04 – 27/04/44	"Operation Immergrün" in the Chelmno – Krasnytav area, together with: *SS-Polizei-Regiment* 25 *Landesschützen-Bataillon 991*
08/06 – 23/06/44 with:	"Operation Vagabund" in the area NE of Lublin (Radzyn Podlaski — Wlodawa – Kholm Parczew) *SS-Polizei-Regiment4* and *25* *Landesschützen-Bataillone 991* and *992*
Summer 1944	Disbandment of the regiment

Feldpostnummern

I./Polizei-Schützen-Regiment 32	42 144
II./Polizei-Schützen-Regiment 32	none assigned
III./Polizei-Schützen-Regiment 32	none assigned

Polizei-Schützen-Regiment 33

The order for the formation of the regiment within the command of the Commander of *Ordnungspolizei* Ukraine was issued on 21 April 1943. *I./SS-Polizei-Regiment 20* formed the regiment's *I. Bataillon*, while the 2nd and 3rd battalions were to be formed from Ukrainian *Schutzmannschaften*. In addition to general police duties in the security area, in January 1944 the regiment was sent to *Polizei-Kampfgruppe "Prützmann"* under the *Wehrmacht* Commander "Ukraine" and subsequently fought in the Brody area. The remnants of *I. Bataillon* were attached to *SS-Polizei-Regiment* 10, and on 25 March 1945 the regiment was disbanded.

Feldpostnummern

Stab	58 390
I./Polizei-Schützen-Regiment 33	46 467
II./Polizei-Schützen-Regiment 33	57 556
III./Polizei-Schützen-Regiment 33	56 785

Polizei-Schützen-Regiment 34

The regiment was created in Bialystok on 21 April 1943, with *I./SS-Polizei-Regiment 21* becoming the unit's *I. Bataillon*. The 2nd and 3rd battalions were made up of Ukrainian *Schutzmannschaften*. Elements of the regiment took part in the following actions:

00/03 – 00/08/43	Action to liquidate and put down the uprising in the Bialystok ghetto
00/02/44	Action in *Polizei-Kampfgruppe "Prützmann"* east of Brody under the *454. Sicherungs-Division*
00/03/44	Action in *Polizei-Kampfgruppe "Prützmann"* east of Brody under the *36. Infanterie-Division* in the *XIII. Armee-Korps*
08/08 – 21/09/44	Attached to *SS-Polizei-Regiment 17* and action as part of *Polizei-Brigade "Anhalt"* with: *SS-Polizei-Regiment* 2 *SS-Polizei-Regiment 4* (*I.* and *III. Bataillon*) attached to the *VI. Armee-Korps* (*4. Armee*) in the area Grodno – Bialystok – East Prussian border.
21/09 – 06/10/44	"Operation Herbstoffensive" in the Kielce – Konskie area under the command of *Korück 532* with: *Kosaken-Schutzmannschafts-Bataillon 209* *SS-Sonder-Regiment "Dirlewanger"* *Ostmuselmanisches SS-Regiment 1* *Ost-Reiter-Abteilung 580* *Kosaken-Abteilung 572* *Aserbaidschanisches-Bataillon I/111* *Korück 585* with *Sicherungs-Regiment "Ostland"* *Kalmücken-Kavallerie-Korps*
26/09 – 30/09/44	"Operation Sternschnuppe" in the area of the Campino Forest northwest of Warsaw under the command of *Korück 532* together with: *Kosaken-Schutzmannschafts-Bataillon 209* *SS-Sonder-Regiment "Dirlewanger"* *Ostmuselmanisches SS-Regiment 1* *Ost-Reiter-Abteilung 580* *Kosaken-Abteilung 572* *Aserbaidschanisches-Bataillon I/111*

Polizei-Schützen-Regiment 34 was disbanded on 5 February 1945, by which time it consisted solely of the German *I. Bataillon.*

Feldpostnummern	
Stab	59 330
I./Polizei-Schützen-Regiment 34	59 891
II./Polizei-Schützen-Regiment 34	58 676
III./Polizei-Schützen-Regiment 34	57 879

Polizei-Schützen-Regiment 35

The order for formation of the regiment was issued on 21 April, and the unit was established in Litzmannstadt. *III./SS-Polizei-Regiment 24* became the *I. Bataillon*, while the 2nd and 3rd battalions were formed from Ukrainian *Schutzmannschaften*. After use in the Warthegau (*Wehrkreis XXI*), in December 1943 the regiment was transferred to Galicia to reinforce the *XIII. Armee-Korps*. Attached to *Kampfgruppe "Messinger"* (*Arko XIII*), the unit was soon all but wiped out in the Dubno area. The remnants joined *Polizei-Kampfgruppe "Prützmann"* near Kremenets. *Polizei-Schützen-Regiment 35* was disbanded on 30 April 1944.

Feldpostnummern

Stab	56 940
I./Polizei-Schützen-Regiment 35	03 963
II./Polizei-Schützen-Regiment 35	59 701
III./Polizei-Schützen-Regiment 35	58 422

Polizei-Schützen-Regiment 36

The regiment was created at the end of July 1943 for use in the sector of the Senior SS and Police Commander "Russia Center and White Ruthenia," and became operational in autumn 1943. *II./SS-Polizei-Regiment 1* became the *I. Bataillon*, while the 2nd and 3rd battalions were made up of Ukrainian *Schutzmannschaften*. The regiment took part in the following actions:

16/04 – 12/05/44	"Operation Frühlingsfest" in the Ushatshi area
08/07/44	Retreat to Lida as part of *Polizei-Kampfgruppe "von Gottberg,"* together with: *SS-Polizei-Regiment 17* *Polizei-Schützen-Regiment 31*
14/07/44	Retreat into the area 20 km E of Grodno as part of *Polizei-Kampfgruppe "von Gottberg"* together with: *SS-Polizei-Regimenter 2, 17* and *22* *Polizei-Schützen-Regiment 31*
17/07 – 26/07/44	Retreat as part of the now *Korpsgruppe* or *Korps-Abteilung "von Gottberg,"* attached to *VI. Armee-Korps*, through Grodno into the area west of Lipetsk.[91]
04/08/44	Briefly attached to the *52. Sicherungs-Division*, elements of the regiment were sent to the *5. Panzer-Division* near Olita.

Virtually destroyed in the fighting withdrawal, the regiment was disbanded on 30 August 1944. The remnants were incorporated into the reformed *SS-Polizei-Regiment 2*.

Feldpostnummern

Stab	57 850
I./Polizei-Schützen-Regiment 37	56 055
II./Polizei-Schützen-Regiment 37	58 227
III./Polizei-Schützen-Regiment 37	58 066

Polizei-Schützen-Regiment 37

The regiment was created at the end of November 1943 in southern Russia under the Commander of *Ordnungspolizei* Rovno and consisted entirely of Ukrainian *Schutzmannschaften*. Even before it was properly established, in January 1944 the regiment was sent to the *454. Sicherungs-Division* and employed at the front near Rovno. The unit was decimated in fighting there, and in April 1944 was disbanded.

Feldpostnummern

Stab	59 650
I./Polizei-Schützen-Regiment 37	56 055
II./Polizei-Schützen-Regiment 37	58 227
III./Polizei-Schützen-Regiment 37	57 861

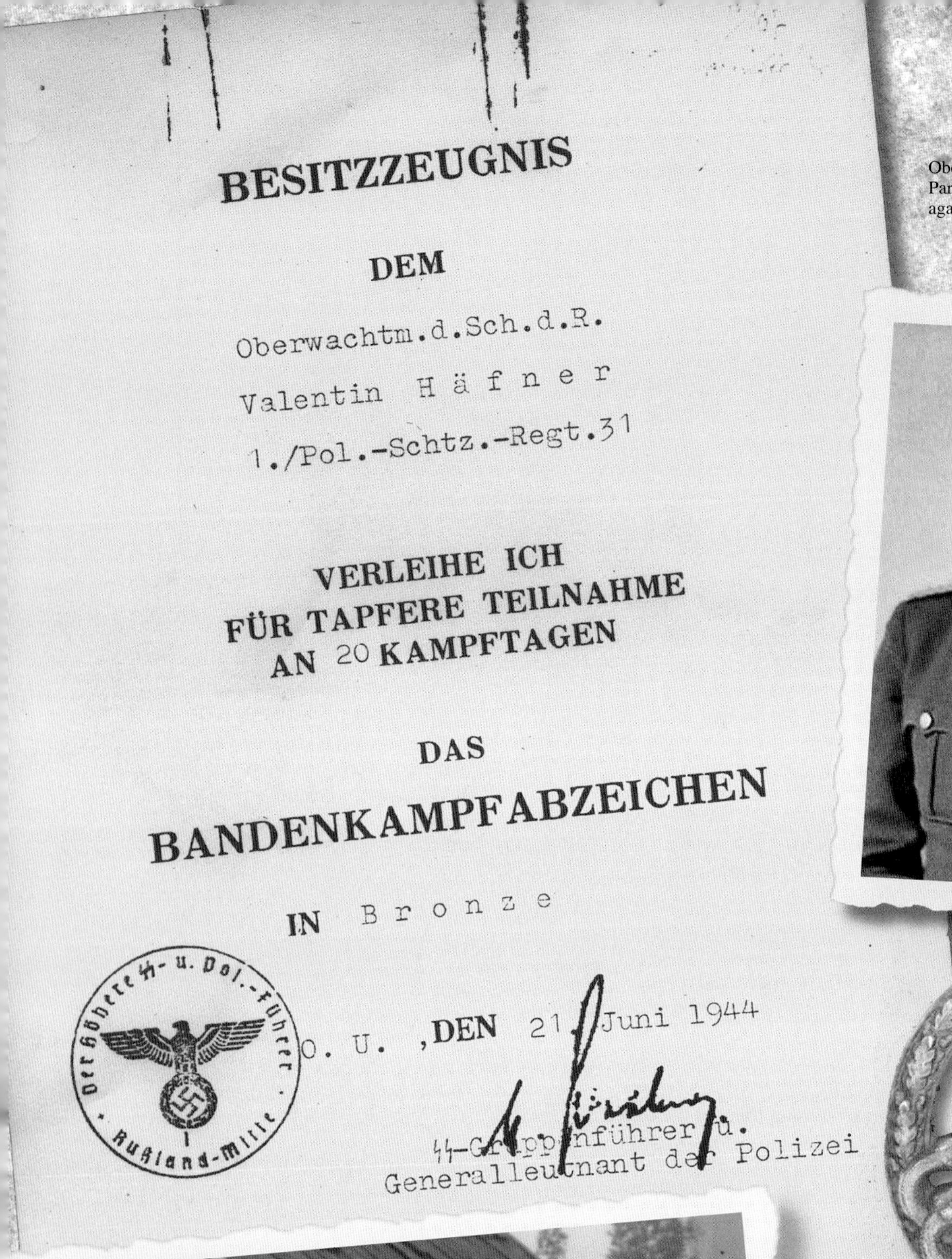
BESITZZEUGNIS

DEM

Oberwachtm.d.Sch.d.R.

Valentin H ä f n e r

1./Pol.-Schtz.-Regt.31

VERLEIHE ICH
FÜR TAPFERE TEILNAHME
AN 20 KAMPFTAGEN

DAS

BANDENKAMPFABZEICHEN

IN B r o n z e

O. U. ,DEN 21. Juni 1944

SS-Gruppenführer u.
Generalleutnant der Polizei

Oberwachtmeister Häfner was awarded the Anti-Partisan Badge in Bronze for 20 days of combat against partisans.

In addition to the Iron Cross and the War Merit Cross, Oberst der Schupo Griep also wore the Danzig Cross First Class, the Infantry Assault Badge, and the Anti-Partisan Badge in Silver.

Situation briefing during an operation against partisans.

Polizei-Schützen-Regiment 38

The regiment was supposed to be created in August 1944 by the Senior SS and Police Commander "Black Sea" based in Galatz; however, the collapse of *Heeresgruppe "Südukraine"* prevented this from happening. The regiment was disbanded in November without having been established.

Feldpostnummern	
Stab	33 719
I./Polizei-Schützen-Regiment 38	26 510
II./Polizei-Schützen-Regiment 38	35 625
III./Polizei-Schützen-Regiment 38	27 668

Polizei-Regiment 50

In February 1945 *Polizei-Regiment 50* was formed from the remnants of decimated SS police regiments in the sector of *Heeresgruppe "Weichsel"* (Army Group Vistula).[92] Together with *SS-Polizei-Regiment 18* it was transferred from the "Protectorate of Bohemia and Moravia" to the Oder Front, and it formed the *1. Polizei-Jäger-Brigade* under the command of *Oberst der Schupo* von Braunschweig. Attached to the *Oder-Korps*, the brigade initially occupied positions on either side of the *Reichsautobahn* south of Stettin, west of the Oder. On 6 April 1945 the corps was organized as follows:

Division 610 z.b.V. with:
- *I./Polizei-Regiment 50*
- *I./SS-Polizei-Regiment 8 (Ungarn)*
- *II./SS-Polizei-Regiment 8*
- *10./SS-Polizei-Regiment 8*
- 2 *Volkssturm* battalions
- 2 construction pioneer companies

Directly attached to the corps were:

Stab/1. Polizei-Jäger-Brigade with the remaining units of the two police regiments
Fallschirmjäger-Ausbildungs- und Ersatz-Regiment 1
Sturmgeschütz-Brigade 284

On 20 April 1945 the Soviet 65th Army succeeded in crossing the Oder south of Stettin and established a bridgehead in the Niederzahden area, where *Polizei-Regiment 50* was deployed. In a daily report from 21 April 1945 the *3. Panzer-Armee* noted:

"*Because of the failure of Polizei-Brigade 1 the enemy gained a foothold east and north of Parnow, and expanded the bridgehead on both sides of the autobahn through attacks with artillery and air support in the direction of Kolbitzow, Hohenzahden, and Kurow.*"

While the fighting strength and morale of many *Wehrmacht* units had dropped by this time, *Polizei-Regiment 50* demonstrated no operational capability. Failures in command of the corps and of the attached police units resulted in *SS-Obergruppenführer und General der Polizei* von dem Bach being relieved of command. The regiment was in disintegration and had to be viewed as destroyed at the end of April 1945.

Feldpostnummern	
Stab	40 863
I./Polizei-Regiment 50	41 852
II./Polizei-Regiment 50	42 585
III./Polizei-Regiment 50	43 298

Polizei-Regiment "Nord"

The regimental headquarters was formed in the summer of 1941 to command *Polizei-Bataillone 22, 53,* and *319* in the coming eastern campaign, and on 22 June it was placed under the Commander of Rear Army Area 101 (later Commander of Rear Army Area "North"). On 7 October 1941 the headquarters moved from Pskov to Opochka. In response to the Soviet winter offensive, on 10 January 1942 the regiment was attached to the *X. Armee-Korps* for service at the front as *Gruppe "Keuper."* It fought alongside the *81. Infanterie-Division* in the Kalikevo – Nagovo – Raschucha – Yevakhnovo – Bubkovchchina area until March 1942. From April to June 1942 the regiment was attached to the *18. Infanterie-Division (mot.)* in the Staraya-Rusa area. On 18 June 1942 the regimental commander reported that the regiment was incapable of further operations at the front and the unit was subsequently withdrawn. In July 1942 it became ***Polizei-Regiment 15***.

Feldpostnummer:
Stab 38 968

Polizei-Regiment "Mitte"

The regimental headquarters was formed in Warsaw in the summer of 1941 to command *Polizei-Bataillone 307, 316,* and *322* in the coming eastern campaign, and at the beginning of July it was placed under the Commander of Rear Army Area 102 (later Commander of Rear Army Area "Center"). Initially used for traffic control and the guarding of camps housing Soviet POWs (e.g. Dulag 185 in Bialystok), from 19 to 22 August 1941 the regiment was attached to the *221. Sicherungs-Division* to guard *Rollbahn 1* in the Mogilev – Bobruisk – Borki area. This it accomplished through the use of motorized patrols and fixed machine-gun posts. Attached to *Korück 580* until 1 September, it subsequently took part in repeated searches for weapons and equipment left behind by the Soviets and checked villages for partisans, communists, and Jews. These could be legally shot with no need for detailed reports.[93] On 19 October 1941 the regiment helped murder just under 4,000 Jews in Mogilev together with *Einsatzkommando 8* of *Einsatzgruppe "B."* At the end of November, *II.* and *III. Bataillon* were tasked with guarding the Smolensk – Vyazma railway line. In July 1942 the regiment was renamed ***Polizei-Regiment 13***.

Feldpostnummer:
Stab 42 307

Polizei-Regiment "Süd"

The regimental headquarters was formed in Cracow in May 1941 to command *Reserve-Polizei-Bataillone 45, 303,* and *314* in the coming eastern campaign, and at the beginning of July it was placed under the Commander of Rear Army Area "South." On 26 July 1941 the latter ordered two of the regiment's battalions to stand ready for a clearing action by the *1. SS-Infanterie-Brigade* in the area between Rovno and Berdichev (Zwiahel – Slutsk – Miropol – Shepetovka – Zazlavl – Ostrog). Beginning August 1941 there were daily executions of Jewish inhabitants of the area. In September 1941 there followed mass executions in the Kamenets-Podolsk area. Elements of the regiment probably took part in the shooting of 18,000 Jews in Vinnitsa on 19 September 1941, and in late September the unit participated in the shooting of Kiev's Jews at Babi Yar. At the beginning of October the regiment was assigned to deal with Soviet stragglers in the Brody – Busk – Pereyaslav area. In mid-October 1941 *Polizei-Bataillon 314* executed Jews, probably more than 1,000, in Dnepropetrovsk. In October and November 1941 *1./Polizei-Bataillon 303* assisted in the execution of 1,000 Jews in Solotonoha. Other shootings were carried out in Zhitomir and Miropol. Beginning on 26 December 1941, approximately 15,000 Jews were executed in the Drobitsky Ravine near Kharkov by elements of *Einsatzgruppe "C"* and *Polizei-Bataillon 314*. On 23 January 1942 *Polizei-Bataillon 314* took part in the shooting of several thousand Jews near Kharkov. At the end of January 1942 the regiment moved to Kremenchug, and in July 1942 became ***Polizei-Regiment 10***.

Feldpostnummer:
Stab 36 524

Polizei-Regiment "z.b.V."

The regimental headquarters was established in the summer of 1941 for the Senior SS and Police Commander "Special Purpose," which was earmarked for the Caucasus and commanded *Polizei-Bataillone 304*, *315*, and *320*. Attached to *Einsatzgruppe "D"* for a time, in September 1941 elements of the regiment took part in the executions of about 5,300 Jews in Starokonstantinov, Vinnitsa, Kirovograd, Uman, and Kiev. In March 1942 the regiment was transferred to White Russia and attached to the *707. Infanterie-Division* for "Operation Bamberg" (area: SW of Bobruisk). In July 1942 the regiment became ***Polizei-Regiment 11***.

Feldpostnummer:	
Stab	44 870

SS-Polizei-Regiment "Bozen"

On 1 October 1943 a police regiment was formed by the Commander of *Ordnungspolizei "Bozen."* Initially consisting of about 2,000 ethnic German volunteers from South Tyrol (age classes 1900 – 1912), the regiment was first given the title *"Südtirol."* A few days later, however, it was renamed ***Polizei-Regiment "Bozen,"*** and on 16 April 1944 the prefix ***"SS"*** was added.

At the beginning of March 1944 the *I. Bataillon* moved from Meran to Fiume, and in March 1944 to Abbazia (west of Fiume). In April 1945 it was transferred to Gorizia, and in May 1945 surrendered to U.S. forces in Tarvisio.

The *II. Bataillon* remained in Bozen until February 1944, when it moved to Belluno. In August 1944 the battalion, together with the *Waffen-SS* High Mountain School in Predazzo and elements of the *Division "Hermann Göring,"* shot 44 suspected partisans and destroyed (sic!) about 245 homes in the Valle del Biois area. Two companies were transferred back to Bozen in September 1944, and in March 1945 they took part in a reprisal action near Travazzoi (S of Bozen).

The *III. Bataillon* transferred to Rome, and on 18 October 1943 it took part in the deportation of about 900 Italian Jews on behalf of the commander of the *Sicherheitspolizei* in Rome. On 22 March 1944 Italian partisans ambushed the *11. Kompanie* and seven policemen were killed. There was another attack the next day and 26 more police were killed. As a reprisal 270 Italian hostages were shot, and shortly afterwards another 335 were killed in the Adriatic caves. The *III. Bataillon* briefly saw action against the American 36th Infantry Division, and in June 1944 withdrew to Lecco. In September 1944 it was ordered to Bologna, and in December to San Stefano di Cadore (Piemont). At the beginning of 1945 the *II.* and *III. Bataillon* were concentrated in Bozen, and at the end of the war they marched toward Schluderbach, about 60 km to the northeast.

A *IV. Bataillon* was formed in Gossensass in April 1944, but in May it was released to become part of the new *I./SS-Polizei-Regiment "Alpenvorland."*

Feldpostnummern	
Stab	00 496
I. Bataillon	03 272
II. Bataillon	01 351
III. Bataillon	02 801
IV. Bataillon	02 589

Polizei-Regiment "Alpenvorland"

Polizei-Regiment "Alpenvorland" was established in May 1944 as the second regiment formed from ethnic Germans from South Tyrol. *IV./SS-Polizei-Regiment "Bozen,"* in Gossensass, became the regiment's *I. Bataillon*, and the South Tyrol *Ordnungsdienst* provided the remaining personnel. Training ended in October 1944, and the regiment was transferred to the Edolo (approx. 70 km W of Trient) – Feltre (approx. 60 km E of Trient) – Belluno (approx. 80 km NE of Trient) area, where it participated in "Operation Monte Grappa" (1,779 m, S of Feltre). The *I. Bataillon* was decimated in fighting with partisans in January 1945. According to a directive dated 29 January 1945, the regiment was supposed to be renamed ***SS-Polizei-Regiment 9***.

Feldpostnummern	
Stab	41 721
I. Bataillon	02 589
II. Bataillon	46 190
III. Bataillon	35 758

SS-Polizei-Regiment "Brixen"

In October 1944 *SS-Polizei-Regiment "Brixen"* was created from the remnants of *SS-Polizei-Regiment 26* and South Tyrolean recruits from Bozen, Belluno, and Trento. On 29 January 1945, while stationed in the Brixen area, the regiment was given the prefix ***"SS,"*** and at the end of February was sent to the *31. SS-Freiwilligen-Grenadier-Regiment* in the Striegau area (S of Jauer). It was subsequently taken into the *Waffen-SS* as *SS-Freiwilligen-Grenadier-Regiment 80*. The regiment, which lacked any combat experience, was sent to the front in mid-March 1945, and in a matter of days was destroyed by the Red Army. A former member from South Tyrol recalled his service and documents the lack of motivation among the regiment's personnel:

"In November 1944 I was called up to serve in Polizei-Regiment 'Brixen.' Brixen was also where our training took place. When Gauleiter Hofer showed up for our swearing-in at the end of February 1944, many had already muttered something to themselves along the lines of 'I'm not taking the oath!' The very next day we were put on a train and sent to Upper Silesia. The train was forced to stop repeatedly on account of air raids, and finally we had to get off and walk. We reached the Schneekoppe area, and I can still remember the villages of Arnsdorf (near Liegnitz) and Böhmisch Leipa. Initially billeted in private quarters, we were then supposed to relieve the Wehrmacht at the front for 14 days. Many had blisters on their feet from the long marches. Despite express orders not to open them, I did so, whereupon my foot swelled so badly that I was no longer fit for duty. That was my big break! When the surrender came I pretended to be an Italian working on anti-tank barricades and, riding a woman's bicycle, I headed for home, arriving there in May 1945. At the district office I was released from military service along with all the others who had made it back."

Feldpostnummern	
Stab	31 464
I. Bataillon	01 773
II. Bataillon	18 524
III. Bataillon	05 010

SS-Polizei-Regiment "Schlanders"

Polizei-Regiment "Schlanders" was formed from members of the South Tyrol *Ordnungsdienst*[94] in October 1944. On 29 January 1945, in Schlanders, it received the prefix ***"SS"*** and was transferred to the 80 x 80 x 80 km triangle Trient – Belluno – Vicenza. Employed mainly to guard objects and Italian POWs, in mid-April 1945 the regiment marched into the Cortina d'Ampezzo area about 80 km to the north. It then headed west to Bozen, where it surrendered to the Allies.

Feldpostnummern	
Stab	11 480
I. Bataillon	21 500
II. Bataillon	17 938
III. Bataillon	00 548

Appendices

Areas of Operation of the
Police Battalions and SS Police Regiments in the Generalgouvernement.

Areas of Operation of the
Police Battalions and SS Police Regiments
in Russia.
©Michaelis-Verlag Berlin, July 2008
Finnischer Busen
Lehingrad
Puschkin
Krasnogwardeisk
Narwa
Ljuban
Wyriza
Wolchow
Reval
Estland
Peipus-See
Luga
Nowgorod
Ilmen-See
Staraja Russa
Pleskau
Ostrow
Lowat
Cholm
Goldingen
Riga
Lettland
Libau
Mitau
Opotschka
Rshew
Sebesh
Welikije Luki
Moskau
Newel
Schaulen
Dünaburg
Litauen
Düna
Polotzk
Raseinen
Wjasma
Uschatschi
Witebsk
Kauen
Lepel
Smolensk
Kaluga
Wilna
Beresino
Orscha
Dnjepr
Tula
Molodetschno
Borissow
Lahoisk
Radoszkowicze
Roslawl
Lyck
Augustow
Lida
Minsk
Mogilew
Sowjetunion
Grodno
Nalibocki
Njemen
St. Bychow
Slonim
Brjansk
Lomza
Bialystok
Bobruisk
Baranowitschi
Bialowiecza
Sluzk
Bez. Bialystok
Beresina
Gomel
Morocz
Woronesh
Luninetz
Brest-Litowsk
Pinsk
Mosyr
Lachwa
General-Gouvernement
Pripjet-Sümpfe
Pripjet
Konotop
Desna
Kowel
Olewsk
Alexiejewka
Bjelgorod
Luzk
Kostopol
Oskol
Rowno
Donez
Dubno
Shitomir
Kiew
Ukraine
Schepetowka
Charkow
Brody
Kremenez
Kupjansk
Lemberg
Starokonstantinow
Berditschew
Poltawa
Nikolajew
Tscherkassy
Dnjestr
Isjum
Winniza
Dnjepr
Krementschug
Losowaja
Kamenez Podolsk
Uman
Pawlograd
Dnjepropetrowsk
Kirowo
Kriwoj Rog
Taganrog
Bug
Ungarn
Bessarabien
Asowsches Meer
Galatz
Rumänien
Schwarzes Meer

Areas of Operation of the Police Battalions and SS Police Regiments.

in Upper Italy under the SS and Police Commander "Bozen"
in the coastland under the Senior SS and Police Commander "Adriatic Coastland"
in the Krain under the Senior SS and Police Commander "Alpenland" (Wehrkreis XVIII)

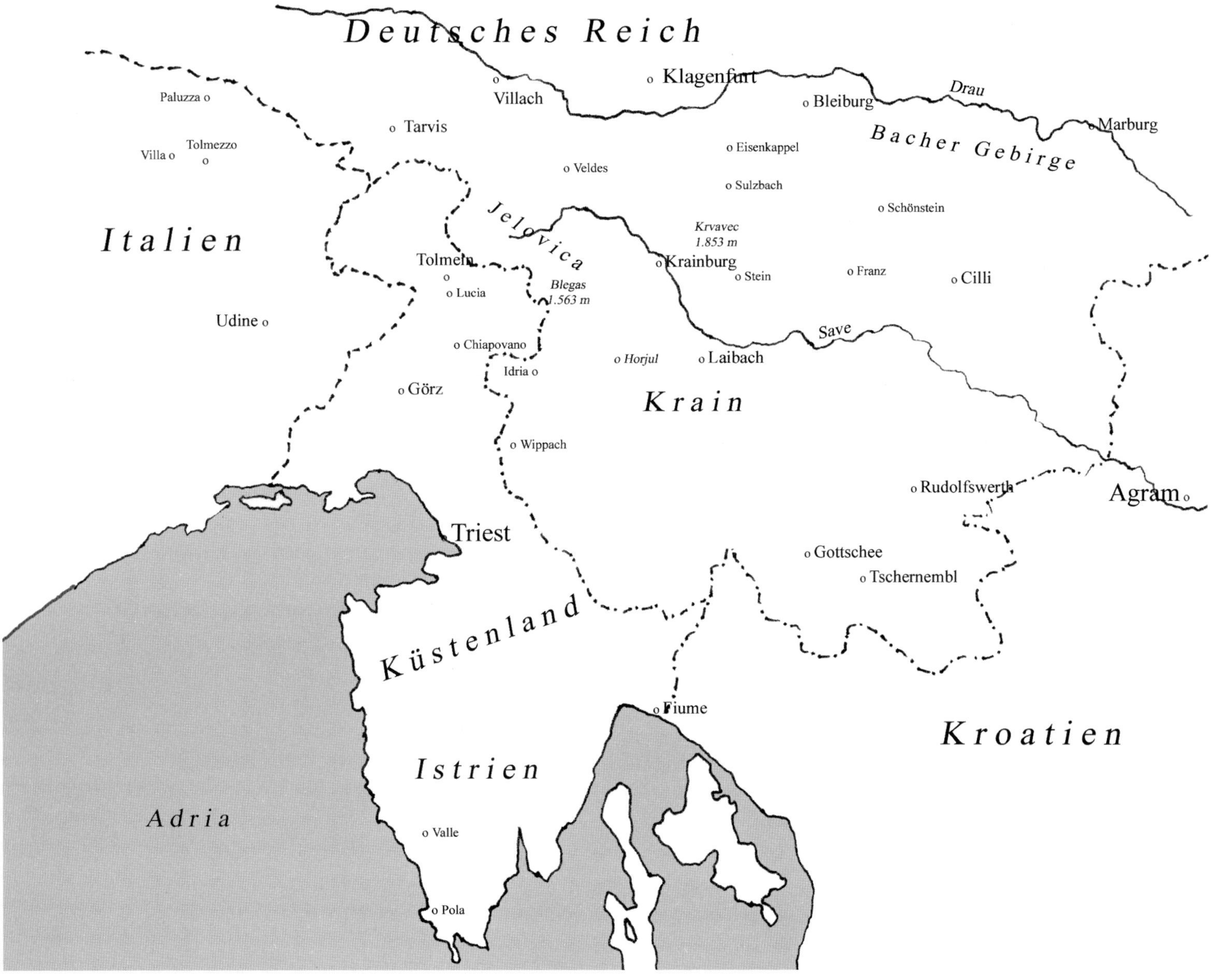

Command Relationships of the *Polizei-Bataillone* and *SS-Polizei-Regimenter*

After all uniformed police of the 17 German *Länder* (states) were centralized in the *Hauptamt Ordnungspolizei* (Order Police Central Office), making control and command exclusively a state function; 1936 saw the creation of the so-called Inspectors of the *Ordnungspolizei* (IdO), which were directly subordinate to the *SS-Oberabschnittführer* of the respective *Wehrkreise*. They oversaw the establishment and training of the uniformed police and had command of operations within their areas of responsibility.

From the end of 1937, the IdO within the Reich were subordinate to Senior SS and Police Commanders, successors to the *SS-Oberabschnittführer*. The appointing of *Ordnungspolizei* Senior Commanders (BdO), responsible for active security tasks in the special areas of the German Reich —some of them incorporated—began in 1938. For example, *Ordnungspolizei* Commanders were employed in the "Protectorate of Bohemia and Moravia" and in the districts of Danzig-West Prussia and Wartheland, as well as in the *Wehrkreise* of Königsberg and Salzburg, because of the partisan uprisings in Bialystok and Slovenia. Interestingly, this also happened in the *Wehrkreise* Hamburg, Münster, Wiesbaden, and Stuttgart, whose inspectors were renamed commanders on account of the Allied air raids.

In the territories occupied from 1939—for example the later *Generalgouvernement* (Poland)—as many as 10 SS and Police Commanders (disciplinary authority of a regimental commander) were subordinate to the Senior SS and Police Commander (disciplinary authority of a division commander). They in turn were subordinate to the *Ordnungspolizei* Commander (KdO) in each locality.

There was no completely standard organization, however. Not only did the number of individual posts in each administrative area vary, but in some cases posts were not established at all, and consequently the hierarchy *de jure* could look quite different.

The following is an attempt to list the positions to which the *Polizei-Bataillone* and *SS-Polizei-Regimenter* were subordinated for employment in the rear areas. When sent to the front, the units were as a rule attached directly to the *Wehrmacht*—usually an infantry division or an army corps.

Reich Territory

Senior SS and Police Commander (*Wehrkreis*)	IdO/BdO
Nordost (I)	Königsberg
Nord, from 1940: Ostsee (II)	Stettin
Ost, from 11/39: Spree (III)	Berlin
Elbe (IV)	Dresden
Südwest (V)	Stuttgart
West (VI)	Münster
Süd (VII)	Munich
Südost (VIII)	Breslau
Fulda-Werra (IX)	Kassel
Nordwest, from 6/40 Nordsee (X)	Hamburg
Mitte (XI)	Hanover
Rhein (XII)	Coblenz
Main (XIII)	Nuremberg
Donau (XVII)	Vienna
Alpenland (XVIII)	Salzburg
Weichsel (XX)	Danzig
Warthe (XXI)	Posen

Outside the Reich

"Protectorate of Bohemia and Moravia"
- Senior SS and Police Commander "Bohemia and Moravia"
  - BdO/KdO Prague

Generalgouvernement
- Senior SS and Police Commander "Ost"
  - SS and Police Commander "Cracow"
    - BdO/KdO "Krakau"
  - SS and Police Commander "Radom"
    - BdO/KdO "Radom"

SS and Police Commander "Lublin"
BdO/KdO "Lublin"
SS and Police Commander "Warsaw"
BdO/KdO "Warschau"
SS and Police Commander "Lvov"
BdO/KdO "Lvov"

Reichskommissariat "Ostland"
Senior SS and Police Commander "Russia North"
SS and Police Commander "Reval"
BdO/KdO "Reval"
SS and Police Commander "Riga"
BdO/KdO "Riga"
SS and Police Commander "Kauen"
BdO/KdO "Kauen"
SS and Police Commander "Minsk"[95]
BdO/KdO "Minsk"

Senior SS and Police Commander "Russia Center"
SS and Police Commander "Mogilev"
BdO/KdO "Mogilev"

Senior SS and Police Commander "Russia South"[96]
SS and Police Commander "Wolhynia"
BdO/KdO "Wolhynia"
SS and Police Commander "Zhitomir"
BdO/KdO "Zhitomir"
SS and Police Commander "Kiev"
BdO/KdO "Kiev"
SS and Police Commander "Nikolayev"
BdO/KdO "Nikolayev"
SS and Police Commander "Dnepropetrovsk"
BdO/KdO "Dnepropetrovsk"
SS and Police Commander "Chernigov"
BdO/KdO "Chernigov"
SS and Police Commander "Kharkov"
BdO/KdO "Kharkov"
SS and Police Commander "Taurien"
BdO/KdO "Taurien"
SS and Police Commander "Stalino"
BdO/KdO "Stalino"
SS and Police Commander "Rostov"
BdO/KdO "Rostov"
SS and Police Commander "Pripyat"
BdO/KdO "Pripyat"

Serbia and Montenegro
Senior SS and Police Commander "Serbia"
Ordnungspolizei Commander-in-Chief "Belgrade"

Greece
Senior SS and Police Commander "Greece"
Ordnungspolizei Commander-in-Chief "Greece"
Ordnungspolizei Commander "Athens"

Ordnungspolizei Commander "Salonika"
Ordnungspolizei Commander "Larissa"
Ordnungspolizei Commander "Peloponnese"
Ordnungspolizei Commander "Arta"

Albania
Ordnungspolizei Commander-in-Chief "Tirana"

Croatia
Ordnungspolizei Commander-in-Chief "Croatia"
Ordnungspolizei Commander "Agram"
Ordnungspolizei Commander "Esseg"
Ordnungspolizei Commander "Sarajevo"
Ordnungspolizei Commander "Banja-Luka"
Ordnungspolizei Commander "Knin"

Italy
Senior SS and Police Commander-in-Chief "Italy"[97]
Ordnungspolizei Commander-in-Chief "Italy"
Senior SS and Police Commander "Upper Italy West"
SS and Police Commander "Upper Italy"
SS and Police Commander "Central Italy"
SS and Police Commander "West Emilia"
Senior SS and Police Commander "Adriatic Coastland"
Ordnungspolizei Commander-in-Chief "Trieste"
Ordnungspolizei Commander Bozen

Hungary
Senior SS and Police Commander "Hungary"
BdO/KdO "Budapest"

Slovakia
Senior SS and Police Commander "Slovakia"
BdO/KdO "Bratislava"

Norway
Senior SS and Police Commander "North"
BdO/KdO "Oslo"

Denmark
Senior SS and Police Commander "Denmark"
BdO/KdO "Copenhagen"

Netherlands
Senior SS and Police Commander "Northwest"
BdO/KdO "The Hague"

France
Senior SS and Police Commander "France"
BdO/KdO "Paris"

Belgium
Senior SS and Police Commander "
Northern France and Belgium"

The Duties of the Armed *Ordnungspolizei* as Defined by the Police Service Manual

"1. The armed uniformed Ordnungspolizei is, alongside the Wehrmacht and Waffen-SS, the arms-bearing representative of the state. Together with the Sicherheitspolizei and the Waffen-SS, it is responsible for the guarding and protection of the Reich's internal well-being, especially preventing and combating violent infringements of the law, protection of the state and its assets, as well as prevention of and defense against attacks on the folk community, the folk comrades, and their possessions. In time of war, in addition to its expanded responsibilities in the home war zone, additional special duties fall to the Ordnungspolizei in the area of operations, in the rear war areas, and in occupied enemy territories. Its principal duty is the pacification and securing of areas conquered by the Wehrmacht and incorporated into the territories of the Reich.

2. As a rule, the armed uniformed Ordnungspolizei fulfills its executive duties through its daily order service. As well, tasks fall to it that can only be carried out by employing concentrated police units (police troops). The rules for the employment of the Ordnungspolizei in daily order service are contained in PDV 27. The following manual contains the command principles for actions by the police troops and the air-defense police with the exception of concentrated units of the fire-defense police. Some of the army command principles laid down in HDV 300 were incorporated into this manual to enable police units to carry out combat assignments. Deviations from these regulations were determined by the differences in roles, organization, armament, and equipment between the Ordnungspolizei and the army.

3. For tasks which are beyond the capabilities of individual members of the Ordnungspolizei, the force has available units and formations organized, armed, and equipped along army lines. These include:

police regiments
police battalions
police mounted battalions
police signals battalions
police companies and platoons, motorized companies and platoons
police cavalry troops, platoons and sections
police armored companies and platoons
police gun platoons
police pioneer platoons
motor transport sections
workshop platoons and special and escort detachments

Their organization and equipment is determined by the Chief of the Ordnungspolizei.

4. Missions that are large in scope can require the combination of several formations and units into larger police units. In addition to their special operational use, units of the Ordnungspolizei also train and educate the next generation of police personnel.

5. For budgeting, police units belong to a police administration (home garrison) where they are under the Schutzpolizei Commander. Gendarmerie units (rural police) are under the Gendarmerie Commander. In the case of special missions, the formations and units of the police force can, by order of senior officials, be attached to other command authorities, which temporarily assume responsibility for their tactical employment and supply (foreign action).

6. In contrast to the units of the Wehrmacht, which as a rule fight within large, combined-arms formations against a similar enemy, the units of the Ordnungspolizei can find themselves tasked with missions whose complexity and diversity challenge to the utmost the skill and flexibility of their officers, non-commissioned officers, and enlisted men.

The foundation of the police force is the superbly-trained individual fighting man. The mastering of purely military tasks is a condition for every unit, every officer, non-commissioned officer, and enlisted man of the police force. Based on this foundation, specialized training and education, with emphasis on the role of the police and ideology, enable the officers, NCOs, and men of the police force to carry out their numerous missions, which are likewise divided into the fields of military and police combat operations, special protection (site defense), supervision duty, catastrophe defense, and air defense.

7. In exceptional cases when police units are attached to units of the Wehrmacht for military combat assignments, the relevant Wehrmacht manuals apply for the duration of the secondment. When engaging in combat as part of the Wehrmacht, police formations and units will be assigned heavy infantry weapons as required. Providing support from other arms (artillery, tanks, aircraft, engineers, etc.) is the responsibility of the Wehrmacht unit to which they are attached.

8. In war and times of tension, special security tasks are frequently assigned to the units of the Ordnungspolizei. They serve either to temporarily prevent attacks on particularly vulnerable (state, war, or vital to life) installations and sites, or to protect the folk community in general. Specifically, the units are assigned the following tactical missions:

- guarding of buildings, sites, and terrain (site defense in the expanded sense)

- border security

- guarding of special construction sites (e.g. of roads, fortifications, military sites)

- guarding of Wehrmacht supply lines (military roads) and railway lines on special occasions (passage of special trains)

- guarding of material dumps and captured equipment dumps, POW camps and the like

- sealing off of city quarters (ghettos), quarantines (outbreak of epidemics), mined areas, etc.

In addition to the guarding of individual sites and installations, special circumstances can make it necessary for the responsibility of guarding entire areas (e.g. occupied areas) to be transferred to a larger unit of the OrPo. In this case security zones and sectors are to be divided among individual police units. These will be responsible for guarding the individual sites and installations in their area based on their degree of importance and the threat level.

9. Special areas of unrest, especially areas where fighting has taken place, are to undergo thorough pacification. The task of pacification is to render harmless all remaining enemy personnel who escaped the fighting, the securing of enemy weapons and war materiel, the capture of enemy command documents, propaganda materials, and evidence, and the destruction of the enemy supply system.

10. The purpose of employing OrPo units in large-scale supervisory duty is to fulfill peacetime police missions which, on account of their size and scope, cannot be accomplished by individual members of the Ordnungspolizei. As a rule, large-scale security operations are triggered by large-scale events, parades and the like. In addition to crowd control and other order-related tasks, the duties assigned to the police in these operations include guarding traffic, directing the masses of people, the maintenance of order and general security in the event area.

The tasks associated with large-scale supervisory duty are expanded in time of war. Traffic control in the army's marshalling and operations zones, the carrying out of evacuations in areas threatened by the enemy, care of human transports of all types (e.g. resettlements, foreign workers, etc.) can make necessary the employment of Ordnungspolizei units or sub-units."

Members of the *Ordnungspolizei* Awarded the Knight's Cross of the Iron Cross

Anhalt, Günther	*SS-Standartenführer*	20/08/44
Bach von dem, Erich	*SS-Obergruppenführer General der Polizei*	19/10/44
Engelbrecht, Wilhelm	*SS-Hauptsturmführer und Hauptmann der Schupo*	19/01/45
Gottberg von, Curt	*SS-Gruppenführer und Generalleutnant der Polizei*	20/07/44
Griese, Bernhard	*Major der Schupo*	13/10/42
Hannibal, Heinrich	*Oberst der Schutzpolizei*	23/08/44
Jeckeln, Friedrich	*SS-Obergruppenführer und General der Polizei*	15/09/44
Landwehr, Paul	*SS-Sturmbannführer und Major der Schupo*	27/02/45
Reinefarth, Heinz	*SS-Gruppenführer und Generalleutnant der Polizei*	22/10/44 (EL)
Walden, Bruno	*SS-Sturmbannführer und Major der Schupo*	15/02/45

The *4. SS-Polizei-Panzergrenadier-Division*

The *Polizei-Division*

On 18 September 1939 Hitler directed the Chief of the *Ordnungspolizei* to establish a horse-drawn infantry division from members of the police. Formation of the division began at Camp "Waldern," near Frankfurt/Oder, under the command of *Generalleutnant der Polizei* Pfeffer-Wildenbruch. Designated the *Polizei-Division*, the unit was to be organized as follows:

Division Headquarters
Police Rifle Regiments 1 – 3 (I to III Battalions)
Police Bicycle Troop (reconnaissance unit)
Police Anti-Tank Battalion
Police Pioneer Battalion
Police Supply Services
Police Medical Battalion
Police Veterinary Battalion

The division, whose "soldiers" remained members of the *Ordnungspolizei*, and which was only established within the army, was also sent:

Artillerie-Regiment 300 (artillery, army)
3 battalions (105-mm light field howitzers)
1 battalion (150-mm heavy field howitzers)
Nachrichten-Abteilung 300 (signals, army)
1. Kompanie (field telephone)
2. Kompanie (radio)

The police personnel assigned to the division were given army ranks and uniforms (including the Reich cockade on the cap). While the ranks were retained, a special type of uniform was introduced soon after the division's formation: the police eagle returned to the cap, and the collar patches and belt buckle were also police issue; however, in keeping with Himmler's wishes the national emblem was the *Waffen-SS* model and was worn on the upper right sleeve. Members of the SS also wore the embroidered version of the *Sig-Runen* beneath the left breast pocket.[98] Following these changes, about the only outward indication that the unit was part of the army was provided by vehicle identity plates which bore the WH (*Wehrmacht-Heer*) title instead of Pol (*Polizei*) or SS (*Waffen-SS*).

After three months of existence, in January 1940 the *Polizei-Division* was moved from Wandern to the *Westwall* (Siegfried Line), where it relieved the *205. Infanterie-Division*, part of the *XXV. Armee-Korps*. Soon after the start of the Western Campaign the division was attached to the *XVII. Armee-Korps* and took part in the fighting in France. The units crossed the Ardennes Canal, which links the Maas and the Aisne, southwest of Sedan and advanced toward Vouziers. After sporadic fighting the troops reached Les Islettes (southwest of Verdun) on 14 June 1940. The division crossed the Rhine-Marne Canal east of Bar le Duc and pursued retreating French troops through Neufchâteau and Besançon in the direction of the Swiss border. It was there that it received news of the ceasefire on 22 June 1940. On 10 July the units were transferred to the St. Dizier area as occupation troops and on 2 August to Camp Suippes (50 km NW of St. Dizier).

At Camp Suippes the unit was reorganized and renamed the *SS-Polizei-Division*. Personnel strength was halved, principally by removing the older members. The army elements were removed and replaced by newly-created police units. In addition to the new *Polizei-Artillerie-Regiment* (artillery) and the *Polizei-Nachrichten-Abteilung* (signals), a *Polizei-Aufklärungs-Abteilung* (reconnaissance) was created from the former *Polizei-Radfahr-Schwadron* (bicycle troop) and a *Polizei-Flak-Abteilung* was formed.

The "SS" prefix was a reflection of Himmler's desire as *Reichsführer-SS* and Chief of the German Police to show a close relationship between the SS and the police. On 12 November 1940 *Generalleutnant der Polizei* Mülverstedt took command of the *SS-Polizei-Division*. In mid-March 1941 *General* Halder advised that the division would be taking part in "Operation Barbarossa." After discussions between *SS-Obergruppenführer* Daluege, *SS-Gruppenführer* Jüttner, and the *Reichsführer-SS*, on 17 April 1941, with a strength of approx. 17,000 men, the *SS-Polizei-Division* was attached to the *Waffen-SS*. Two months later orders were issued for the division to move from France to the *L. Armee-Korps* in the east. The first transport trains reached East Prussia on 26 June 1941.

As had been the case in the Western Campaign, when the Russian Campaign began on 22 June 1941 the division was not deployed at the front, and it was not until 30 June that it crossed the Lithuanian border. Most of the advance roads were completely blocked, delaying the division's progress in the fierce summer heat. The division lost 600 of its 5,000 horses within a few days, and in Latvia horses were requisitioned or rented with their owners.

On 14 July 1941 the division crossed a pontoon bridge over the Dvina near Dryssa. Two days later the artillery regiment received battle orders, the first element of the division to do so. During the night of 23-24 July the division marched through Ostrov, as yet having seen no action. It then moved into swampy old-growth forest. Attached to the *LVI. Armee-Korps*, on 1 August 1941 the division—under its new commander *SS-Brigadeführer und Generalmajor der Polizei* Walter Krüger—set out to take a key position near Luga. The enemy had fortified the Luga position extremely well, setting up bunkers, mine fields, anti-tank barricades, and barbed wire in the complex terrain of swamps, lakes, and forest. Part of the area was a former army training camp, which also proved an advantage to the enemy. The powerful enemy defenses inflicted heavy casualties on the *SS-Polizei-Division*. Again and again attacks had to be called off, the troops falling back to the start line. As Luga could not be taken by frontal assault, on 22 August the division moved south past Sopolye in order to attack from the flank. Faced with the threat of encirclement, on 1 September the Red Army abandoned the city. By that time the *SS-Polizei-Division* had lost 1,000 men killed and 2,000 wounded.

The division was once again attached to the *L. Armee-Korps*, and 9 September 1941 saw the start of the battle for Krasnogvardeysk, one of the main blocking positions before Leningrad. Five days later the *SS-Polizei-Division* took the city. Once known as the "Paris Guard Division," the unit boasted a good fighting strength. Hitler halted the advance on Leningrad, however, to avoid having to feed the civilian population of the Russian metropolis. On 18 October 1941 the division received 3,000 replacements to make good its losses. The division—now under the command of *SS-Brigadeführer und Generalmajor der Polizei* Wünnenberg—remained in the siege ring around Leningrad in the Pushkin – Pulkovo area until February 1942.

On 13 January 1942 units of the Red Army broke through the German front on the Volkhov (approx. 40 km N of Novgorod) at the boundary between the *16.* and *18. Armee*. Leaving the *Polizei-Artillerie-Regiment* behind, on 19 February 1942 the division handed its positions in front of Leningrad over to the *121. Infanterie-Division* and marched into the Chudovo area. Attached to the *I. Armee-Korps* the division, which had been absorbed into the *Waffen-SS* on 10 February 1942, was supposed to restore contact with the *XXXVIII. Armee-Korps*. Concerning the takeover, Himmler noted in his duty calendar the persistent difficulties with the *Ordnungspolizei* Headquarters and Daluege's constant interference with the command of the division. With incorporation into the *Waffen-SS*, the division's personnel were given corresponding *Waffen-SS* ranks. Thus, for example, a *Gefreiter* became an *SS-Sturmmann*.

The *SS-Polizei-Division* attacked on 15 March 1942, and four days later was able to close the so-called Volkhov Pocket. When the pocket in the heavily forested area was closed at the end of June 1942, the division was again attached to the *L. Armee-Korps* and moved north into the Sablino area.

From there the unit returned to the front before Leningrad and occupied positions near Krasny-Bor. The Red Army launched a major attack on 23 July. After the costly defensive fighting died down, on 8 August 1942 one battalion from each of the three regiments was ordered to SS Training Camp "Heidelager" for reformation. Just one week later the troops still in the main line of resistance had to face another Soviet attack in the Kolpino area. To make good losses, on 20 August 1942 the division received 2,000 replacements.

In mid-October 1942 the SS police rifle regiments were renamed SS police infantry regiments and the SS Police Reconnaissance Battalion was renamed SS Police Bicycle Battalion.

In November 1942 the unit, consisting of three infantry regiments each with two battalions, reported a strength of:

Officers	Other Ranks	Total
322	10,157	10, 479
3.1%	96.9%	100%

As well, the three infantry battalions undergoing reformation at SS Training Camp "Heidelager" reported:

Officers	Other Ranks	Total
48	2,872	2,290
1.6%	98.4%	100%

The *SS-Polizei-Division*'s total strength of 13,400 members represented more than 80% of its authorized strength of approximately 16,500.

On 12 January 1943 the Soviets launched their winter offensive on the northern front. Enemy troops penetrated the XXVI. *Armee-Korps*' front to the southeast, and four days later the *SS-Polizei-Division* received orders to fight its way into Schlüsselburg, rescue the German troops encircled there, and at the same time re-close the ring around Leningrad. The German troops had nothing to match the tremendous artillery and tank forces deployed by the enemy. Schlüsselburg had to be abandoned. The *SS-Polizei-Division* was almost wiped out in the fierce fighting in the Sinyavino area. The battalions were down to 30 to 50 men. When the battle rose to an inferno pitch on 28 January 1943, some of the division's troops fled in panic. The next day what was left of the unit was pulled out of action and transferred back to the LIV. *Armee-Korps*. Assembled in Sablino, three weak battalions were formed from the remnants of the three infantry regiments—designated SS police-grenadier regiments since 1 February 1943. All available personnel, including cooks, laborers, horse-tenders, and stenographers, were incorporated into the fighting units. The *SS-Polizei-Division* had suffered approximately 3,000 casualties in the past few days.

On 9 February 1943 a newly-formed battalion (1,200 men) arrived from SS training camp "Heidelager." The other battalions had been sent to the Eastern Front at the end of 1942.[99]

On 10 February 1943 the Red Army forced its offensive once again, and the German troops, summoning the last of their strength, tried to hold as many areas as possible. The fighting died down at the end of February 1943, and the sector along the Tosna remained quiet until mid-March. Already hard-pressed by the difficult winter conditions, the grenadiers in the area south of Kolpino got no rest. The enemy attacked again on 18 March, committing masses of men and powerful artillery forces. The front held, and after 14 days the Red Army ceased its attacks. For about 1/3 of the *SS-Polizei-Division* this meant withdrawal from the front during April. The forces pulled out of the front were mainly used as cadres in the reformation and reorganization into a Panzergrenadier-Division at the SS Training Camp "Heidelager." Meanwhile, the

SS-Polizei-Artillerie-Regiment
SS-Polizei-Flak-Abteilung
III./SS-Polizei-Grenadier-Regiment 1
I./SS-Polizei-Grenadier-Regiment 2
I./SS-Polizei-Grenadier-Regiment 3

were brought up to strength with personnel from other units and remained in the siege line around Leningrad as *Kampfgruppe/SS-Polizei-Division* under *SS-Standartenführer* Bock. There was no further serious fighting for the time being. From 21 October 1943 the three battalions together were designated *SS-Polizei-Grenadier-Regiment 3*.

In November 1943 elements of the *24.* and *225. Infanterie-Division* took over the positions held by *Kampfgruppe/SS-Polizei-Division* which, attached to the *L. Armee-Korps*, moved to the western front of the Oranienbaum pocket between Kernovo and Gorbovitsy. At the end of 1943 the *III. SS-Panzer-Korps* arrived from Croatia and took over the area. Under this new command the SS battle group boasted a strength of:

Officers	NCOs	Enlisted Men	Total
11	903	4,053	5,067
2.2%	17.8%	89%	100%

With the arrival of the main body of the corps in the Oranienbaum pocket, on 10 January 1944 *Kampfgruppe/SS-Polizei-Division* was pulled out of the line and sent almost 200 km to the east to the front on the Volkhov. Attached to the *XXVIII. Armee-Korps*, it relieved elements of the *96. Infanterie-Division* and occupied positions at the mouth of the Tigoda. There was heavy fighting there on 16 January 1944 after the Soviets launched their latest winter offensive. As one of the main efforts was farther south near Novgorod, the unit, which was also designated "*SS-Kampfgruppe Bock*," was pulled out of the line five days later and ordered to the *XXXVIII. Armee-Korps*. In the subsequent fighting the battle group was virtually destroyed by the Red Army. The men withdrew through Sapalye to Oredesh, losing all their heavy weapons. Together with Latvian volunteers, the survivors of the division defended the town until it was encircled. They managed to break through the enemy lines at the cost of heavy casualties and made their way through Luga—which had been taken by the *SS-Polizei-Division* on 24 August 1941—to Turkoviche, and thus regained the German main line of resistance.

With no possibility of offering organized resistance the troops streamed back in the direction of Pskov, and on 2 March 1944 occupied provisional positions in the "Panther Position." Two days later the Red Army attacked the desolate units along the Velikaya. With no supporting heavy weapons, the final action by *SS-Kampfgruppe "Bock"* was a desperate attempt to prevent the Soviets from breaking through between Pskov and Ostrov on Lake Pskov. Finally recognized as no longer fit for operations, at the end of March 1944 the remnants were ordered through Opochka to SS Training Camp "Kurmark."

The *4. SS-Polizei-Panzergrenadier-Division*

Reorganization of the division — which still relied on horses for transport, into a panzer-grenadier division — began in April 1943. Because of the situation at the front, however, only about 2,500 men were transferred to SS Training Camp "Heidelager" or elsewhere for specialized training (e.g. pioneers or signals personnel). The authorized strength of:

Officers	NCOs	Enlisted Men	Total
520	3,355	13,130	17,005
3.1%	19.7%	77.2%	100%

was to be achieved largely through the use of ethnic Germans from Rumania. While *SS-Kampfgruppe "Bock"* was still fighting with *Heeresgruppe "Nord,"* the formation of frameworks of the new units was begun. The new *SS-Polizei-Panzergrenadier-Division* was to be organized as follows:

SS-Polizei-Panzergrenadier-Regiment 1 (*I. – III. Bataillon*)
SS-Polizei-Panzergrenadier-Regiment 2 (ditto)
SS-Polizei-Panzergrenadier-Regiment 3 (ditto)
SS-Polizei-Artillerie-Regiment
SS-Polizei-Flak-Abteilung
SS-Polizei-Panzer-Abteilung
SS-Polizei-Nachrichten-Abteilung (signals)
SS-Polizei-Panzer-Aufklärungs-Abteilung (armored recon.)
SS-Polizei-Panzerjäger-Abteilung
SS-Polizei-Pionier-Bataillon
SS-Polizei-Wirtschafts-Bataillon

SS-Polizei-Panzergrenadier-Regiment 3 was not established as a new unit at the training camp; instead, the infantry units of *SS-Kampfgruppe "Bock"* formed the third grenadier regiment. In April 1943 the first units were sent from Camp Heidelager straight into action against Polish partisans in the *Generalgouvernement*. In July 1943 Mussolini was removed from power, and it became apparent that the Italians were about to change sides. As a result, German forces were forced to take over large parts of the Balkans. Among the units sent to bolster German forces there were elements of the *SS-Polizei-Panzergrenadier-Division*, which were attached to the *2. Armee*.

At the end of July 1943 *SS-Polizei-Panzergrenadier-Regiment 1* took up quarters in the Valjevo area southwest of Belgrade and *SS-Polizei-Panzergrenadier-Regiment 2* in the Misar/Sabac area (70 km W of Belgrade). When, in the course of the new political situation, the Italian III Army Corps was ordered home from Greece, the two panzer-grenadier regiments received orders to move into that area of operations. Attached to the *XXII. Gebirgs-Korps* together with the *1. Gebirgs-* and *104. Jäger-Division*, the units in Thessaly were supposed to continue training; however, their main task was to combat the Greek partisan groups ELAS and EDES. A large-scale, active effort against the partisans was scarcely possible, however.

As part of the renumbering of *Waffen-SS* units, effective 22 October 1943 the division—now attached to *Oberfeldkommandantur 395* (Commander Salonika-Aegean)—was renamed the ***4. SS-Polizei-Panzergrenadier-Division***.

While the division units were also assigned the number 4, the panzer-grenadier regiments were numbered 7 and 8.[100] The "*Polizei*" title was dropped from all designations except that of the division. On 31 December 1943 the division reported the following strength (not including the battle group still at the front):

Officers	NCOs	Enlisted Men	Total
216	1,399	9,094	10,709
2.0%	13%	85%	100%

Barely a year after the formation of the motorized SS division began, its new commander, *SS-Brigadeführer und Generalmajor der Waffen-SS und Polizei* Schmedes, summed up the situation by declaring that unit training could not yet be completed because of missing weapons and equipment and a shortage of fuel. Apart from that, the division's occupation duties meant that any tactical employment of the entire division was impossible. The units were almost all deployed separately in the area.

On 23 May 1944 *Heeresgruppe "E"* ordered elements of the *4. SS-Polizei-Panzergrenadier-Division* to relieve *SS-Polizei-Gebirgsjäger-Regiment 18* on the Gulf of Corinth. Together with *I./SS-Artillerie-Regiment 4*, *SS-Polizei-Panzergrenadier-Regiment* 7 subsequently moved the approximately 120 kilometers to the south. There was a visible escalation of force as the units carried out their security and pacification tasks there. When a number of civilians were killed in a reprisal action in the village of Distomon—a few kilometers from the sea—the result was a court-martial investigation against the responsible company and battalion commanders.

After the bulk of *SS-Kampfgruppe "Bock"* arrived from SS Training Camp "Kurmark" and joined the units in Greece, on 30 June 1944 the division was able to report the following strength:

Officers	NCOs	Enlisted Men	Total
385	2,491	13,015	15,891
2.4%	15.7%	81.9%	100%

Authorized strength at that time was:

Officers	NCOs	Enlisted Men	Total
557	3,388	12,595	16,538
3.4%	20.5%	76.1%	100%

Approximately 50% of the units' personnel had experience in Russia, while about 50% had a one-year tour of duty as occupation troops, and with the necessary training it proved possible to merge them into an operational division.

In July 1944 elements of the two SS panzer-grenadier regiments were assigned the task of clearing the rear area of the *LXVIII. Armee-Korps* to the south in the southern Pindus Mountains. At the end of August 1944 Rumania changed sides and the situation deteriorated drastically. To shore up the threatened front and prevent German troops in the south from being cut off, the *4. SS-Polizei-Panzergrenadier-Division* was ordered to Werschetz, near Belgrade, about 600 km to the north in the sector of *Heeresgruppe "Südukraine."*

Divided into battle groups, the division—moving mainly by night on account of constant air attacks—began arriving in the Belgrade area on 11 September 1944. Attached to the *LVII. Panzer-Korps*, the *4. SS-Polizei-Panzergrenadier-Division* was supposed to retake Temesvar (German Temeschburg). Because of the situation *SS-Brigadeführer* Schmedes did not carry out the attack. Instead he had his unit, which was under constant enemy pressure, establish a bridgehead over the Theiss near Szeged. Having failed to follow orders, Schmedes, whom Himmler described as a "*weak character*," was soon afterward relieved by *SS-Standartenführer* Harzer. Still under heavy pressure from the Red Army, the division was moved to the Szolnok area, about 100 km away. Ethnic Germans were evacuated with the division as it passed. Beyond the Theiss the Soviet advance on Budapest was supposed to be stopped. After fierce fighting the *4. SS-Polizei-Panzergrenadier-Division* was forced to withdraw into the Jász-Ladany area. Attached to the division was the *18. SS-Freiwilligen-Panzergrenadier-Division "Horst Wessel,"* which proved a complete failure in the fighting on 11 November 1944. Until 25 November the units withdrew through Heréd toward Ecséd. There *SS-Feldersatz-Bataillon* 4 provided replacements, allowing them to at least partially make good their losses in personnel.

The German troops had long since been limited to reacting to Soviet moves, and in the subsequent fighting the division, under the command of *SS-Standartenführer* Harzer, was almost encircled south of Kis-Terenye. Attached to *Panzerkorps "Feldherrnhalle,"* the division moved into the Slovakian-Hungarian border area and in mid-January 1945 was ordered to seal off a Soviet breakthrough in the Divin area (approx. 20 km from the border). There, in the days that followed, the attached elements of the *18. SS-Freiwilligen-Panzergrenadier-Division* left the unit. Having lost most of its heavy weapons during the retreat from Greece, the *4. SS-Polizei-Panzergrenadier-Division* took over the equipment of the attached units, and *I./SS-Freiwilligen-Panzergrenadier-Regiment 40* was incorporated into the division.

In the Schemnitz area, at the end of January 1945 the division received orders to proceed to Pomerania. Soviet units were already advancing toward Berlin along the Netze and Warthe Rivers. The first element of the division, *SS-Polizei-Panzergrenadier-Regiment 8*, arrived in Stargard on 1 February 1945, and it was immediately committed southeast of Greifenhagen. In the first week of February the entire division assembled there—between the Oder and Lake Madü.

In preparation for the planned German offensive in Pomerania, which was to be a drive into the Soviet flank from the north, the *4. SS-Polizei-Panzergrenadier-Division* moved into the area south of Stargard, where it was attached to *XXXIX. Panzer-Korps*. Fighting began on 16 February, and with *SS-Panzer-Abteilung 4*, which was again operational, the division was able to advance toward Dölitz. The offensive was called off on 19 February 1945 in the face of superior Soviet forces. The next day the *10. SS-Panzer-Division* took over the positions of the *4. SS-Polizei-Panzergrenadier-Division*, which was ordered to assume the defense of Danzig because it was "*still very well-equipped.*"

The *4. SS-Polizei-Panzergrenadier-Division* entrained on 24 February 1945 and was transported to the *VII. Panzer-Korps* in the Dirschau area. The division detrained in the Rummelsburg area, short of its destination. The *VII. Panzer-Korps* had been ordered to reestablish contact with the *3. Panzer-Armee*. The *4. SS-Polizei-Panzergrenadier-Division* counterattacked on 28 February and succeeded in at least bringing some relief. Soviet pressure forced the German units to steadily withdraw, however.

To prevent the German front from being rolled up along the coast to Danzig, the *4. SS-Polizei-Panzergrenadier-Division* moved into the Stolp area and withdrew through Lauenburg to Neustadt. As the combined units only possessed the strength of a strong regiment, from then on they were identified only as *Kampfgruppe/4. SS-Polizei-Panzergrenadier-Division*. Consisting of 5 battalions, 1 pioneer battalion, 1 replacement battalion, and three attached companies of French SS members,[101] the unit occupied the area from the Putziger Wiek (Putzig Bay) to Rahmel.

On 20 March 1945 the Red Army succeeded in splitting up the Danzig – Gotenhafen defense zone. Four days later Hitler ordered the fortresses of Hela, Gotenhafen, Danzig, and Königsberg held at all costs. Events soon overtook the order, however, as on 28 March the Soviets occupied Gotenhafen. The situation north of the city on the Oxhöfter Kämpe grew increasingly grave. In order to rescue the approximately 20,000 men of the *VII. Panzer-Korps* and elements of the civilian population from destruction and captivity, on 4 April 1945 commanding general *General der Panzertruppen* von Kessel ordered a withdrawal to Hela. During the evacuation over Putzig Bay all remaining vehicles were destroyed on the airfield at Oxhöfter Kämpe. In a masterful effort, by the following day the *Kriegsmarine* was able to evacuate all of the German soldiers and many civilians on the peninsula.

As part of *Generalkommando Hela*, the *4. SS-Polizei-Panzergrenadier-Division* assumed responsibility for coastal defense in the area around Heisternest, and on 9 April 1945 it reported a fighting strength of 3,110 men and a daily strength of 4,871 men. These numbers included a navy rifle battalion and an air force battalion temporarily attached to the division. The unit no longer had any heavy weapons. Because of the division's still "*considerable*" personnel strength, the OKH ordered it sent to *Heeresgruppe "Weichsel"* (Army Group Vistula).

SS-Kampfgruppe "Harzer"

On 13 April 1945 the *4. SS-Polizei-Panzergrenadier-Division* began boarding ships for transport to Swinemünde, in order to bolster the Oder Front in anticipation of a major Soviet offensive. After disembarking there the next day the units initially assembled near Heringsdorf, and on 18 April were attached to the *III. SS-Panzer-Korps* in the Gramzow area. When *SS-Obergruppenführer und General der Waffen-SS* Steiner, commanding general of *Heeresgruppe "Weichsel,"* ordered the boundary between the *3. Panzer-Armee* and the *9. Armee* between Liebenwalde and Oderberg guarded, the remnants of the *4. SS-Polizei-Panzergrenadier-Division* were reorganized, reinforced by army units, and renamed SS-*Kampfgruppe "Harzer."* The battle group was organized as follows:

Stab (Headquarters)
SS-Panzergrenadier-Regiment 7[102]
SS-Panzergrenadier-Regiment 8
SS-Füsilier-Regiment 4
Heeres-Pionier-Bataillon 630
(Heeres) Panzer-Aufklärungs-Abteilung 115

By the time the first unit, *SS-Panzergrenadier-Regiment 7*, marched into the Eberswalde area, the Red Army had succeeded in breaking through in the direction of Bernau. The rapid advance by enemy armor toward Oranienburg led to the order for the rest of *SS-Kampfgruppe "Harzer"* to proceed immediately to the Oranienburg area instead of the Eberswalde bridgehead. The battle group thus went into action divided. After the Soviets breached the Randow position, *SS-Panzergrenadier-Regiment 7* was ordered to the *XXXXVI. Panzer-Korps* in Mecklenburg – Lower Pomerania. After fierce fighting near Prenzlau and Neubrandenburg, what was left reached Hagenow by way of Waren – Karow and there surrendered to the Americans. After heavy fighting between Oranienburg and Berlin on 25 April *SS-Kampfgruppe "Harzer"* initially withdrew toward the line Kremmen – Behrensbrück – Kuhbrücke forester's house. From there, at the beginning of May 1945 what remained of the former *4. SS-Polizei-Panzergrenadier-Division* proceeded via Kyritz – Perleberg to the Allied demarcation line at Schwerin – Ludwigslust and there surrendered to the Americans.

Originally formed from policemen and police reservists, heavy casualties increasingly changed the unit's makeup. When the *4. SS-Polizei-Panzergrenadier-Division* was established in the spring of 1943, many of the companies consisted of recently recruited ethnic Germans from Rumania. By the end of the war the number of former policemen represented less than 10% of total strength.

Comparison of Ranks

Waffen-SS	Deutsche Polizei	Schutzmannschaft	Heer
SS-Grenadier	Anwärter	Schutzmann	Grenadier
SS-Sturmmann	Unterwachtmeister	Unterkorporal	Gefreiter
SS-Rottenführer	Rottwachtmeister	Vizekorporal	Obergefreiter
SS-Unterscharführer	Wachtmeister	---	Unteroffi zier
SS-Scharführer	Oberwachtmeister	Korporal	Unterfeldwebel
SS-Oberscharführer	Zugwachtmeister	Vizefeldwebel	Feldwebel
SS-Hauptscharführer	Hauptwachtmeister	Kompaniefeldwebel	Oberfeldwebel
SS-Untersturmführer	Leutnant	Leitenant	Leutnant
SS-Obersturmführer	Oberleutnant	Starschy Leitenant	Oberleutnant
SS-Hauptsturmführer	Hauptmann	Kapitan	Hauptmann
SS-Sturmbannführer	Major	---	Major
SS-Obersturmbannführer	Oberstleutnant	---	Oberstleutnant
SS-Standartenführer	Oberst	---	Oberst
SS-Oberführer	kein vgl. Rang	---	kein vgl. Rang
SS-Brigadeführer	Generalmajor	---	Generalmajor
SS-Gruppenführer	Generalleutnant	---	Generalleutnant
SS-Obergruppenführer	General	---	General
SS-Oberstgruppenführer	Generaloberst	---	Generaloberst

Uniforms and Rank badges of the German Police
Shoulder Straps

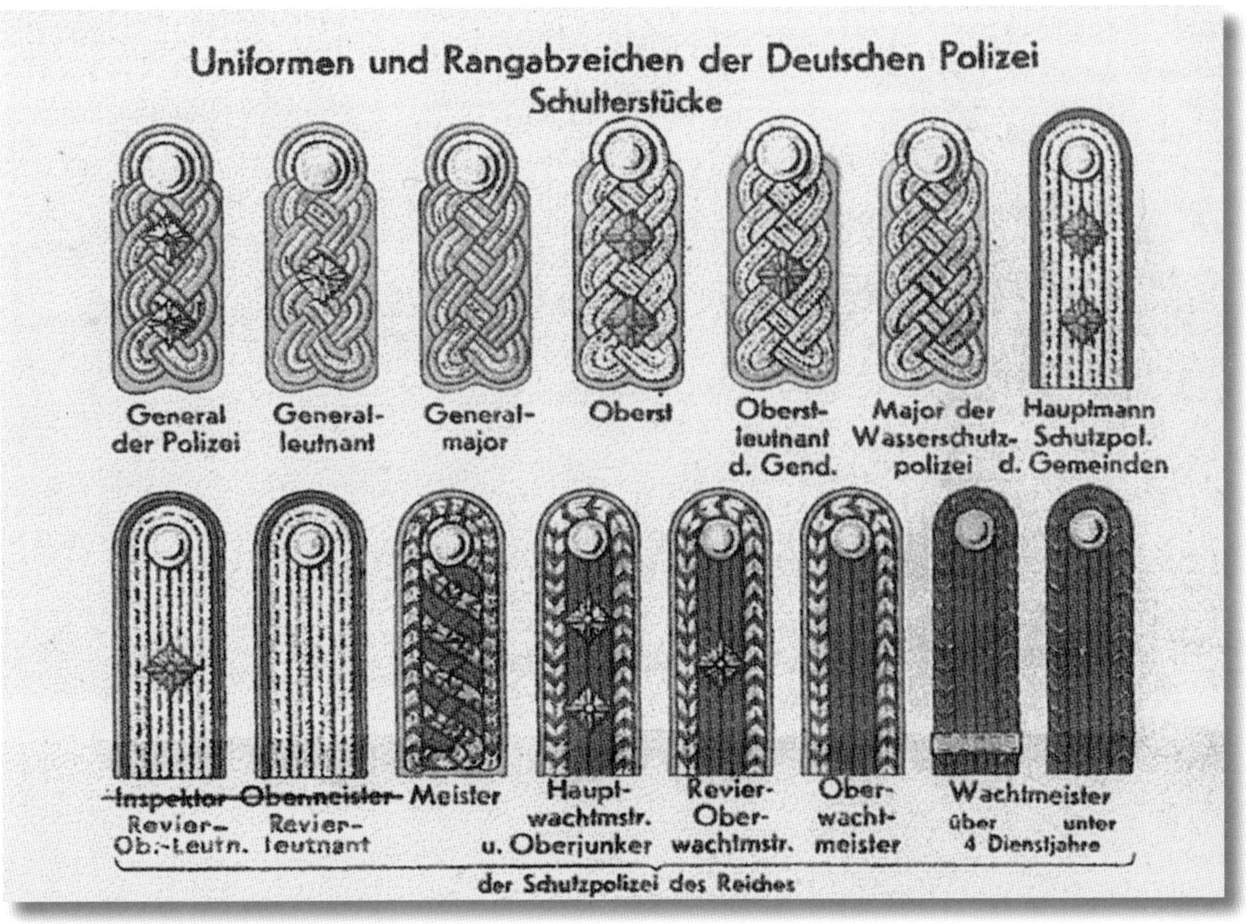

Documents

The following is a selection of original documents intended to convey an impression of the activities in which the police battalions and regiments were involved. They show the types of actions to which these elements of the *Ordnungspolizei* were assigned in addition to their usual patrol duties: guarding supply routes to the front, combating partisans and their sympathizers—a term subject to much interpretation—securing the harvest and the collection of agricultural products, as well as labor forces for German industry, and employment in the changing of the demographic structures in the occupied territories.

Document 1

Report by the company commander of *7./Polizei-Regiment "Mitte"* concerning captured Soviet soldiers designated as partisans, dated 13 September 1941:

In carrying out this action, on 11/9/1941 I advanced from Uboltye to Borki and arrived in the village at 07:50 hours. On leaving the forest west of Borki I observed through my binoculars that the entire population was on the village street. When they sighted us, the people ran into their houses or fled in an easterly direction. The village was immediately surrounded. The village leader who was brought in at first claimed to know nothing about partisans and communists. After sharper measures he admitted that about 20 partisans armed with automatic weapons had emerged from the woods south of Borki at dawn. They passed through the village and then wandered off in an easterly direction. As we were searching the village, two uniformed partisans were sighted coming from the woods to the south. The two partisans fled and fire was opened from long range. The two escaped, however, as they were able to immediately escape into a ravine.

A shepherd then declared that there was a large partisan camp north of the Borki – Kokotovo road.

I deployed the company to search the area north of the road, with eight paces between men. The terrain was extremely difficult, very swampy and in places under ½ meter of water. East of the Borki cemetery two fleeing partisans were sighted in a clearing about 500 meters away. There was no point in shooting because of the heavy growth. While the company advanced in a skirmish line I led my headquarters squad forward. We came upon a large partisan camp consisting of four large, well-built huts with sloped roofs. The camp had just been abandoned (fire pit was still warm), the partisans having fled north into the swamp. Tracks indicated one small party. We found 2 hand grenades, small arms ammunition, transmitter and receiver equipment with accessories, about 100 meters of fuse, and freshly butchered veal and other food. The huts, fuses, food, and radio accessories were burned. Much of the small arms ammunition exploded in the fire.

Pursuit of the partisans was impossible, as leading the company into the swamp was out of the question.

During the subsequent advance toward Kokotovo one partisan was sighted trying to enter Kokotovo. He was shot at and then captured.

He revealed that he had had gone to the above-described camp with two officers. In the morning they had been moving toward Borki, were fired on, and one was wounded. 7 soldiers and 4 officers had stopped in the big camp while on their way to an even bigger camp in Rogi. On 13/9/41 an aircraft wearing German markings came to Dolgoye and brought new orders. He also stated that there was a tank cannon and a radio repair shop in Makovka, and in Chatuschteschi there was a weapons dump, a heavy mortar, and a motorcycle with sidecar and machine-gun.

The prisoner was used as a guide, and I was able to confirm that the information he had given me was reliable. He knew all the routes to the partisan camp. Because of very deep swamp crisscrossed by ditches, some 1½ meters deep, the company operation had to be called off. We detoured through Stolev to Khorov and approached Kokotovo from the west. At about 10:00 on 12/9/41 the other two prisoners were brought in. They raised their hands and surrendered when they realized they were surrounded. All of the initial statements made by these two, especially the supposed parachutist, were untrue, but under cross examination the three admitted that they all belonged to the big partisan group and had hidden weapons. A search revealed 3 hand grenades, a submachine-gun with a full drum magazine, a rifle with 70 rounds, and a pistol.

The prisoners were handed over to the regiment. I request that the weapons remain with the company.

Document 2

Report by *9./Polizei-Regiment "Mitte"* Concerning the Patrolling of the Area between Mogilev – Orsha and the Dniepr on 23 September 1941:

On 23/9/41 the 9. Kompanie searched a 7.1-km strip of land for mines and military equipment of all kinds. The search action began on the Mogilev – Orsha road at the north end of the city and extended due east to the Dniepr. The left boundary extended along the right boundary of the 8. Kompanie's sector.

No mines were found, as the area was mainly cultivated farmland—part freshly-ploughed fields, part potato fields. We also found no mines in an intervening wood. 200 brass casings of various calibers were found in abandoned artillery positions, as well as 3 Russian rifles and 10 Russian helmets. Everything was delivered to the collection point for captured equipment in Mogilev.

Unexploded artillery rounds were discovered near the road. The attached technical personnel were unable to defuse the shells. The location of the unexploded rounds can be seen in the attached sketch.

The removal of further military equipment will continue on 24/9/41.

Document 3

Final report on "Operation Adler," in which *Polizei-Regiment 2* and *II./Polizei-Regiment 8* took part:

Sicherungs-Division 286
"Kampfgruppe Adler"
Division Command Post, 8 August 1942

For months strong enemy partisan bands have been causing unrest in the area of the Mogilev – Beresino – Bobruisk – Mogilev road. These bands are under the unified command of Russian officers and commissars.

The bands have grown in size through the delivery of regular troops by aircraft, through the arrival of parachute troops, and through recruiting of the local population, making it impossible for smaller German units or local economic agencies to enter the area. Their presence and activities represented a constantly growing threat.

The wooded, swampy region in the center of this occupied area was the backbone of the bands. They supplied themselves with weapons and other military equipment from a former Russian training camp in the designated area. Estimates of the bands' strength varied between 2,000 and 5,000 men. Their armament consisted of light and heavy field howitzers, anti-tank guns, light and heavy mortars, light and heavy machine-guns, submachine-guns, and rifles. Marshall Kulik is said to have directed formation of the bands and was their first commander. He was replaced by Colonel Nichipurovich.

Since autumn 1941 several operations have been carried out against these bands by forces of Sicherungs-Division 286, Sicherungs-Division 203, and the Senior SS and Police Commander. Some success was achieved; however, this was insufficient to pacify the area. When engaged, the bands usually fled into the impassible swampy area, thus avoiding destruction. As well, because of inadequate security forces, the commands assigned to pacify the area had to limit themselves to reconnaissance and keeping the main through roads open. More powerful units were needed to destroy the enemy.

After "Operation Maikäfer" by Sicherungs-Division 203, the main body of the enemy withdrew north across the Stary Bykhov – Svishloch road. This resulted in a significant strengthening of the enemy forces in the area Belynichi – Beresino road – Svishloch – Stary Bykhov road to Belynichi on the Drut. The Commanding General of Security Troops and the Commander in Army Area Center subsequently ordered Sicherungs-Division 286 to destroy these bands. The commanding officer of Sicherungs-Division 286 was placed in charge of the operation.

Sicherungs-Division 286 had available the following units with which to carry out the operation:

from the Senior SS and Police Commander "Russia Center"

Gruppe Oberstleutnant Buchmann with
Polizei-Regiment 2 (I. and II. Bataillon)
SS-Sonderkommando "Dirlewanger"
SD detachments

from Sicherungs-Division 203:
Gruppe Major Kopf with:
Sicherungs-Bataillon 420
Sicherungs-Bataillon 473
Sicherungs-Bataillon 642
Kampf-Bataillon "Dnjepr"
8./Artillerie-Abteilung "Smolensk"
GFP detachments
from Sicherungs-Division 286:
Gruppe Oberstleutnant von Geldern
Polizei-Bataillon 134 (II./Polizei-Regiment 8)
Sicherungs-Bataillon 452
Kosaken-Abteilung 102
9./Artillerie-Abteilung "Smolensk"
Bataillon Hauptmann Dr. Knoblauch
GFP detachments
Panzerkampfwagen-Zug 286 (tank platoon)
from other units:
2 light armored cars
Flak-Nachrichten-Zug 6 (mot.) (flak signals platoon)
1 platoon 20-mm light flak from leichte Flak-Abteilung 769[103]
1 platoon 40-mm flak from leichte Flak-Abteilung 715[104]
bombers of 4./Kampfgeschwader 1 from Stary Bykhov
bombers of Kampfgeschwader 51 from Bobruisk

The available forces were divided into four battle groups for the operation. They reached the new line of departure on 20 July 1942 […]

The entire operation was carried out in 7 attack sectors in intervals of 2 – 4 days. This slow pace was made necessary by the extremely difficult terrain conditions. The complex swamp and forest terrain had to be thoroughly and repeatedly searched and combed, as it offered the enemy too many opportunities to hide and allow the attack line to pass by.

The attack usually played out in such a way that the objective was reached by noon of the first day. The rest of that day and, depending on the difficulty of the terrain, the 2nd and 3rd days were thus available for the clearing of captured ground. All reconnaissance and enemy reports from the first day clearly revealed that the enemy was withdrawing everywhere in the pocket, specifically into the extensive area of swamps and forest west of the Olsa and north of the Mogilev – Osipovichi rail line.

This was a maneuver that had saved them from destruction in all previous operations. These enemy movements in the pocket were a lucky break for the command, for, given the size of the area, the available forces were insufficient to close the ring tightly enough so as to prevent enemy units from breaking out.

Except for the area south of Klitchev, where several villages had to be stormed after softening up by the air force, there was limited contact with the enemy in the first days of the operation, usually small patrols. Not until 30 July 1942, after the fourth objective had been reached, did the enemy realize that he was completely encircled and begin attempts to break out. By then, however, the ring had been so reduced in size that the line of security was so tight as to make an enemy breakout impossible.

From statements made by prisoners and deserters it was deduced that the enemy command had ordered the partisans recruited from the nearby villages to return to their homes and act like harmless farmers. It was observed that the male population in the captured areas increased two- to threefold in a few days.

GFP and SD detachments scoured and cleared these villages. The enemy forces left in the pocket were mainly regular partisan battle groups under the command of Colonel Nichipurovich. On 31 July 1942 Colonel Nichipurovich was requested to meet with a special officer of the Smolensk defense office. He was guaranteed free passage. The purpose of the meeting was to offer him the chance to surrender with his units to avoid further bloodshed. The colonel received the letter from the division; however, he failed to show up for the meeting.

Enemy breakout attempts became more frequent as the pocket was reduced. In some cases the attacks were fierce and supported by heavy infantry weapons. In two places small groups succeeded in breaking out, although the enemy left large numbers of dead behind.

Not until the last days, after the 5th objective had been reached, did the enemy order his bands to break up. The men were ordered to try to reach their own lines singly or in small groups. Standing neck-deep in the swamps or sitting high up in tall trees, they tried to evade capture. Small groups frequently made determined efforts to break out. In a number of cases commissars and officers avoided capture at the last minute by committing suicide.

The operation was concluded on 7 August 1942 after the last small pocket had been mopped up. Since the reaching of the 4th objective, the group had discovered numerous small and large camps, some capable of accommodating up to 500 men. Large quantities of weapons, ammunition, and other equipment were captured in these camps, some of which had been hastily abandoned. Three large ammunition dumps were discovered. One of these was fiercely defended and had to be taken by storm. Large quantities of ammunition of all kinds fell into our hands there.

Supply containers, some still full, were found, and it was determined that the bands were supplied with weapons, ammunition, medical supplies, and other equipment mainly by air.

Casualty and captured material figures: see appendix.

Compared to the scale of the enemy losses, the quantity of captured weapons, especially machine-guns and rifles, was small. An explanation for this was found quickly, however, for in this swampy area it is easy for the enemy to make his weapons disappear, even at the last minute. On realizing the situation the enemy buried many weapons, a common Russian tactic.

The willingness and fighting spirit of the troops was exemplary. It must be taken into account that native units like Kampf-Bataillon "Dnjepr" and elements of the Kampf-Bataillon "Wolga" did not take part, as they had only recently been established. Some of the security battalions involved had previously only carried out pure guard duties. Nevertheless, despite their mixed composition and the presence of older age classes, these units carried out all the tasks given to them to the complete satisfaction of the command. Our own minor casualties were unavoidable given the underhanded fighting style of the enemy and the difficult terrain conditions. The division would have been unable to carry out the operation with its own forces and weapons.

The presence of units from outside the division made up for the absence of the division's intervention group. The division's signals resources were also completely inadequate. Because of the size of the area and the poor roads, almost all reports and orders were transmitted by radio. Flak-Regiment 18 and its signals platoon filled the gaps.

The Fieseler Storch generously provided by the Senior SS and Police Commander proved invaluable in maintaining tight control of this operation and for face-to-face meetings with the regimental commanders, which were of vital importance in a concentric attack. It also did valuable service in evacuating the seriously wounded.

If the division is able to report that it has accomplished the task of destroying the enemy as ordered by the commander-in-chief, it is in large part due to the efforts of all the troops involved in this operation.

Document 4

Propagandistic Summons by the Commander of *Polizei-Regiment* 14 to Villages in the Area of "Operation Regatta":

Before the departure of the troops, the populations of Moshkova, Rekotka, and Dobraya are to be summoned and the following read out to them by interpreters:

The German armed forces have occupied the villages and searched the surrounding forests, because in recent months there have been frequent ambushes against German troops carried out by gangs in outlying areas of the forest. In these ambushes German trucks and columns have been shot at, telephone lines and bridges destroyed, and roads attacked.

The German Reich is waging war with its forces against the army of the Soviets; however, anyone found carrying arms behind the German front is a robber and bandit and will be dealt with ruthlessly.

Anyone who aids these bandits and their officers and commissars is equally guilty, and this accusation applies to the villages that were occupied here.

It is known that the bandits were fed and supplied from this village. The village's cattle are available to the bandits. The bandits have entered and left this village. It was learned that two days ago they had a party in Moshkova.

Camps have been set up near the villages, as at Rekotka. Residents of the village helped in their construction and their location absolutely must be known in the village.

In spite of requests by the German authorities, unlike the other villages occupied by the German armed forces this village has not made a single delivery of cattle or wheat. The residents must come to terms with the fact that the Soviets have lost the war and that the country must deliver cattle and grain.

All cows have therefore been driven out of the villages and assembled in Gorki. As soon as the requested quantities of grain have been delivered the cows will be returned to their owners.

The men who take part in bandit activities will be shot according to military law. Suspected [bandits] will be sent to a prison camp. Women directly involved in bandit activity will also be shot.

Nothing will happen to those who stay away from the bandits and who inform German commanders in the villages in the area outside the forest as soon as bandits show themselves, or to those who, like the German armed forces and police and the administrations and agricultural authorities, do everything they can to allow the country folk to carry out their activities in peace. News occasionally smuggled in by commissars, Jews, and agents from Moscow is false. It is nonsense to claim that the German front has been breached or threatened somewhere. Anyone who doesn't believe this only needs to travel to Leningrad, to Rzhev, to Stalingrad, or to Moscow and see for himself where the German troops are. For the Soviets the war is lost and here—many hundreds of kilometers from the fronts—there is nothing to be seen of the war. The only threats to your agriculture are the band members, and it is in your interest to help defeat them.

We will now leave you in peace for the time being, but we tell you:

If there is another attempt in this village to take up arms against German forces, if the German forces are not immediately notified as soon as new band members appear here, the village will be burned to the ground and its entire population shot.

Document 5

Mission order issued by *Sicherungs-Regiment 36* for "Operation Regatta," in which *Polizei-Regiment 14* took part. For this operation the *I. Bataillon* was designated *Polizei-Bataillon "Nord"* and the *II. Bataillon Polizei-Bataillon "Süd."*

Sicherungs-Regiment 36
Gorki, 3 October 1942
514/42 secret

1) Enemy: A partisan band about 400 strong has long been active in the forest around and south of Rekotka (12 km SW of Gorki). Its core unit, about 80 men strong, wears Russian uniform coats and leather caps. The band is well-led and has heavy weapons. In recent weeks it undertook attacks in the local villages. Most of its men wear civilian clothes. Camps were reported between Rekotka and Ryabki and 4 km southeast of Rekotka. The villages of Rekotka and Moshkova appear to be the band's support bases.

2) The Rekotka Forest will be surrounded on Sunday, 4 October 1942 and attacked early on 5 October. The encirclement will consist of a ring of combat outposts which must be in place by 14:00 hours on 4 October 1942 and positioned as follows:

Road bridge over the Golsha Brook, just east of the village of Chutor Debryj Dvor (8 km S of Gorki) – south edge of Sakharovka – then along the road which, 1 km west of this village, leads southwest through the forest to Ryabki – east edge of the group of houses just south of Point 201.1 – east end of Sastenki Beloy – east end of Shateva, then veering to the southeast, along the south edge of the projecting forest corner east of Gubari – north of the Skvan to the road from Korvtchino to Bir, along this road north around the village of Bir to the forest corner in which the word Gubin is found, bordering the forest along the road from the south – then turning northeast 600 m west of Point 200.9 through Point 197.2 to the north – 600 meters west past the church in Gorodets to the bend in the road southwest of Yasychkova – then along the road to Yermaki and northwest to the bridge at Chute Dobryj Dvor.

The blocking ring will be manned by:

a) Polizei-Bataillon "Süd" (approaching from Mogilev via Suchari – Mabye Buschkovo – Zhdanovichi – Korovchino) with the right wing on the forest corner west of Point 200.9 (SW of Novy Pribush), with the left on the southeast corner of Shateva. Headquarters in Bir.

b) Polizei-Bataillon "Nord" (approaching from Mogilev via Sloboda, Litvinovichi – Timokhovka) with the right wing on the southeast corner of Shateva, with the left wing at the Chutor Dobry Dvor bridge – headquarters in Ryabki.

c) Kompanie Ickes of Sicherungs-Bataillon 664[105] with two anti-tank guns with the right wing at the Chutor Dobry Dvor bridge, with the left west of the Gorodets church. Company headquarters northwest edge of Gorodets.

d) Kompanie Dietel of Sicherungs-Bataillon 664 from Drubin with 1 anti-tank gun with the right wing 500 m west of the Gorodets church, the left on the forest corner 600 m west of Point 200.9. Company headquarters – west corner of Novy Pribush.

The Ickes Company will begin patrolling its later sector early on 4 October 1942 to prevent band members from fleeing the villages in its sector and to the east, with which the bands appear to have contact. While this reconnaissance is going on, the village of Gorodets is to be surrounded until the Ickes Company arrives, which for specific reasons will not arrive until 11:00 hours.

e) Concerning the use of a proposed combat company from Nachrichten-Regiment 537, orders will follow as soon as a decision has been made on its participation. The units a), b), and d) will report the completion of attack preparations to regiment by radio, the Ickes Company by field telephone. The companies are to make their attack preparations in such a way that the blocking ring's combat outposts prevent band members from fleeing until the various sectors are manned. In doing this the villages and open fields are to be relatively weakly manned, difficult and wooded terrain more strongly. Frequent patrols between posts are envisaged during the night, equipped with flare pistols and, whenever possible, dogs. Battalions and companies will maintain intervention squads immediately behind the line of outposts which can be moved forward to a threatened point at any time.

There will be no local bivouac on the night of the operation. In order to maintain the integrity of the line of outposts, the troops must remain alert and close to the enemy for the 1-2 nights of the operation. The trains, which must remain outside the forest during the subsequent advance, especially in the southern sector, will assume hedgehog positions, for contact with the enemy will be possible at any time, especially south of the forest.

5) After the line of outposts is established, all units will actively patrol the forest in front of them to scout the terrain and search for the enemy, specifically Polizei-Bataillon "Süd" in its attack sector for 5 October 1942 as per paragraph 6), Polizei-Bataillon "Nord" in the west end of this sector, feeling its way no farther than about 1 km into the forest, to the north, to the extent that the enemy situation permits, if possible to the Moshkova – Rekotka – Dobrya road, including villages. The Ickes and Dietel Companies will not send their patrols any farther than about 1,500 meters into the forest, during which the Dietel Company will not set foot in the later attack sector of Polizei-Bataillon "Süd" (see Paragraph 6). It is necessary to send a few strong and capable patrols to all sides to avoid ambushes.

6) On Monday, 5 October 1942, Polizei-Bataillon Süd will attack from south to north—its right and left wings brushing along the eastern and western edges of the forest—and reach as the objective of the day the west-east forest lane, which leads along Points 195.4, 197.3, 190.4 (S of Moshkova), and 192.8. Reaching of the objective is to be reported by radio. Polizei-Bataillon "Nord" will move the screening forces on its right wing, and the Dietel Company the outposts of its left wing, to the north, keeping pace with the northwards attack by Polizei-Bataillon "Süd." On 5 October 1942 Polizei-Bataillon "Nord" and the Ickes and Dietel Companies will remain stationary with the bulk of their forces and continue patrolling for the enemy. Should the development of a serious battle ahead of their fronts make it appear advantageous to advance the blocking line, this will be done on orders from the regiment, which will be transmitted by radio before striking. If the enemy offers serious resistance and radio somehow fails, the closest unit will attack and advance the blocking ring independently, and report to the regiment as soon as it is able. Further attack orders will be issued as soon as Polizei-Bataillon "Süd" reaches its objective. Throughout the operation the integrity of the ring must be maintained despite isolated combats. All units must therefore ensure that contacts are maintained day and night.

7) Conduct of Battle: Within the daily target areas, which have yet to be issued to Polizei-Bataillon "Nord" and the Ickes and Dietel Companies, the enemy is to be located and destroyed in every wood, and later in the villages in the core of the forest area. The burning of villages is forbidden unless the population is observed taking part in the fighting. Weapons and captured cattle, as well as prisoners, are to be assembled by the sectors and later sent to Dobrya via Moshkova and Rekotka. Caution when using flare pistols in the presence of thatched roofs and granaries! The attached agriculture officers will take charge of the captured cattle.

8) GPF detachments, of which only a few can be provided by Gorki, will be sent to the villages as soon as the troops approach them. The GPF will take over the villages from Novy Pribush to Yermaki on 4 October 1942.

9) Communications: The Senior SS and Police Commander is requested to provide the two police battalions with 100-watt radio sets. The division's 100-watt set is being used by the regiment. The Senior SS and Police Commander is requested to assign frequencies and codes. Polizei-Bataillon "Nord" will tap into the telephone line between Sacharovka and Dushki to enable telephone contact with regimental headquarters, which will make a similar connection. Regimental signals platoon will establish telephone links with the Ickes and Dietel Companies. Radio communications will also be established, with the latter using 5-watt sets. Battalions and companies will keep the regiment constantly informed of the progress of the fighting and will report the events of the night each morning at 07:00, and then the events of the day at 19:00.

10) The regiment is to submit proposals when the use of aircraft against certain worthwhile targets appears warranted. The regiment will submit requests for such support to division.

11) Regimental command post in Yermaki from 12:00 hours on 4 October 1942.

Document 6

Mission order issued by *Kampfgruppe Kutschera* for "Operation Franz," in which *III. Bataillon Polizei-Regiment 2* took part:

Kampfgruppe Kutschera
4 January 1943
1a Diary No. 1513/42 secret

1) Enemy bands in considerable strength, with significant fighting power and considerable will to fight, are present in the area southeast of Cherven. All observations to date suggest that these enemy forces form the core of the band movements in central Russia. Their activities radiate widely in all directions. Based on information gathered by the SD and reconnaissance by SS-Sonderbataillon Dirlewanger, it is a force of 2,000 – 2,500 men under a unified leadership housed in three main camps in the area Pirunoff Most – Veselov – Grodsyanka – Kolsyna. In the area surrounding this core unit there are smaller bands with an average strength of 100 – 200 men, which have placed lookouts in the nearest villages. Machine-guns have been observed, also artillery. The core unit is also said to have mounted units. The security outposts are believed to have built numerous well-concealed and camouflaged field positions. The bridges on the roads leading into the area held by the bands have been destroyed in many places. The farmers in the villages in the area occupied by the bands either fight with the bands voluntarily or at least have been forced to cooperate. The presence of many Jews in the bands must be expected. It is likely that bandits will be encountered in German uniforms (Wehrmacht, Waffen-SS or police). Recently bands have reappeared in the previously pacified area north of the Beresino – Cherven road.

2) Conduct of "Operation Franz" is under the command of the temporary deputy of the RF-SS' Plenipotentiary for Anti-Partisan Operations, SS-Brigadeführer und Generalmajor der Polizei von Gottberg, in Minsk. I have been placed in command of Kampfgruppe Kutschera.

3) Forces of the battle group:

a) Headquarters: Oberstleutnant der Gendarmerie Köllner (chief-of-staff) Hauptmann der Schupo Schlecht (Pol. Nachrichten-Kp. 112) as signals officer

Oberleutnant der Schupo Boeddecker (12. Pol. Panzer-Kp.) as deputy commander

Leutnant der Schupo Weise (SS and Police Commander Mogilev)

one stenographer, one interpreter (Abt. Gendarmerie attached to HSSPF)

2 special missions officers provided by the 12. Polizei-Panzer-Kompanie

2 drivers and 2 automobiles, supplied by the motor pool

b) Operational Forces:

III./Polizei-Regiment 2

Schutzmannschafts-Bataillon 57

SS-Sonderbataillon "Dirlewanger"

Kommandeur der Osttruppen 700 z.b.V. with

Ost-Bataillonen 633 and 634[107]

1 battery from Schutzmannschafts-Artillerie-Abteilung 56 (76.2-mm short)

(the battery is to be transported by 12. Polizei-Panzer-Kompanie)

4. Polizei-Panzer-Kompanie

12. Polizei-Panzer-Kompanie (without tanks)

Polizei-Nachrichten-Kompanie 112

Brückenbau- und Minensuchtrupp der TeNo. Abt. II (bridging and mine-detector squad)

c) Special Forces:

Attached to each battalion will be one special detachment of the SD and one man from SS-Kriegsberichterstatter-Zug 9 (war correspondent platoon). The forces fall under the command of the battle group effective 5 January 1943.

4) The battle plan for "Operation Franz" is as follows:

The main enemy force will be encircled by a surprise attack from the north (Kampfgruppe "Kutschera"), and from the south and west (Kampfgruppe "Gottberg"), and subsequently destroyed. The digging out of secondary forces, which initially will be bypassed, and the mopping up of the area will follow. Boundary between Battle Groups "Kutschera" and "Gottberg" runs from east to west: Teshacha (on the Beresina) – forester's house N of Lyadetskaya – lane leading past Point 171.1 to the west – in a northwesterly direction Senenpolye – Gorki – Kommisarski – Sad. The named villages to Kampfgruppe "Gottberg." Specific orders for the execution of the battle plan:

a) III./Polizei-Regiment 2 will reach Chutor (on the Beresino – Cherven road) on 5 January 1943 and take over defense of the village. 5 trucks and one staff car from III./Polizei-Regiment 2 will be made available to Schutzmannschafts-Bataillon 57 for transport from Belynichi on 6 January 1943. The vehicles are to be returned to III./Polizei-Regiment 2 as soon as the task is completed. III./Polizei-Regiment 2 will remain in Chutor at my disposal as a reserve. One platoon is to be provided to guard the battle group command post.

b) Assembly of the remaining forces will take place on 6 January 1943 on the Beresino – Cherven road. Scouting of roads to the assembly areas is to be carried out on 6 January 1943.

c) All available forces of the 12. Polizei-Panzer-Kompanie (without tanks) are to be attached with transport to SS-Sonderbataillon "Dirlewanger" for the duration of the operation. Report to SS-Sonderbataillon "Dirlewanger" in Beresino on 6 January 1943. On 5 January 1943 six trucks and one staff car are to be made available to Schutzmannschafts-Artillerie-Abteilung 56 for transport of the battery. As well, the company will provide Schutzmannschaften-Bataillon 57 with 2 motorcycles and 2 motorcycles with sidecar for the duration of the operation. Vehicles are to report to Schutzmannschafts-Bataillon 57 in Belynichi on 6 January 1943.

d) 4. Polizei-Panzer-Kompanie. Two of the company's armored cars will be attached to the Kommandeur der Osttruppen for the duration of the operation. Three of the company's tanks will be attached to Schutzmannschafts-Bataillon 57 for the duration of the operation. Report to Schutzmannschafts-Bataillon 57 in Belynichi on 6 January 1943. Two of the company's tanks will be attached to SS-Sonderbataillon "Dirlewanger" for the duration of the operation. Report to SS-Sonderbataillon "Dirlewanger" in Beresino on 6 January 1943. Four of the company's armored cars (including those attached to III./Polizei-Regiment 2 for 5 January 1943) will begin guarding the Beresino – Cherven road at 07:00 hours on 6 January 1943. Their mission is to protect the assembly of forces on the Beresino – Cherven road against ambush. Afterwards the four tanks will be at my express disposal. Leader to report to the battle group command post at 13:00 hours on 6 January 1943, and with 2 tanks of the 4. Polizei-Panzer-Kompanie area south of New Niva. Schutzmannschafts-Bataillon 57 with 3 tanks of the 4. Polizei-Panzer-Kompanie and bridging and mine-detecting squad of the TeNo. Abt. II village of New Niva. Commander of Osttruppen with Btl. 633 and 634 and 3 tanks of the 4. Polizei-Panzer-Kompanie in the area in and south of Bogushevichi. Attack preparations must be completed by 06:30 hours on 7 January 1943.

g) All units deployed in the front line will advance simultaneously from the assembly areas to an encirclement line beginning at 07:00 hours on 7 January 1943 with the following objective for the day: right wing of SS-Sonderbataillon "Dirlewanger" contact with the boundary with Kampfgruppe "Gottberg" near Senenpolye – via south edge of New Lyady – to edge of forest 1 km south of Old Lyady (including village). Schutzmannschafts-Bataillon 57 with right wing in contact with SS-Sonderbataillon "Dirlewanger" via south edge of Tahulichi – to southwest edge of New Retchki (including village). Commander of Osttruppen with right wing in contact with Bataillon 57 via road from Old Retchki – in southerly direction to forester's house near Point 162.9 (800 m N of Lyadetskaya) with left wing in contact with Kampfgruppe "Gottberg" at the boundary line.

Conduct of Operations: The advance must be made rapidly, employing powerful point forces. Resistance on the advance roads must be overcome swiftly through the use of sufficient heavy weapons. Smaller camps and nests beside the approach roads are to be bypassed. The main objective is to swiftly envelop the core band from all sides and encircle it. After the line of the objective of the day is reached, all units must establish close contact with each other and prepare to resist possible breakout attempts. In dealing with especially strong nests of resistance, support can be requested from the Bobruisk Bomber Training Squadron. Requests are to be passed to the battle group command post with precise information on target location and attack timing. Our own units must have a safety distance of at least 1 kilometer from the target. The position of resistance nests or camps in forests must be carefully marked, as it is difficult for the bomber crews to pick out targets in the forest.

h) The destruction of the main bands begins on 8 January 1943 at 07:00 hours with the attack from the encirclement line against the fortified bandit camp. Detailed orders for this main attack will follow if required. In the event that there is no change in the enemy situation, the attack is to be carried out with the following objectives: depending on the enemy situation, SS-Sonderbataillon "Dirlewanger" will support the left wing of Kampfgruppe "Gottberg" by attacking the enemy forest camp near Pirunoff Most, or by attacking in a southeasterly direction toward the main camp near Sekenyj Les. Attack lane for SS-Sonderbataillon "Dirlewanger" right demarcation line with Kampfgruppe "Gottberg," left demarcation line with Schutzmannschafts-Bataillon 57 from southeastern edge of Old Lyady in southerly direction through Yasvenki – Makovye (including village).

Depending on the situation, Schutzmannschafts-Bataillon 57 will advance via Kurganok – Belenyj Les in a southwesterly direction toward Yasvenji – Makovye and there seek contact with Kampfgruppe "Gottberg" or via Polyanki – Koleyna in a southerly direction toward Grodsyanka and there establish contact with Kampfgruppe "Gottberg." Attack lane for Schutzmannschafts-Bataillon 57: right demarcation line with SS-Sonderbataillon "Dirlewanger" (as above); left demarcation line from southwest edge of New Retchki in a southwesterly direction (including village) – in a southerly direction from Koleyna to Grodsyanka to Point 171.1 on the demarcation line with Kampfgruppe "Gottberg."

Commander of Osttruppen: advance from the line of encirclement in a southwesterly or westerly direction toward the road from Koleyna to Grodsyanka, and together with the neighboring unit of Kampfgruppe "Gottberg" attack the bandit camp northeast of Grodsyanka. Enemy bands are to be stopped from breaking out through the forest in an easterly direction. Attack lane for Commander of Osttruppen: right demarcation line, see above for Schutzmannschafts-Bataillon 57; left demarcation line with Kampfgruppe "Gottberg".

i) Mopping up of the band area to begin the day after the destruction of the main bands. Advancing from within to without, the units will comb the bandit area to the line Beresino – Cherven road. The attack lanes remain to be designated.

k) After the mopping-up, several yet to be designated units will remain in the bandit zone to pacify the area, in order to protect the subsequent collection of the harvest and workers.

l) During the operation all forces, including those in the encircling ring, are to conduct armed reconnaissance constantly and extensively in all directions. The purpose is to prevent our forces from being ambushed or missing enemy hiding places. After questioning, prisoners and deserters are to be sent to III./Polizei-Regiment 2's prisoner collection point in Chutor if it is felt that there are sufficient reasons to continue holding them. Otherwise proceed as per orders.

m) Booty:

a) Weapons, ammunition, and equipment not captured during combat operations are to be buried in the subsequent mopping-up action. Only those things that cannot be taken away are to be destroyed on the spot.

b) During the advance, agricultural products found in the camps are to be given an initial inspection by the agricultural officer attached to the headquarters of each battle group. Preparations are to be made for a planned recovery during the later mopping-up.

c) All bandit quarters are to be completely destroyed. The decision to destroy entire villages I reserve to myself.

7) Supply of Ammunition and Fuel. At the beginning of the operation all units must take their complete initial allotment of ammunition and fuel with them. Fuel and ammunition distribution points are in Beresino, with fuel available from 7 January 1943 at 12:00 hours and ammunition from 8 January 1943 at 08:00 hours. Further orders to follow.

8) Rations: The police units are to take with them the rations issued until 10 January 1943 and field kitchens. From 11 January 1943 rations are to be received at the rations distribution point to be set up in Beresino. Further orders to follow. The battle group headquarters will assign a ration detail of 15 men to III./Polizei-Regiment 2 and Nachrichten-Kompanie 112 one of 12 men. Beginning 6 January 1943, rations for the battle group headquarters are to be ready at noon.

9) Medical Services: the units are to set up their own dressing stations with their own doctors and first-aid personnel. Those battalions without their own first-aid personnel are directed to seek medical services from the neighboring units, specifically:

SS-Sonderbataillon "Dirlewanger" to III./Polizei-Regiment 2 in Chutor

Schutzmannschafts-Bataillon 57 to III./Polizei-Regiment 2 in Chutor

a foreign doctor will be assigned to care for foreign men

doctor to report to Schuma.Btl. 57 in Belynichi on 6 January 1943

An ambulance is to be standing by at the battle group command post in Chutor from 6 January 1943 at 13:00 hours to evacuate the wounded. If serviceable, a medical evacuation Storch will be kept available, and requests are to be directed to the battle group command post.

10) Identification Features, Signal Flares, Code words, and Maps:

All participants in the operation will wear a broad white stripe on their left shoulder strap as an identification feature. Other identification features are forbidden. Signal flares:

white vertical = we are here
white in specific direction = enemy resistance there
green = shift fire forward
Air identification symbol: to identify the front line: swastika flags

Code word:

from 5 January 16:00 hours – 6 January 1943 16:00 hours "Roma"

From 6 January 16:00 hours – 7 January 1943 16:00 hours "Agram"

From 7 January 16:00 hours – 8 January 1943 16:00 hours "Pilsen"

From 8 January 16:00 hours – 9 January 1943 16:00 hours "Paris"

From 9 January 16:00 hours – 10 January 1943 16:00 hours "Stettin"

From 10 January 16:00 hours – 11 January 1943 16:00 hours "Palermo"

Additional code words may be assigned, if considered necessary, by the Commanding General of Security Forces and Commander in Army Area Center.

Maps will be assigned to units from existing stocks. Special Issue Russia 1:100,000 Cherven Compilation, Page No. N-35-XII (West), is to be used for drawings accompanying orders.

11) Communications: Using currently available equipment, Nachrichten-Kompanie 112 will establish and maintain radio contact between the battle group command post and the units.

a) Radio communications to be established: from battle group command post to SS-Sonderbataillon "Dirlewanger" and Commander of Osttruppen 700 z.b.V. through the use each of one large police radio squad.

b) from Schutzmannschafts-Bataillon 57 to SS-Sonderbataillon "Dirlewanger" and from the Commander of Osttruppen to one of the deployed battalions through the use each of one backpack radio line. The large police radio squads at the specified command posts will convey radio traffic from the backpack radio lines to the battle group command post.

c) Signals Platoon III./Polizei-Regiment 2 will second two backpack radio squads to the Commander of Osttruppen. The radio squads will report to the Commander of Osttruppen in Beresino on 6 January 1943 at 09:00 hours.

d) Radio plan and code tables will be specially issued to signals unit leaders.

12) Reports:

a) The battalions and independent companies and batteries will report their battle and rations strengths to the battle group command post by 6 January 1943. After the objective of the day is reached, on 7 January 1943 the units up to battalion level will each dispatch a dispatch rider on a motorcycle or motorcycle-sidecar to the battle group command post in Chutor to receive orders. The driver must be briefed on the location of the regiment and battalion command posts and the routes there.

b) The regiments and battalions will simultaneously report the locations of their command posts and see to it that the command posts are identified by air identification panels for possible landings by Fieseler Storch aircraft.

c) To be reported to the battle group command post by radio:

Reaching of the objective of the day on 7 January 1943

Completion of attack preparations on 8 January 1943

Capture of important enemy camps, camp complexes, agricultural products, and all special and important events

Further situation reports from 09:00 to 10:00 hours, from 15:00 to 16:00 hours, and from 20:00 to 21:00 hours.

13) Battle group command post in Chutor (on the Beresino – Cherven road, 24 km west of Beresino) from 6 January 1943, 13:00 hours until further advised. Transfer forward to Krasnaya Sloboda on 7 January 1943.

Document 7

Final report on "Operation Erntefest," in which elements of Polizei-Regimenter 2, 13, and 23 took part:

"Operation Erntefest" proceeded according to orders in my sector. The objectives of the day and the final objective were achieved on schedule.

The final reports contained in the situation report of 2 January 1943 are accurate with respect to the camp south of Krugloye. However, other camps in this sector were not found. All tracks that could be found in the fresh snow led in the direction of this camp. According to statements by local residents, during the night of 25-26 January 1943 approximately 200 men arrived in the camp from the northwest. Their tracks made it simple to locate the camp on 26 January 1943. The camp was capable of accommodating about 500 men.

The living barracks, which were sunk deep in the ground, contained rooms for 20 men each and were covered with several layers of tree trunks, covered with earth and thus well camouflaged. At important points there were bunkers with firing slits.

The horse barns were large enough to accommodate a large number of horses. The camp also contained all of the installations necessary for living, such as a butchery, bakery, armory, and hospital.

The diameter of the camp was 300 – 400 meters. Rifle pits had been dug all around. There was also a smaller outer camp about 200 meters to the southwest. The camp was also surrounded by swamp. According to local residents, after the bombing raid there was a certain mood of panic among the bandits in this camp. Prisoners stated that late in the evening on 26 January 1943 a band of about 500 men approached from the area southwest of Minsk for the purpose of reinforcing the camp and reached the area of Stalin Brod at about 22:30. There they saw that the camp was already burning.

After a run-in with our forces they became dispersed. The majority had broken through between Stalin Brod and

Shantarovtschchina and, as I was able to determine from sleigh tracks the next day, turned west again approx. 2 km south of Shantarovtschchina.

This shows that the sectors assigned to the battalions were too broad, making it impossible to completely watch over them, especially at night. As well, the Radjanoff Battalion had reached the attack objective one day earlier and, in my opinion, failed to seal off the road from Stalin Brod to the east, as contact could not be established with Beresinets until well after nightfall. A patrol that was supposed to make contact came under fire from Beresinets between 12:30 and 14:30 hours.

In my opinion this operation showed that:

1) Combat missions must not be preceded by collection actions, for this gives the enemy time to determine the strength of our forces.

2) As the abandoned camp shows, all stores can be taken to safety in time to prevent capture.

3) That objectives of the day laid down in the orders must absolutely be kept internally.

4) That during an encirclement, a battalion's sector must be significantly reduced the nearer it comes to the objective.

That the enemy abandoned his camp prematurely and without resistance, I credit to the use of tanks, which proved themselves well in action. Concerning the high loss rate, I agree with the opinion of a tank platoon leader that the machines could not handle the change of weather (thaw and cold). With the exception of one case, where a tank burned out (see report by Oberleutnant Heuschkel).

The artillery also made a significant contribution to the abandonment of the camp. These are the only weapons the bandits fear. In my opinion they are our equal in every other arm. Perhaps they also expected to be bombed again, for this one camp had been spotted from the air and was bombed. Bomb craters were found, but in the deep snow they were not particularly evident. Tracks indicated that the bandits fled to the northwest.

Communications: The radio squads assigned to me carried out their assignments; however, on 27 January 1943 a backpack radio went unserviceable due to battery failure, followed on 28 January 1943 by the large radio, because the set had been in use for five months without being serviced. Because one cannot get by in such a large sector without this means of communication, and command is only really in a position to command when it has accurate information, it is entirely reasonable to have spare batteries available for such tasks. The assignment of small backpack radio squads for at least two lines per battalion to allow timely reporting is absolutely essential. Communications with neighboring units existed throughout the operation. The assignment of S.D. forces proved advantageous, as they were able to immediately provide the information needed for decoding.

Unfortunately this operation was cancelled so suddenly that a search of the entire forest area for stragglers was not possible.

Collection: In my opinion, the collection of labor forces, cattle, and grain by the agricultural officers was not conducted with the necessary sharpness. First of all they should have brought specific directions with them. In particular, it is essential that they know what levies have been placed on each community and what has been delivered. As well, the seizure of labor forces must go hand in hand with the seizure of agricultural products, for the levies and what was actually delivered form the basis for not unimportant decisions.

I assume that if the destruction of the band could not be achieved, it was at least scattered and will not be capable of further attacks for some time.

The collection of labor forces, cattle, and grain was a complete success.

Document 8

Letter from Polizei-Bataillon 72 to the Headquarters Chief-of-Staff of the Reichskommissar for the Strengthening of the German Race, SS-Gruppenführer Greifelt, concerning the removal of Polish undesirable persons from Carinthia:

Concerning the progress of the Carinthia Action, it is reported:

That the removal of Polish unreliable elements from the District of Carinthia assigned to Resettlement Headquarters Altreich has been carried out according to plan and without incident during the period from 14/4 to 16/4/1942.

To prevent some of the persons being deported from avoiding their resettlement duty through flight, the deportation had to be carried out abruptly, meaning it had to be completed in no more than two days.

That was only possible if an increased number of police troops, buses, and trucks, a correspondingly large transit camp, and the trains necessary for an accelerated removal could be provided.

Only after repeated futile attempts did we succeed in convincing the Reichsbahn (state railway) administration to provide two special trains on two consecutive days, which were absolutely vital for the quick execution of the resettlement, in spite of the heightened transport restrictions and the current shortage of rail cars.

The Reich Labor Service command in Berlin declared its readiness to hand over to us a RAD camp in Klagenfurt to temporarily house the deportees. We took over the camp on 7/4/42 and increased its capacity from 200 to 1,000 persons by removing the beds and setting up straw quarters, thus allowing both the deportees and working staff to be accommodated.

By order of the Senior SS and Police Commander "Alpenland," the Commander of Ordnungspolizei made it possible to commit an entire Ordnungspolizei battalion for the quick execution of the resettlement, despite the heavy burden this placed on the police units under his command, and the local traffic administrator in Salzburg promised to provide the buses and trucks needed for the action.

After quarters were made for the police and drivers in two Klagenfurt schools, the police battalion arrived in Klagenfurt on the afternoon of 13/4/42, and the 22 buses and 28 trucks arrived at the same time.

Meanwhile, the maps needed for the carrying-out of the deportation and the file cards for the individual deportees were prepared by the office of our agent in Klagenfurt and of the head of the Secret State Police.

The officers of the police battalion attached to us for the operation were briefed on their assignments on the morning of 13/4/42 and the necessary maps and file cards were handed out.

The deportation began at about 3 o'clock in the morning on 14/4/42 and was completed by noon on 15/4/42, with the exception of a few stragglers who had to be picked up from outlying and difficult to access areas and were brought in the next day. Refer to the appendix for details of the action and the whereabouts of the individual deportees.

Based on the file cards given us by the head of the Secret State Police, the original number to be deported: 1,220 persons.

Of these, removed from the list by our agent in consultation with the head of the Gestapo were: 123 persons

Resulting total to be deported: 1,097 persons

Fled or failed to show up were: 22 persons, so that deported by the police and transported to the camp were: 1,075 persons.

Of these, released from their resettlement obligation by our agent in consultation with the head of the Gestapo prior to the departure of the transport trains were: 158 persons.

The actual number of those resettled: 917 persons

Also taken out of the Upper Krain on the same train for resettlement: 201 Slovenes

Total: 1,118 persons

Delivered to the camps by the 1st train:

Forth	*104 persons*
Spalt	*97 persons*
Hesselberg	*322 persons*
Hegenbüchach	*89 persons*
Markt-Bibart	*96 persons*

to the camps by the 2nd train:

Glasow	*211 persons*
Frauenaurach	*199 persons*

The deportees who arrived in the Spalt and Forth camps were Slovenes from the newly-acquired areas who had to be treated exactly the same as the deportees from Lower Styria, while the Ethnic German Mittelstelle must still receive special instructions for the handling of the Reich Germans being resettled from Carinthia, who are housed in the camps at Hesselberg, Hagenbüchach, Markt-Bibart, Frauenaurach, and Glasow.

Following the departure of the remaining deportees, the 158 persons released by our agent in consultation with the head of the Gestapo prior to the deportation were released from the camp, and to avoid unnecessary attention and talk they were transported by us back to their districts of origin.

Apart from that, all of the deportees were processed in the same manner we employed in Lower Styria, mustered in the camp, and given numbers and number plates and personal identification papers.

In keeping with procedure, their property was picked up by the agent of the German Settlement Society in the camp and immediately after their deportation it was transferred on the spot to agents of the party or the local head farmer, in order to avoid damage.

The resettlement trains arrived at their destinations on the 16th, 17th, and 18th of April 1942. The transport lists and file cards went with the transport officers, who gave them to the responsible camp commanders.

The copies of the transport lists and file cards still in our possession were passed to our agent in Klagenfurt.

The Altreich Settlement Staff has thus completed the special mission given to it.

Document 9

Special Order from the Commander of *Ordnungspolizei "Alpenland"* to the commanders of *Reserve-Polizei-Bataillone 93*, *322*, and *181* dated 19 July 1942 concerning "Punishment Measures" in his security area:

Special Order No. 1

1. The population of the villages

a. Hrastnigg (4 km NE of Moräutsch)

b. Kanker (7 km E of Höflein)

c. Zavoden (8 km SW of Goreinawass)

have for a long time taken in or supported bandits.

2. As a punishment measure the male population over the age of 15 years is to be shot on the spot and the bodies thrown in the fire. The villages are to be destroyed by fire. The remaining population is to be deported and taken to the resettlement camp in St. Veit (Save).

3. Assigned to carry out this order are:

to a) C.O. Res.Pol.Btl. 93

to b) C.O. Pol.Btl. 322

to c) C.O. Res.Pol. Btl. 181

The actions are to begin in the early morning hours of 20/7/1942.

4. The deportees are to be given a brief opportunity to take with them clothing, underwear, bedding, jewelry, money, documents etc., and food for several days as may be packed in hand luggage. The deportation is to take place in such a way that all persons leave their homes with the above-named items. The homes are to be guarded during this period. This will be followed by a detailed search for weapons, food, etc, and all valuable equipment, such as agricultural machinery, is to be seized.

The forces assigned to this action must expect to find bandits in the structures, houses, and barns being searched or encounter harassment from the bandits. Therefore the necessary security measures are to be taken.

5. The representative of the Reichskommissar will see to the collection of cattle, stores, and other inventory and the associated guarding and evaluation.

Easily spoiled foods such as meat, butter, fats, eggs, etc. are to be collected by the battalions and a list is to be made. These foodstuffs are to be used by the participating battalions and forces of the security police as supplemental rations.

6. The Stapo. Field offices in Stein, Krainburg, and Laak have been ordered to make contact with the battalion commanders and provide forces for the actions.

7. The order is to be revealed to the operational forces shortly before the start of the action.

8. A written report about the conduct of the resettlement is to be submitted to me.

Selected Sources and Literature

Bundesarchiv Berlin: Aktenbestand des Höchsten SS- und Polizeiführers Italien
Bundesarchiv Koblenz: Aktenbestand Reichsführer-SS
Zentrale Stelle der Landesjustizverwaltungen: diverse Ermittlungs- und Verfahrensakten
Birn, Ruth: Die Höheren SS- und Polizeiführer, Tübingen 1985
Brin, Ruth: Die Sicherheitspolizei in Estland 1941 – 1944 – Eine Studie zur Kollaboration im Osten, Paderborn 2006
Browning, Christopher: Ganz normale Männer – Das Reserve-Polizei-Bataillon 101 und die "Endlösung" in Polen, Reinbek 2002
Curilla, Wolfgang: Die deutsche Ordnungspolizei und der Holocaust im Baltikum und in Weißrußland 1941- 1944, Paderborn 2002
Dallin, Alexander: Deutsche Herrschaft in Russland, Düsseldorf 1958
Forschungsstelle für Zeitgeschichte (Hrsg.): Der Dienstkalender Heinrich Himmlers 1941/42, Hamburg 1999
Heiber, Helmut (Hrsg.): Lagebesprechungen im Führerhauptquartier, München 1964
Klemp, Stefan: Nicht ermittelt – Polizei-Bataillone und die Nachkriegsjustiz, Essen 2005
Meissner, Gustav: Dänemark unterm Hakenkreuz, Frankfurt am Main 1990
Meyer, Hermann Frank: Von Wien nach Kalavryta – Die blutige Spur der 117. Jäger-Division durch Serbien und Griechenland,
Möhnesee-Wamel 2001
Neubacher, Hermann: Sonderauftrag Südost, Göttingen 1956
Neusüss-Hunkel, Ermenhild: Die SS, Hannover 1956
Rauchensteiner, Manfried: Der Krieg in Österreich '45, o. O. 1995
Reitlinger, Gerald: Die SS – Tragödie einer deutschen Epoche, München 1957
Richter, Hans, Einsatz der Polizei, Berlin 1943
Rumler, Günther, Holzmann, Otto: Freigemachtes Grenzland, Berlin 1942
Schramm, Percy (Hrsg.): Kriegstagebuch des OKW, München 1982
Tessin, Georg: Die Stäbe und Truppeneinheiten der Ordnungspolizei in:
Neufeldt, Hansjoachim u. a.: Zur Geschichte der Ordnungspolizei 1936 – 1945, Koblenz 1957
Wegner, Bernd: Hitlers Politische Soldaten, Paderborn 1982
Wilhelm, Friedrich: Die Polizei im NS-Staat – die Geschichte ihrer Organisation im Überblick, Paderborn 1999
ohne: Die Wehrmachtberichte 1939-1945, München 1985

Notes

1 Rumler, Günther, and Holzmann, Otto: Freigemachtes Grenzland, Berlin, 1942

2 Not covered in this book are the units formed by the *Ordnungspolizei* with foreign troops—e.g. the *Schutzmannschafts-Bataillone* or *Polizei-Freiwilligen-Regimenter*—the *Polizei*-Wach-*Bataillone*, which as a rule were not employed in the occupied territories, or the *Gendarmerie* units, which were small in terms of personnel. These may be covered in a later publication.

3 These 56,000 men were equivalent to three infantry divisions.

4 This was the "Decree to Guarantee the Required Forces for Tasks of Special National-Political Importance of 15 October 1938 (Emergency Service decree)"

5 Rumler, Günther, and Holzmann, Otto: Freigemachtes Grenzland, Berlin, 1942

6 In the beginning the battalions lacked supporting combat arms, such as armored cars, anti-tank guns, and infantry guns. These were not supplied until the start of the Russian Campaign, and from 1942 were generally supposed to be a part of every battalion. The 37-mm anti-tank gun, however, was practically useless as a front line weapon. The issuing of captured weapons, such as the 45-mm gun, could only be characterized as an improvised measure.

7 See the extract from the police service manual in the appendices.

8 See the related article in the appendices.

9 Of these, about 46 battalions with about 24,000 men were in the occupied territories.

10 The desertion by elements of the *Schutzmannschafts-Bataillone* to the partisans was a regular occurrence. In some cases, when combing wooded areas foreign volunteers failed to report finding partisans or civilians taking refuge there.

11 On 27 February 1942, for example, persons from German National List III were called up to serve in the police battalions in the new Defense Districts XX and XXI. From the summer of 1943, even larger contingents came from the ethnic German settlement areas in southeastern Europe (e.g. Croatia, Rumania, and Hungary) in the course of "general mobilization" there to serve in existing or new police regiments. Most of these were from the older age classes; as a rule the younger men were drafted into the *Waffen-SS*.

12 In fact, the organizations often differed greatly. Not every regiment had a panzer company, for example. Some regiments were also bolstered by the addition of a police artillery battalion, which consisted of three so-called police gun companies equipped with captured submarine 76.2-mm field guns.

13 While police rifle regiments whose *I. Bataillon* at least was made up of German police personnel are covered in this book, the police volunteer units from Croatia, Albania, Greece, and elsewhere made up entirely of foreign personnel are not. These are to be dealt with in a separate publication.

14 See Michaelis, Rolf: Die Waffen-SS – Mythos und Wirklichkeit, Berlin 2006 (The *Waffen-SS* – Myth and Reality)

15 See Michaelis, Rolf: Die Waffen-SS – Mythos und Wirklichkeit, Berlin 2006 (The *Waffen-SS* – Myth and Reality)

16 Ostap Hladkiwskyj, who later volunteered for the 14. Waffen-Grenadier-Division der SS (ukrainische Nr. 1), recalled the *Ordnungspolizei*'s "seizure" of Ukrainian civilians for service as laborers in Germany:

"I was born in Galicia in 1926, and we Ukrainians suffered greatly under Polish rule. My father, who worked for the Polish state, was forced to convert from the Greek-Orthodox to the Roman Catholic faith in order to keep his job. When the Soviets came many were imprisoned, and so the German Wehrmacht was welcomed with flowers as a true liberator. Disenchantment slowly set in, however. Young Ukrainians were initially called up for two years labor service. Poor food and hard labor led to rising resistance. Finally the German police began seizing ordinary civilians at train stations and deporting them to Germany to work. It was particularly bad in our village when, during a party in the town hall, the entire population was surrounded and taken away! And so many began to hate the Germans."

17 Between November 1939 and January 1941 more than 400,000 Poles from West Prussia, Zichenau, Upper Silesia, and the Warthe District were resettled in the *Generalgouvernement*.

18 Richter, Hans: Einsatz der Polizei, Berlin 1943

19 On 6 October 1939 Himmler was named Reich Commissar for the Strengthening of the German Race. In this capacity he was supposed to oversee the "return home" of ethnic Germans living abroad, eliminate "foreign racial" influences within the Reich, and create settlements for the returnees in the new eastern areas (provinces lost to Poland in 1918 and the Lodz region). There were approximately 650,000 Jews in the new areas, about 550,000 of whom were supposed to be resettled in the *Generalgouvernement* in the first wave of deportations, along with members of the Polish intelligentsia. Many Jews and Poles lost their lives in these deportations, which were temporarily halted in March 1940.

20 In autumn 1940 the former police battalions were replaced by newly-established units, consequently the regiments were organized as follows:

Polizei-Regiment "Warschau" (became Polizei-Regiment 22 in 1942)
Polizei-Bataillon "Warschau I" (H.Q. Bochum) (Polizei-Bataillon 301)
Polizei-Bataillon "Warschau II" (H.Q. Chemnitz) (Polizei-Bataillon 304)
Polizei-Bataillon "Warschau III" (H.Q. Duisburg) (Polizei-Bataillon 307)
Polizei-Regiment "Radom" (became Polizei-Regiment 24 in 1942)
Polizei-Bataillon "Radom" (H.Q. Cologne) (Polizei-Bataillon 309)
Polizei-Bataillon "Tschenstochau" (H.Q. Berlin) (Polizei-Bataillon 310)
Polizei-Bataillon "Kielce" (H.Q. Hamburg) (Polizei-Bataillon 305)
Polizei-Regiment "Krakau" (became Polizei-Regiment 23 in 1942)
Polizei-Bataillon Krakau I" (H.Q. Jena) (Polizei-Bataillon 311)
Polizei-Bataillon"Krakau II" (H.Q. Breslau) (Polizei-Bataillon 321)
Polizei-Bataillon "Tarnow" (H.Q. Bremen) (Polizei-Bataillon 303)
Polizei-Bataillon "Reichshof" (H.Q. Vienna) (Polizei-Bataillon 314)
Polizei-Regiment "Lublin" (became Polizei-Regiment 25 in 1942)
Polizei-Bataillon "Lublin" (H.Q. Frankfurt/Main) (Polizei-Bataillon 306)
Polizei-Bataillon "Zamosc" (H.Q. Stettin) (Polizei-Bataillon 313)
Polizei-Bataillon "Biala-Podlaska" (H.Q. Lubeck) (Polizei-Bataillon 308)

21 Wehrkreis XX (Danzig-West Prussia) Polizei-Bataillone 13, 64, 71, and 91) Wehrkreis XXI (Wartheland) Polizei-Bataillone 41, 101, and 132

22 Richter, Hans: Einsatz der Polizei, Berlin 1943

23 Rumler, Günther, and Holzmann, Otto: Freigemachtes Grenzland, Berlin 1942

24 Richter, Hans: Einsatz der Polizei, Berlin 1943

25 Although several battalions had already been detached for the formation of the Polizei-Division, the numbering sequence was maintained for new battalions. As there could not have been an 11th or 12th Battalion (these already existed in Wehrkreis I), a second numbering sequence was now introduced in Berlin, this time beginning with the number of the Wehrkreis.

26 In fact, however, "only" 72,000 Jews were brought to the Warsaw ghetto, which subsequently numbered 430,000 people!

27 At the end of October 1941 Jews were transported from the German Reich and the "Protectorate of Bohemia and Moravia" to the ghetto and to work camps in Minsk and Riga.

28 Concerning this, on 29 August 1941 the Senior SS and Police Commander "Russia South" reported to the *Reichsführer-SS*:
"*Activities: 1. SS-Infanterie-Brigade continues clearing action north of Korosten – Bialokurowicz. General line Ignatpol reached in the evening. Destroyed bridges partially repaired by pioneer platoons. Polizei-Regiment "Süd" continues road guard duty without change. Otherwise no reports. H.Q. Company HSSPF Russian-South has concluded action in Kamenets Podolski under the direction of SS-Obergruppenführer Jeckeln.*
Results: 1. SS-Infanterie-Brigade took 18 prisoners and shot 77 Jews. H.Q. Company HSSPF Russia South shot another 7,000 Jews, bringing the total number of Jews liquidated in the action at Kamenets Podolski to around 20 thousand. Change in activity reports of 26 and 27/8/1941: replace Polizei-Bataillon 320 with H.Q. Company. In the report of 27/8, instead of 5 thousand 11 thousand, Polizei-Bataillon 320 was only employed in barricading."
As in most numbers of statistics, the numbers were obviously "colored" to make an impression on Himmler.

29 Because of the emotional stress on the German police members, most executions were relatively soon handed over to mainly Lithuanian, Latvian, and, in part, Ukrainian auxiliary police and Schutzmänner. This ultimately led to the plans to abandon shootings and kill the victims with poison gas.

30 For more information see the individual battalion histories.

31 In addition, the deportation of Jews from France, Holland, and Belgium—mainly to Auschwitz—began in July 1942.

32 At the beginning of March the battle group, which existed until mid-August 1942 and was attached to the L. Armee-Korps, was organized as follows:

Infanterie-Regiment 310 (212. Infanterie-Division) with attached
Polizei-Bataillonen 121 and 306
H.Q./Infanterie-Regiment 409 (122. Infanterie-Division) commanding:
V./Leibstandarte-SS "Adolf Hitler"
Polizei-Bataillon 56
Polizei-Bataillon 305
Polizei-Bataillon 310
Freiwilligen-Legion "Norwegen"
Aufklärungs-Abteilung 158 (58. Infanterie-Division)
Panzerjäger-Abteilung 158 (58. Infanterie-Division)
elements of the Panzerjäger-Abteilung of the SS-Polizei-Division
2 light infantry gun platoons of the SS-Polizei-Division
2 heavy infantry gun platoons of the SS-Polizei-Division
5 light infantry gun platoons of the 58. Infanterie-Division
3 heavy infantry gun platoons of the 58. Infanterie-Division
Artillerie-Regiment 158 (58. Infanterie-Division)
artillery regiment of the SS-Polizei-Division

33 While Polizei-Regiment 14 and 15 received personnel from other units, enabling them to be brought back up to strength at least in numbers, Polizei-Regimenter 6 and 8 were not formed until autumn 1944 in Hungary.

34 The gradual merging of the SS and police actually began in 1937, when Himmler ordered "*the personnel renewal of the Schutzpolizei from the ranks of the SS members.*" In 1939 members of the police who joined the SS were immediately given the corresponding SS rank, and promotions in police service were automatically matched.

35 SS-Polizei-Regiment "Griese" in Marseille.

36 SS-Gebirgs-Polizei-Regiment 18 in Karelia.

37 This was a regiment created by combining Schutzmannschafts-Bataillonen 276, 277, 278, and 312.

38 A planned Polizei-Schützen-Regiment 32 was not established.

39 The regiments were:

SS-Polizei-Regiment 1	disbanded (July 1943)
SS-Polizei-Regiment 2	action in northern Russia
SS-Polizei-Regiment 3	occupation unit in the Netherlands
SS-Polizei-Regiment 4	occupation unit in the Generalgouvernement
SS-Polizei-Regiment 5	occupation unit in Serbia
SS-Polizei-Regiment 6	disbanded (January 1943)
SS-Polizei-Regiment 7	occupation unit in Norway
SS-Polizei-Regiment 8	disbanded (January 1943)
SS-Polizei-Regiment 9	action in Russia – disbanded July 1944
SS-Polizei-Regiment 10	action in southern Russia
SS-Polizei-Regiment 11	action in southern Russia
SS-Polizei-Regiment 12	home garrison
SS-Polizei-Regiment 13	action central Russia
SS-Polizei-Regiment 14	occupation unit in France
SS-Polizei-Regiment 15	occupation unit in Italy
SS-Polizei-Regiment 16	action in northern Russia
SS-Polizei-Regiment 17	occupation unit in Generalgouvernement
SS-Polizei-Gebirgsjäger-Regiment 18	occupation unit in Greece
SS-Polizei-Regiment 19	occupation unit in Slovenia
SS-Polizei-Regiment 20	"Protectorate of Bohemia and Moravia"
SS-Polizei-Regiment 21	"Protectorate of Bohemia and Moravia"
SS-Polizei-Regiment 22	occupation unit in Generalgouvernement
SS-Polizei-Regiment 23	occupation unit in Generalgouvernement
SS-Polizei-Regiment 24	action central Russia
SS-Polizei-Regiment 25	occupation unit in Generalgouvernement
SS-Polizei-Regiment 26	action in southern Russia
SS-Polizei-Regiment 27	occupation unit in Norway
SS-Polizei-Regiment 28	occupation unit in France
Polizei-Schützen-Regiment 31	action in central Russia
Polizei-Schützen-Regiment 32	not established
Polizei-Schützen-Regiment 33	action in southern Russia
Polizei-Schützen-Regiment 34	occupation unit in *Generalgouvernement*
Polizei-Schützen-Regiment 35	action in southern Russia
Polizei-Schützen-Regiment 36	action in central Russia
Polizei-Schützen-Regiment 37	action in southern Russia
Polizei-Schützen-Regiment 38	action in southern Russia
SS-Polizei-Regiment "Bozen"	action in Italy

40 Lettisches Freiwilligen-Polizei-Regimenter 2 (elements), 3, and 5 (Latvian volunteer police regiments), plus two Estonian police battalions.

41 Lettisches SS-Grenzschutz-Regimenter 2, 4, and 6 (Latvian border protection regiments).

42 Lettisches Freiwilligen-Polizei-Regimenter 1 and elements of 2.

43 These were:

SS-Polizei-Regiment 2	*Polizei-Kampfgruppe* "Hannibal" East Prussia
SS-Polizei-Regiment 3	occupation unit in the Netherlands
SS-Polizei-Regiment 4	*Polizei-Kampfgruppe* "Hannibal" East Prussia
SS-Polizei-Regiment 5	disbanded (December 1944)
SS-Polizei-Regiment 7	occupation unit in Norway
SS-Polizei-Regiment 9	disbanded (July 1944)
SS-Polizei-Regiment 10	occupation unit in Adriatic coastland
SS-Polizei-Regiment 11	disbanded (December 1944)
SS-Polizei-Regiment 12	*III. Bataillon* only: Italy
SS-Polizei-Regiment 13	occupation unit in Slovenia
SS-Polizei-Regiment 14	occupation unit in Slovenia
SS-Polizei-Regiment 15	action in Italy
SS-Polizei-Regiment 16	disbanded (December 1944)
SS-Polizei-Regiment 17	occupation unit in Generalgouvernement
SS-Polizei-Regiment 18	occupation unit in the Balkans
SS-Polizei-Regiment 19	Western Front
SS-Polizei-Regiment 20	action in Italy
SS-Polizei-Regiment 21	"Protectorate of Bohemia and Moravia"
SS-Polizei-Regiment 22	disbanded (December 1944)
SS-Polizei-Regiment 23	III. *Bataillon* only: Generalgouvernement
SS-Polizei-Regiment 24	reformed in Upper Silesia
SS-Polizei-Regiment 25	I. Btl. Slovenia, II./III. Btl. Generalgouvernement
SS-Polizei-Regiment 26	disbanded (November 1944)
SS-Polizei-Regiment 27	occupation unit in Norway
SS-Polizei-Regiment 28	occupation unit in Slovenia

Polizei-Schützen-Regiment 31	*Polizei-Kampfgruppe* "Hannibal" East Prussia
Polizei-Schützen-Regiment 33	disbanded (March 1944)
Polizei-Schützen-Regiment 34	occupation unit in Generalgouvernement
Polizei-Schützen-Regiment 35	disbanded (April 1944)
Polizei-Schützen-Regiment 36	disbanded (August 1944)
Polizei-Schützen-Regiment 37	disbanded (April 1944)
Polizei-Schützen-Regiment 38	disbanded (November 1944)
SS-Polizei-Regiment "Bozen"	action in Italy
SS-Polizei-Regiment "Brixem"	action in Italy
SS-Polizei-Regiment "Schlanders"	action in Italy
SS-Polizei-Regiment "Alpenvorland"	action in Italy

44 See Michaelis, Rolf: "Die Waffen-SS – Mythos und Wirklichkeit," Berlin 2006

45 It is believed that a total of about 8,000 members of the Ordnungspolizei were killed.

46 It is interesting that, because of the great emotional stress that these shootings caused the German "folk comrades," Himmler's representatives soon reassigned this task in large part to foreign auxiliary police, mainly Lithuanian or Latvian. Another consequence was the creation of so-called "gas vans."

47 This had already shot Jews and Poles in Bromberg at the beginning of September 1939 on orders from the Sicherheitspolizei.

48 German Ostenburg – approx. 56 km north of Warsaw at the confluence of the Narev and Rozoga Rivers.

49 Between 7 April and 13 December 1941, a total of 5,807 Polish families, 24,912 persons altogether, were forced to move to the Generalgouvernement.

50 See the chapter "In Action 1942."

51 For a time it was attached to Oberfeldkommandantur 670.

52 11 officers, 1 medical officer, 3 administrative officials, 72 NCOs, and 70 enlisted men.

53 The dates concerning the police regiments established in the Protectorate and in Norway appear in the chapters "In Action 1939" and "In Action 1941."

54 By the summer of 1942, of the 100 battalions that existed in 1940 only 75 remained. Nine battalions had to be reestablished in order to achieve the required number of 84 for 28 regiments of 3 battalions each.

55 Polizei-Lehr-Bataillone (police instruction battalions) were formed to serve as replacement and training units for the new regiments. The battalions were each responsible for a number of regiments:
Polizei-Lehr-Bataillon I Dresden-Hellerau for Polizei-Regimenter 3, 4, 7, 10, 11, 12, 26, 27, and 28
Polizei-Lehr-Bataillon II Iglau for Polizei-Regimenter 5, 8, 9, 14, 16, 18, 19, 20, and 21
Polizei-Lehr-Bataillon III Adlershorst for Polizei-Regimenter 1, 2, 6, 12, 15, 22, 23, 24, and 25
Polizei-Lehr-Bataillon IV Maastricht for Polizei-Schützen-Regimenter 31, 32, 33, 34, 35, 36, 37, and 38
In August 1943 the Lehr-Bataillone were renamed Polizei-Waffen-Schule I – IV.

56 Rumler, Günther, and Holzmann, Otto: "Freigemachtes Grenzland," Berlin 1942

57 The unit was now temporarily designated Polizei-Regiment "Griese" or "Marseille."

58 See: Michaelis, Rolf: "Die Waffen-SS – Mythos und Wirklichkeit," Berlin 2006

59 On 10 January 1944 the I. Armee-Korps assumed command over all troops deployed in the Polotsk – Yasno Lake sector. Among these was Polizei-Kampfgruppe "von Gottberg."

60 Also see: Michaelis, Rolf: "Die Waffen-SS – Mythos und Wirklichkeit," Berlin 2006

61 Elements of the division were at the SS Training Camp "Heidelager" in Debica, about 100 km away, for reformation.

62 The ethnic German recruits were first sent to Polizei-Ausbildungs-Bataillon "Oranienburg," and on 5/11/1942 returned to Serbia.

63 They had relieved Polizei-Bataillone 45, 303, and 314, formerly part of Polizei-Regiment "Süd."

64 They had relieved Polizei-Bataillone 307, 316, and 322, formerly part of Polizei-Regiment "Mitte."

65 They had relieved Polizei-Bataillone 22, 53, and 65, formerly part of Polizei-Regiment "Nord."

66 Lettische-Freiwilligen-Polizei-Regimenter 2 (elements), 3, and 5 (Latvian volunteer police regiments), plus two Estonian police battalions.

67 Lettische SS-Grenzschutz-Regimenter 2, 4, and 6.

68 Lettische-Freiwilligen-Polizei-Regimenter 1 and elements of 2.

69 SS-Brigadeführer und Generalmajor der Polizei Walter Schimana was awarded the German Cross in Gold for "Operation Weichsel" against partisan bands. The operation was described in a rather bold style in the award recommendation:
"*For the exemplary* ***execution of the major "Operation" "Weichsel"*** *(Vistula) between the Pripyat and the Dniepr, and for his personal actions during this operation, I recommend SS-Brigadeführer und Generalmajor der Polizei Schimana for the award of the German Cross in Gold.*
Schimana kept his iron nerve during the various crises that arose during the operation. He was always present at the critical points of the battle, and through his personal example inspired his men to attack. Of his various acts of personal bravery one is deserving of special mention:
When the attack against the enemy encircled in the swamps bogged down in one place because the swampy terrain was impassible, Schimana took horses from the ***SS-Polizei-Regiment 10****'s train for himself and six other men of the regiment. Leading this mounted patrol, he galloped toward the enemy bandit camp. The enemy allowed the mounted patrol to come within 30 meters before opening up with withering machine-gun fire. The horses were immediately hit. For hours, Brigadeführer Schimana lay behind a fallen horse close to the enemy lines, firing his machine-gun at the enemy. This exemplary act inspired the entire regiment to advance. Wading*

through the swamps in hip-deep water, the men worked their way toward the enemy and, following their Brigadeführer, stormed the bunker positions shouting the battle cry."

70 The cattle collection brought in 6,450 cows and calves, 227 oxen, 696 horses, and 5,390 sheep.

71 Battle strength of Polizei-Kampfgruppe "Prützmann" (4 February 1944):

Stab von Braunschweig	41
I./SS-Polizei-Regiment 11	358
III./SS-Polizei-Regiment 11	468
Lettisches Polizei-Bataillon 23	178
Gendarmerie-Züge 3 and 5	42
III./Polizei-Schützen-Regiment 35	324
SS-Polizei-Reiter-Abteilung I	141
I./SS-Polizei-Regiment 10	486
Gendarmerie-Züge 8, 16, 45, 55, 65	
Total	2,103
Stab Koellner	53
II./SS-Polizei-Regiment 10	340
III./SS-Polizei-Regiment 10	229
Polnisches Schutzmannschafts-Bataillon 202	60 and 260 Eastern people
Gendarmerie-Züge 5, 44, 60	45
II./SS-Polizei-Regiment 11	330
Total	1,317

72 On 26 January 1945 the commander of III./SS-Polizei-Regiment 10 made the following comments concerning the recommendation for the awarding of the German Cross in Gold to the commander of the 9. Kompanie, Leutnant der Schutzpolizei Bertet:
"Worthy of particular mention is the fact that he achieved great success while keeping casualties down. In addition to the purely numerical successes achieved by his company, its tactical success was also of great significance. Since July 1944 Ltn. Bertet and his company have fought 32 battles with bandits, achieving the following total results:
294 counted enemy dead, whose number is undoubtedly much higher, as the bandits carried away many dad and wounded.
207 prisoners (armed bandits), as well as numerous bandit helpers and suspected bandits.
3 heavy machine-guns, 18 light machine-guns, 1 medium mortar, 1 bazooka, 14 submachine-guns, 206 rifles, 5 automobiles, 2 trucks, 1 motorcycle, 5 drums of fuel, 1,500 liters of diesel fuel, and 1 brigade and 1 battalion office, as well as numerous items of equipment.
Many captured weapons and much equipment also had to be destroyed as it could not be transported out.
Our own losses were minimal compared to those of the enemy:
2 dead, 25 wounded, 16 of them minor."
Leutnant Walter Bertet was awarded the German Cross in Gold on 30 March 1945.

73 See SS-Polizei-Regiment 10.

74 On 10 January 1944 the I. Armee-Korps took over command of all the units in the Polotsk – Yasno Lake sector. Among these was SS-Polizei-Regiment 13 with a strength of 2,239 men, part of Polizei-Kampfgruppe "von Gottberg" (total strength: 8,132 men).

75 During this they shot the family living there for supporting the partisans.

76 On 10 April 1943 the unit, temporarily designated Polizei-Regiment "Griese" or Polizei-Regiment "Marseille," reported the following strength in serviceable tanks:
6 Panzer II
2 Panzer III (flamethrower)
3 Panzer IV (short-barreled gun)

77 On 5 October 1943 the regiment was advised that it was to take part in an operation under the CIC Southeast against a partisan force in the Italian-Croatian border region which had grown to 10,000-12,000 men armed with equipment captured from at least two Italian divisions. The regiment was to advance into the Fiumi area, where it would be attached to Heeresgruppe "B."

78 Also see: Michaelis, Rolf: "Die Waffen-SS – Mythos und Wirklichkeit," Berlin 2006

79 In fact, the battalion did not arrive until February 1943, in the midst of the regiment's reestablishment.

80 Also see: Michaelis, Rolf: "Die Waffen-SS – Mythos und Wirklichkeit," Berlin 2006

81 ebenda

82 The corps reported:
"05:00 hours, situation: Attack by approximately 1,000-man partisan unit with mortars and machine-guns against rail line 15 km northeast of Ivye (approx. 40 km NE of Lida). Polizei-Schützen-Regiment 17 and 36 repulsed the attack and, with police tanks, drove into the bandit group. Two anti-tank guns were destroyed and numerous machine-guns, mortars, and rifles captured."

83 On 22 April 1945 fighting developed in the Kocevje (in German Gottschee) against Tito partisans. On 26/4/45 the commanding general of Rear Army Area "E" reported to HGR "E" that SS-Polizei-Regiment 17 was deployed in the line Göttenitz – Gottschee to the Gurk River.

84 The II. Bataillon was surrounded by French rebels in Limoges. It broke out on 19 August 1944 and *SS-Hauptsturmführer* Engelbrecht was awarded the Knight's Cross.
85 Among its units was Sicherungs-Regiment 200.
86 It may have been a battle group under the command of the former Brunswick Police President, *Oberstleutnant* Aug, who had first been summoned to Berlin in May 1944.
87 Altogether about 110,000 Poles were deported and approx. 60,000 ethnic Germans moved in. Some Poles able to work were sent to Germany as laborers while others went to Auschwitz.
88 Mass executions of Jews in Maidanek, Travniki, and Poniatova.
89 Elements of the division were in the SS Training Camp "Heidelager" in Debica, about 100 kilometers away, for reestablishment.
90 See: Michaelis, Rolf: "Die Waffen-SS – Mythos und Wirklichkeit," Berlin 2006
91 The corps reported: *"05:00 hours, situation: Attack by approximately 1,000-man partisan unit with mortars and machine-guns against rail line 15 km northeast of Ivye (approx. 40 km NE of Lida). Polizei-Schützen-Regiment 17 and 36 repulsed the attack and, with police tanks, drove into the bandit group. Two anti-tank guns were destroyed and numerous machine-guns, mortars, and rifles captured."*
92 Interestingly, according to military postal number records the unit did not receive the "SS" prefix.
93 Only the total number shot had to be reported.
94 The South Tyrol *Ordnungsdienst* was formed in September 1943 by members of the *Deutsche Volksgruppe* (formerly The Association of Optants for Germany) under *Volksgruppenführer* Peter Hofer). (Optant = non-Italian-speaking South Tyrolean). Equipped mainly with captured Italian weapons, it numbered almost 20,000 members. Many of these were men unfit for military service or boys too young to be drafted.
95 From 1 April 1943 the SS and Police Commander "Minsk" was subordinate to the Senior SS and Police Commander "Russia Center and White Ruthenia."
96 Following the establishment of an additional Senior SS and Police Commander "Black Sea" in the area of Heeresgruppe "A," in March 1944 the Senior SS and Police Commander "Russia South" also became Supreme SS and Police Commander Ukraine.
97 After the Senior SS and Police Commanders "Upper Italy West" and "Adriatic Coastland" were subordinated to him, in June 1944 he was given the title Supreme SS and Police Commander "Italy."
98 This was also adopted by the 7. SS-Freiwilligen-Gebirgs-Division "Prinz Eugen."
99 As part of SS-Kampfgruppe "Fegelein," the II./SS-Polizei-Infanterie-Regiment 3 was transferred into the Boguchar area (NW of Stalingrad) in December 1942. In February 1943, with just 200 of its original approximately 1,000 men, it was transported back to Debica from Valuiki.
In December 1942 the I./SS-Polizei-Infanterie-Regiment 1 was likewise ordered to the hard-pressed HGR "B." The companies were attached to various battle groups southwest of Stalingrad. Not until 19 February 1943 was the battalion united as *SS-Kampfgruppe* "Schuldt." It consisted of:
SS-Wach-Bataillon "Berlin"
I./SS-Panzergrenadier-Regiment "Der Führer"
I./SS-Polizei-Infanterie-Regiment 1
SS-Kampfgruppe "Schuldt" was disbanded after heavy fighting near Millerovo and Uktino. The *I./SS-Polizei-Infanterie-Regiment* 1 moved back to the SS Training Camp "Heidelager" (Debica) with 84 of its original 527 men.
100 The division was listed as having two panzer-grenadier regiments. *SS-Polizei-Panzergrenadier-Regiment* 3, which was still deployed in Russia, was later divided among the first two regiments.
101 The three companies were under the command of *Waffen-Hauptsturmführer* Obitz. After he was wounded, *Waffen-Hauptsturmführer* Martin led what was left. From Hela, by way of Copenhagen, on 10 April 1945 the Frenchmen reached Neustrelitz, where the 33. *Waffen-Grenadier-Division der SS "Charlemagne" (französische* Nr. 1) was supposed to be reformed.
102 The SS panzer-grenadier regiment was reorganized on 16/4/45 and merged with *SS-Feldausbildungs-Regiment* 103. It was sometimes also called *SS-Panzergrenadier-Regiment* 103.
103 Flak-Regiment 35
104 Flak-Regiment 35
105 286. *Sicherungs-Division*
106 *SS-Brigadeführer und Generalmajor der Polizei* Franz Kutschera was SS and Police Commander "Mogilev."
107 The men of the *Ost-Bataillone* (eastern battalions) wore Soviet uniforms and steel helmets.